FIELD & STREAM

THE TOTAL OUTDOORSMAN MANUAL

T. EDWARD NICKENS
AND THE EDITORS OF *FIELD & STREAM*

WITH SPECIAL CONTRIBUTIONS BY
PHIL BOURJAILY, KIRK DEETER, ANTHONY LICATA,
KEITH McCAFFERTY, JOHN MERWIN,
AND DAVID E. PETZAL

weldon**owen**

CONTENTS

CAMPING

FISHING

HUNTING

SURVIVAL

Foreword

Try to imagine your favorite hunting and fishing moments–those memories big and small that stick in your brain and work their way into your heart, bringing a smile to your face long after they've passed. I bet you can't keep the list to fewer than twenty.

If it's April, one of the first things that may come to mind is a morning in the turkey woods. You climb through the timber in the pitch black, with the whip-poor-wills droning, and as you stand on the point of a ridge listening to the woods wake up you hear it: that first gobble rolling across the hollow like thunder. It makes the hair on your neck stand on end, no matter how long you've been turkey hunting.

A month later the top of your list may be when you're standing waist-deep in a cold river, the current pushing against your legs, as you stare at a bit of feather and steel as intensely as you've ever looked at anything in your life. You watch it drift next to fluttering mayflies as a shadow surges to the surface and turns into the fist-size head of a brown trout. It inhales your fly, which is always the goal, but when it happens it's always a surprise.

Come fall there is the instant when there was nothing but thick brush and then suddenly, undoubtedly, there's a buck—steam pluming from his nose and the sun glinting off his antlers. Or when a flock of mallards, on a two thousand-mile journey from northern Canada, cups wings and glides in to your decoys.

You can probably conjure up hundreds of these glory moments, but I'll bet some of the things you think of are more mundane. A smushed sandwich pulled from your hunting coat, eaten on a stump and washed down with lukewarm coffee. The bouncing cherry of your buddy's cigar as he launches into his one musky story for the 100th time while you wait for a channel cat to take the bait. Seeing a kid catch a frog with as much enthusiasm as he catches bass. The trembling of your dog right before the hunt. Watching the sun rise and set from the same tree. Staring at the dying flickers of the campfire and waiting to see who will be the first to break the spell, swallow the last mouthful of whiskey, and head to the tent. A good cast. The wind in the pines. The sun on the lake. Fresh snow.

The rewards of hunting, fishing, and camping are endless, and *Field & Stream*'s mission is to make sure you drink deeply from these great activities. *The Total Outdoorsman Manual* is here to help you do that—to learn how to cast a fly line in the wind or set up the perfect camp. To call in a buck or land a truly big fish. Because the more that you can do, the more fun you can have.

This book fulfills this mission the way *Field & Stream* magazine has been doing it every month for over 115 years: by using great writing, photography, art, and design to capture the great big outdoors, the wildlife and wild places, the laughs and the drama, and the knowledge that often only comes from years in the field.

The vast amount of collected knowledge in this book comes from a team with true expertise and experience and the skills to share it. First is the book's editor, T. Edward Nickens, *Field & Stream*'s editor-at-large, who contributed three quarters of the material for this book. He writes the magazine's annual "Total Outdoorsman" cover story, relying on a network of guides across the country and his own deep experience. There isn't much that this outdoorsman can't do. From paddling remote rivers catching walleye or salmon to decoying antelope and chasing rabbits with beagles, Nickens explores every corner of the outdoors and comes back with hard-won knowledge and great stories to share.

Next, is outdoor skills editor Keith McCafferty. If I could pick one person to bring with me into the wilderness it'd be McCafferty. This survival expert could get out of nearly any jam. He's also a great hunter and fishermen and a heck of storyteller, so getting lost with him might actually be kind of fun.

Shooting editors David E. Petzal and Philip Bourjaily are *Field & Stream*'s Total Gun Nuts, and they've forgotten more about rifles, shotguns, and shooting than most people will ever know. John Merwin and Kirk Deeter can catch any fish anywhere on any tackle, and following their advice will put more fish in your boat.

Finally, what turns all this great knowledge into a beautiful book is the vision of our photographers, illustrators, and designers. Many of the stunning images come from photographers Dusan Smetana, Bill Buckley, and Dan Saelinger; the illustrations of Dan Marsiglio make even complicated skills look beautiful.

We hope what you hold in your hands adds up to more than a book. Think of it as a tool that can take you into the backcountry and help you find the great experiences that come from hunting, fishing, and camping. Keep it on hand and return to it often, and I promise you'll always be able to add to your list of favorite moments.

—*Anthony Licata, Editor*
Field & Stream

The Next Level

The deer I remember the most wasn't my first whitetail buck nor my last, and it wasn't a big deer, not by the standard units of measurement: antler size or body weight or a wilderness residence tucked into soaring mountains. It was a 7-point buck dropped with a .30-30 lever-action rifle. My "cowboy gun." But days earlier I'd found the subtle trail that buck used to cross a patch of open woods between a tangled ridge of oaks and pines and a line of bramble thickets along a river. I'd figured out the tree that afforded me the best shot of the crossing, and I'd hiked the three-quarters of a mile through the woods, an hour-and-a-half before sunrise, stopping a few hundred yards downwind to completely change clothes, stowing my sweaty duds in a plastic bag beside a swamp, then dousing myself in scent killer in the dark.

After the deer was down, I dragged it to the riverbank, tied a hind leg to an ironwood sapling, and gutted it. I remember hiking to the barn to retrieve the deer cart—another three-quarters of a mile there, and the same back—and man-handling that deer over cypress knees and muddy bottoms. All told, three miles of hard work for one deer. My arms were shaking when I finally made it back to the truck.

But more than the sight of the buck slipping into the open, or the shot, or the still form on the ground, this is what I most remember: Pushing that deer cart through the woods, stealing glances at the buck's polished antlers and long, muscular back, and revelling in the feeling that I had done this all alone. All by myself. I would haul that deer home and age it for five days, butcher it in the basement, package it in the kitchen. This deer would nourish my family over the next year, and each time I pulled a package of deer meat from the freezer, I would reflect on that feeling I had months earlier, hauling my deer out of the woods. That's what I remember, more than the deer: A sense of confidence and a feeling of competence that I had gone to the woods and pulled it off. Sound crazy? Not to the person who would read this book.

The person who would read this book wants to know that feeling, or loves knowing the feeling that comes from taking their skill level up a notch.

< The author with his daughter, Markie, and son, Jack.

This is the kind of hunter or angler who never wants to be just good enough to just get by in the woods or on the water. They want to have the confidence to go where the trout and elk and deer and bass live, and come home with a trout or elk or deer or bass— or a cherished memory of a wild place.

Because being good enough isn't good enough anymore. Few of us have time to waste. We don't want to lose a fish because we tied a sorry knot. We don't want to lose sleep because we pitched a tent in the wrong place. If you're reading this book, I'm betting that you couldn't care less about being a pretty good angler. Or a decent hunter. Or the kind of camper who gets just a little wet when the storms pound your tent. After all, being pretty handy with survival skills gets you only part of the way back to the truck. Then you die.

We don't think you approach the outdoors with half-hearted enthusiasm. And quite frankly, we aren't so interested in doing things half-way, either. Which is why you hold in your line-cut, wood-singed, blood-stained, and calloused hands a guide to getting you to the next level of outdoorsmanship. This is a mix of timeless skills, from lashing to finding survival water, and ingenious ways to use cutting-edge technology. Can you cast a flyline upside-down? Use a computer to calculate shot range? They'll give you what you need to know to get it done all by yourself.

So what, exactly, is this book? And where did it come from? Most of these skills come from a special cover story published each May in *Field & Stream* called "The Total Outdoorsman," which I've had the enormous good fortune to write, in part or the whole

shooting match, for eight years. Pound for pound— or column inch for column inch—the "Total Outdoorsman" package packs in more know-how, more tricks to more trades, than any other publication out there. Many of those skills come from my own field experiences, but plenty are straight from the mouths of other experts—hunting and fishing guides, survival experts, accomplished hunters from every part of the country, and, of course, other editors and writers for *Field & Stream*.

In some ways, the Total Outdoorsman concept isn't all that new, really. It's just a new way to follow footsteps into the woods and out on the water. After all, most of us have followed a well-defined set of tracks into the places where we hunt and fish and camp. Most of us were blessed with a father, an uncle, a mother, friend—a mentor who showed us

how to launch a boat down a dark, skinny ramp and shoot a rifle and build a fire. Most of us followed someone around a farm pond or squirrel bottom like a puppy dog, hanging on their every word, taking in every movement and gesture.

My mentor was a man named Keith Gleason, and I remember to this day following him in the snow, placing my feet in the dark depressions of his own boots as we tracked a fox that was trailing a rabbit through a chunk of the North Carolina oak woods. I was thirteen years old, Keith was twenty-five, and I would have walked with him across fire and jagged steel knives.

That's how we learned. That's how the spark grew into a passion. There are plenty of mentors still out there, taking their kids or a neighbor's kids or a coworker hunting and fishing. And plenty more

are needed, because no one needs to tell you that this world is changing.

I'd like to think this book is a part of that tradition, that handing down of hard-won experience and know-how. Maybe it's not as alluring as a night by a campfire, or a trout rise, or cathead biscuits and gravy at a deer camp breakfast. But the skills and insights in these pages represent the collected wisdom of some of the best outdoors experts alive in the world today. I've just been lucky enough to follow a few of their tracks.

But there's more to this book than a how-to manual that helps folks learn how to tune lures and patch tents and get home in the dark. We're laying down tracks to follow. If just one kid lies in a bunk-bed late one night—after the homework, of course—and thumbs through these pages to find a tiny spark that lights his eyes and ignites his spirit with a passion for the outdoors, that'd be a legacy to savor, wouldn't it? If just one kid reads about how to catch the biggest trout in the stream or how to make fire in the rain and grows up to lay down tracks for his kids to follow—then this book will have been worth the months of work by a team of editors and writers, and the years of accumulated experience poured between these book covers. One kid who starts following tracks. There could be no better paypack.

Eleven times a year, 1.5 million copies of *Field & Stream* land in mailboxes, bookstores, doctor's offices, country diners, and libraries across the country. On the cover are photographs of deer and bass, elk and trout, mountain men and American presidents. Inside, month to month, readers never know what they're going to get, except they know there will be stories of amazing trips to the far corners of the world and to woodlots just down the

road. There will be honest reports of gear. And there will be sage advice about how to get a deer out of the woods. Or how to paddle a canoe or sharpen a knife or tie a fly for short-striking salmon.

Part of the pleasure of this book, we hope, is like that. Sort of like paddling a winding creek, pleasantly surprised with the view around each bend. While scratching your noggin over the three steps involved in hoisting a heavy food bag or elk quarter out of a bear's reach you might see a quick tip on jump-shooting ducks and think: Hey, maybe I should try that some time. Fine by us.

So coming up are a few more stories, a few more adventures—and nearly 400 ways to make your own outings more adventurous. And fodder for even better stories of your own. Learn them, and you'll catch more fish, down more birds, and build better fires. But more importantly, you'll sit a little taller in the saddle knowing that just getting by just doesn't get it. Not for the kind of person who would read this book.

—*T. Edward Nickens*
Editor-at-Large, Field & Stream

Roughing It

It was at the end of a long, long day of fishing, at the end of a long, long week on the water. For six days we had portaged falls and paddled through rapids as northern Ontario's Allanwater River mutated from gentle stream to wind-frothed lake to plunging whitewater rapids and back again. Cruising through the skeletal forest burns, we'd watched sandhill cranes flying overhead. Rounding walls of lichen-crusted granite, we'd searched for pictographs and trailed a woodland caribou across the river.

Now the northern lights danced above our campsite, sending green and blue waves across a star-spangled black sky. I dragged a canoe to the edge of the water, climbed in, and set it adrift. A loon cried. My stomach bulged with pike and walleye. As I lay in the bottom of the boat, I could hear the purl of distant whitewater, the crackling of our campfire. This was our last night in the woods and every icon of boreal Canada—sky, fish, bird, water— was in cahoots to make it an unforgettable one.

Oddly enough, I've had that very feeling—that this is as good as it gets—many times, in campsites from Canada to Louisiana's Cajun country, from the wild shores of Alaska to the uninhabited barrier island beaches of the Carolina Outer Banks. Pair a hunting or fishing trip with a tent and a sleeping bag, or with a deep-woods cabin whose sooty windows are smudged with wood smoke, and every moment seems to be the best there ever was. Every trip is the trip of a lifetime.

Camping and outdoor sports do share a lot of common ground. Perhaps it's because of history: For untold centuries Native Americans gathered at prime fishing grounds, be they Pacific Northwest salmon rivers or the shad shoals of Southeastern streams. Entire villages struck their tepees and longhouses and wigwams to follow buffalo and elk and geese, a symbiotic migration that was as much about knowing how to pitch a perfect camp as knowing how to shoot a bird with an arrow. Perhaps the connection has to do with the visceral response of the human senses to yellow flames licking at a spitted fish or fowl. Or the fact that the best hunting and fishing frequently occurs in those places far from the madding crowd. Not to mention cell phones.

For a host of reasons, a lot of folks can't conceive of taking a camping trip that doesn't involve a fishing rod. Or a hunting trip that doesn't end with a campfire and a cozy tent or backwoods cabin. If you're camping, you sack out mere steps from the pool where last night's white-fly hatch—and smallmouth bass—roiled the water. In the morning, you can lay out a cast while the coffee perks. I once shot a pair of wood ducks while standing on the

edge of a sandbar campsite in my pajamas, not 15 feet from my frost-covered sleeping bag. You can't do that if you wake up at home.

But there are a lot of ways to go about sleeping on the ground, and not every camping trip requires you to give up all creature comforts. There's no question that backpacking into remote country is the epitome of the wilderness experience. Every decision—where to camp, when to rise, how long to fish, how far to trail the elk—is yours alone. In return for a tacit agreement to work with what the land and the weather offer, you have vespers of firelight and overhead stars. There might be planked salmon for supper and deer loin for breakfast. And then there are the people you meet in the backcountry: If you're lucky, there will be none of them.

Car camping, on the other hand, celebrates the best of both sides of the American travel spectrum—a little bit of Yellowstone, a little bit of Route 66. It's a fine way to find yourself in fish country. And let's be honest: Having a vehicle makes it much easier to restock the potato chip stash. Done well, with enough good-neighborliness and aluminum lawn chairs with dry-rotted seats, car camping is a great way to nudge into wild country.

And then there is *the* camp. The family fish camp. The friend-of-a-friend's hunting camp.

The cabins and cottages at the end of the road, at the edge of the big woods, on the far side of the river. Maybe yours is merely a humble pile of bricks and boards. Maybe yours is a high-dollar getaway. Doesn't matter. What matters is the thing that all great hunting and fishing camps share: an accumulation of legend and lore, dusty window grime, and rusty cans of beans that turns a simple structure into a shrine.

The door's open. Kick off your boots. You must understand: You're walking on sacred ground.

So here's the trick. No matter your preference—whether a flat patch of ground 15 miles in or a deer camp beloved by your daddy and his daddy and his—most campers tend to fall into one of two, shall we say, camps. There is the Good Enough Camper who figures that just getting by is good enough. This type thinks this way: "It's only a couple of nights, so why do I need to pack an extra lighter?" This is the guy who forgets to bring any rope. He's the one whose tent always leaks, and the only thing weaker than his flashlight batteries are his excuses. And to make matters worse, this guy is always borrowing your knife.

And then there's the guy who always seems to have the knots tied correctly and the fire banked properly—just in case. Part of it is knowing how, sure. But a big part of it is appreciating every moment in the woods and on the water as a gift. Who wants to be drying clothes by the fire when the trout are biting? Who wants to miss first light in the elk woods because you couldn't light wet wood? This guy always has the sharp knife. The right knot. The guylines taut as banjo strings. This guy has a name too: the Total Outdoorsman.

I want to be that guy. We all want to be that guy.

—*T. Edward Nickens*

1 PITCH CAMP LIKE A WOLF

Wild animals know how to pick the right spot to sleep. You'll know it, if you know what to look for. The perfect campsite is a blend of the haves and the have-nots. It should have a view that makes you want to leap from the tent and high-five the rising sun. Good water within 100 yards. It should be sheltered from the worst winds but not so cloistered that the skeeters like it, too. Give bonus points for rocks and logs that double as chairs. Double reward miles for a pair of trees that will anchor a tarp. The ground should not be squishy.

The wolf and the dog turn in circles before choosing a bed, possibly to scan for danger, and so should you, at least, metaphorically. Study overhead trees for "widow makers"—the dead branches that could fall during the night and crush or skewer the hapless camper. Pace off the ground that will be under the tent, clear it of rocks and roots, fill the divots with duff. Sleep with your head uphill and your heart filled with gratitude for the call of the cricket and the shuffling sounds of unseen feet beyond the firelight. —T.E.N.

2 MAKE A CAMP COFFEE CUP

Durn. You left your coffee mug at home again. But there's a tall can of beans in the camp cupboard and a hammer and tin snips in the shed. Get to it.

STEP 1 Remove the top of the can. Empty and wash the can.

STEP 2 Make a cut around the can's circumference (a) about 2 inches down; leave a vertical strip of can 1 inch wide.

STEP 3 Tap small folds over the sharp edges. Tamp them down smooth so you won't slice your lips.

STEP 4 Bend the strip down into a handle (b). Smirk at your buddies while you sip. —T.E.N.

3 PUT UP A CAMP GUN RACK

Your guns are unloaded in camp—of course—but that still doesn't mean you want them leaning precariously against trees and walls. You can create an outdoor gun rack in 10 minutes with a sharp knife and two 5-foot lengths of rope.

STEP 1 Find or trim a downed branch about 6 to 7 feet long. It should have numerous smaller branches to serve as barrel stops; cut these to 2-inch lengths.

STEP 2 Select two trees free from branches to head height, about 5 feet apart.

STEP 3 Lash the support branch to the upright trees about 36 inches from the ground.

STEP 4 Institute a rule that all guns in camp must be placed in the camp gun rack. Violations are punishable by dish-washing and firewood-gathering duties. —T.E.N.

tight ring of coals   Dutch oven

6 to 8 coals

FIELD & STREAM CRAZY-GOOD GRUB

4 MAKE A DUTCH OVEN CHICKEN QUESADILLA PIE

Making a one-pot meal in a Dutch oven is a campfire staple: It frees up the cook to sip whiskey and trade stories while pretending to be hard at work. This chicken quesadilla pie serves 10 to 12, and it's as easy as falling off the log you're sitting on while claiming to cook.

INGREDIENTS

5 lb. chicken breasts, cut into stir-fry–size chunks
2 medium sweet yellow onions, chopped
2 green peppers, chopped
1 large yellow squash, cubed
One 19-oz. can enchilada sauce
25 small corn tortillas
2 lb. shredded cheddar or jack cheese
One 16-oz. can corn kernels
One 16-oz. can black beans
3 boxes cornbread mix
3 eggs
1 cup milk

STEP 1 Sauté chicken, onions, green peppers, and squash until chicken is cooked through.

STEP 2 In a 14-inch Dutch oven, layer enchilada sauce, tortillas, cheese, canned ingredients, and cooked chicken-and-vegetables mixture.

STEP 3 Mix cornbread with eggs and milk according to box instructions and spread over the top.

STEP 4 Bake for 1 hour using 6 to 8 coals on the bottom and a tight ring of coals around the top. —T.E.N.

5 LIGHTEN YOUR PACK

2 TO 3 POUNDS Replace your leather wafflestompers with a pair of midcut boots with synthetic uppers.

½ POUND Ditch the flashlight for a lightweight headlamp. Some models offer both a long-burning LED for doing your camp chores and a high-intensity beam for nighttime navigation.

3 POUNDS Trade your tent for a tarp shelter. You can find some that weigh less than 2 pounds.

1 POUND Leave the hatchet at home. Carry a wire saw.

2 POUNDS Cook with an ingenious wood-burning portable stove instead of a gas burner and avoid having to carry fuel.

1 TO 2 POUNDS Pack only two sets of clothes: one for around camp, the other for hunting or fishing.

1 POUND Repack commercial food items in reclosable plastic bags and lightweight water bottles. —T.E.N.

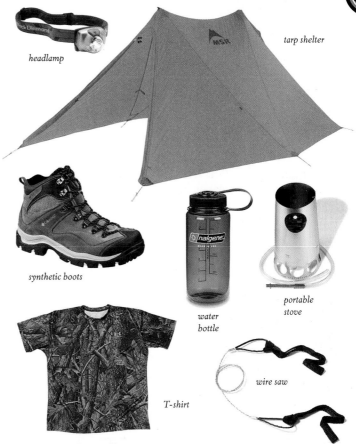

headlamp

tarp shelter

synthetic boots

water bottle

portable stove

T-shirt

wire saw

6 CUT THE CHEESE

Use a 12-inch section of one of the inner strands of parachute cord to slice cheese and salami when you leave your knife at home.
—T.E.N.

7 TIE A CANOE TO YOUR RACKS

To tie down a canoe correctly, follow the rule of twos: two tie-downs across the boat, two bow anchors, and two stern anchors.

STEP 1 Place the boat on the canoe racks upside down and centered fore and aft. Tightly cinch the boat to the racks, using one cam-buckle strap per rack or ⅜-inch climbing rope finished off with a trucker's hitch. Do not crisscross these tie-downs. It's critical to snug the tie-down straps or ropes directly against the gunwales where they cross under the racks.

STEP 2 Run two independent bow anchors by tying two ropes to the bow, and the end of each rope to a bumper or bumper hook. Repeat for stern anchors. Do not use the same rope or strap to create one long V-shaped anchor. Otherwise, if one end comes loose, everything comes loose. Pad these lines wherever they run across a bumper edge.

STEP 3 Test the rig by grabbing the bow and shifting hard left, right, up, and down. You should be able to rock the entire car or truck without shifting the canoe. Do the same for the stern. Repeat after 10 minutes on the road and tighten the rig if needed. —T.E.N.

poll

head

cheek *blade* *edge*

8 SHARPEN A HATCHET OR AXE IN THE FIELD

Assuming that you're savvy enough to have a file and whetstone in the toolbox, here's how to give your axe an edge.

STEP 1 Drive a peg into the ground. Place a wrist-thick stick 4 inches from the peg.

STEP 2 Place the poll of the axe against the peg, resting the cheek of the axe head on the stick so that the bit is very slightly raised. Rasp the file perpendicular to the edge and inward from the cutting edge to prevent burrs. Flip the axe and repeat on the other side.

STEP 3 Finish with a whetstone. Use a circular motion that pushes the stone into the blade. Flip the axe and repeat. —t.e.n.

9 PEE IN A TENT

Nothing says "expert" like answering nature's call inside your tent. (Sorry, ladies. You're on your own here.) Here's the drill.

STEP 1 Roll over on your stomach. Place your pee bottle near the head of your sleeping bag. Sit up on your knees.

STEP 2 Shimmy the sleeping bag down to your knees. Lift one knee at a time and shove the bag below each knee. Your bag should be out of harm's way.

STEP 3 Do your thing. Afterward, thread the cap back on the bottle and store the bottle in a boot so it remains upright. Better safe than soggy. —t.e.n.

10 HANG FOOD FROM A TREE

STEP 1 Tie one end of a 40-foot length of parachute cord to the drawcord of a small stuff sack. Tie a loop in the other end of the cord and clip a small carabiner to it. Fill the sack with rocks and throw it over a branch that's at least 15 feet off the ground (a). Dump the rocks from the sack.

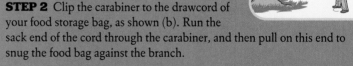

STEP 2 Clip the carabiner to the drawcord of your food storage bag, as shown (b). Run the sack end of the cord through the carabiner, and then pull on this end to snug the food bag against the branch.

STEP 3 Find a sturdy twig and, reaching as high as possible, tie a clove hitch around the twig. Stand on a rock for additional height if possible. Slowly release the rock-sack end of the rope (c). The twig will catch on the carabiner to keep the food bag hanging (d).

STEP 4 When you need to retrieve your food, pull the rope down, remove the twig, and lower the bag. —t.e.n.

11 COOK FISH LIKE AN IRON . . . ER, TINFOIL CHEF

Store-bought reflector ovens work wonders, but they're a little tricky to fit into a fishing vest. All it really takes to turn this morning's fresh catch into a memorable shore meal is a pocketknife and some heavy-duty aluminum foil. Reflector oven cooking is fast because you don't wait for glowing coals. It's easy because you can dress up a trout with whatever herb or spice is at hand. It's tasty because your fish is hot and smoky. And best of all, cleanup is as simple as wadding up the foil.

STEP 1 Cut yourself two branched sticks about 20 inches below the Y. Drive them into the ground at the edge of the fire ring, 18 inches apart. Wrap a 22-inch-long stick with heavy-duty aluminum foil, place it in the forks of the Y-sticks, and unroll foil at a 45-degree angle away from the fire to the ground. Anchor the foil with another stick and unroll a shelf of foil toward the fire. Tear off the foil. Place four dry rocks on the bottom of the shelf. These will hold any baking rack or pan.

STEP 2 To create the oven sides, wrap one of the upright Y-sticks with foil. Unroll the foil around the back of the oven. Tear off the foil. Repeat on the other side. Pinch the two pieces of foil together.

STEP 3 Build a hot fire with flames reaching at least to the top of the foil. You want a tall fire to reflect heat downward from the upper wall of foil. To broil fish, line a baking pan (or simply use the bottom shelf as the baking pan) with onion slices. Add the fillets, seasoned with lemon juice, salt, and pepper. An easy way to punch it up is to slather the fillet with store-bought chipotle sauce. Top with a few more onion slices. Flip once and cook until the fish flakes with a fork. —T.E.N.

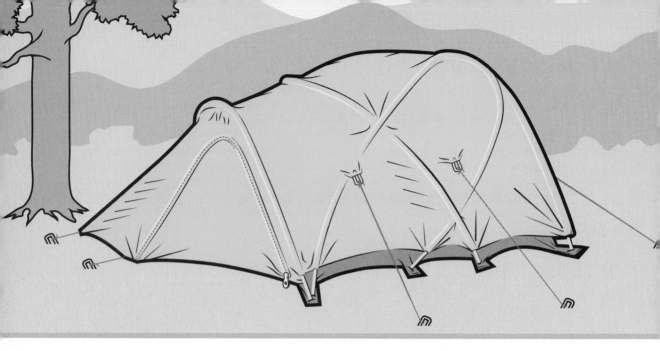

12 RAINPROOF ANY TENT

No matter how much money you doled out for your tent, you still need to take a few steps to make it rainproof. Too many campers fail to properly seal a high-tech shelter's numerous seams and then plop it down on an ill-fitted groundcloth and haphazardly stake out the rain fly. The result: soggy sleeping bags and long, miserable nights. From the floor to the fly, these three simple steps will ensure that you'll stay dry even in a sideways rain. Deal with them now—before the first drops start to land on your head.

SEAL SEAMS Tape-sealed seams, which look as if they have a narrow band of tape sewn in, require no sealing. All others on the floor and the fly do. Pitch the tent, turn the fly upside down, and stake it out tautly to open up the needle holes. Clean the seams with a cotton swab and household alcohol first. Seal tent-floor seams on the inside, so the sealant doesn't abrade off so easily in the field. Apply sealant with even strokes. Let dry for two hours and then reapply.

TIGHTEN LINES A rain fly works best when tightly pitched, but guylines sag in the rain—and you get soaked while retying them in a heavy downpour. To avoid all of this, tie the guylines at home and then use reflective accessory

cord so that the lines are easy to work with in the dark. Attach the guylines to your tent's rain fly with a taut-line hitch knot (see left), which creates an adjustable loop that will allow you to increase tension in a matter of seconds. Be sure to tie the knot at the attachment point to the fly instead of the tent stake. This enables you to adjust the guylines where they attach to the tent, so you won't be stuck scrambling around in the dark trying to find the tent stakes and bent saplings that you used as anchors.

CUSTOMIZE YOUR GROUNDCLOTH In the rain, a groundcloth keeps your tent floor from soaking up water. If the cloth extends beyond the edge of your shelter, however, it catches rain and funnels it beneath your tent. Prevent this by tucking under all protruding edges of the groundcloth. Or better yet, before you leave home, make a custom groundcloth. Set up the tent body (without the fly) on a piece of plastic or waterproof fabric. Stake it out and then trace the outline of the tent with a marker. Strike the tent and cut the plastic 2 inches smaller than the outline. Now no material will stick out from the edges to funnel rain under the floor. —T.E.N.

13 HOIST STEW

One of the classic skills of the backcountry cook is slow-simmering stew in a massive black pot. To do this, you'll need to make a tripod of three poles and cord to hold your kettle over the fire. Place three poles (each roughly 6 feet long) on the ground with two end to end, and the third perpendicular. Tie a clove hitch on the left pole. Wrap seven turns over, under, and around the poles. Finish with another clove hitch. Raising the tripod will tighten the lashings. Now you can start a fire and get that pot of squirrel stew bubbling. —T.E.N.

14 CROSS OBSTRUCTIONS ON A CREEK

Blowdowns and beaver dams are common on many small streams, but they don't have to block your way to the fine fishing and hunting grounds that lie beyond them. Two paddlers in a canoe or johnboat can easily and safely cross such obstacles and stay as dry as toast—if they know how. With a little practice, you can accomplish this maneuver in two minutes or less.

STEP 1 As you approach the fallen log or beaver dam, secure any loose items—fishing rods, guns, daypacks—that will shift as you tilt the craft over the obstacle. If you're not wearing your life jacket, put it on.

STEP 2 Turn the boat parallel to the obstacle. One at a time, each paddler carefully steps out of the boat and onto the dam or log (a). Keeping a hand on the boat aids in stability. If the footing on a blowdown is particularly slippery, try straddling it. In streams with high flow, be very careful not to tilt the boat upstream or the water may catch the gunwale and flip it.

STEP 3 Face each other and then turn the boat perpendicular to the obstacle (b), with the bow between you. Lift the bow onto the log or dam. Work together to pull the boat up and over the obstacle.

STEP 4 Turn the boat parallel to the blowdown or beaver dam and board carefully (c). —T.E.N.

15 DRIVE AN ATV (ALMOST) ANYWHERE

The modern four-wheel all-terrain vehicle (ATV) is a great tool for hunters who want to get far from the pavement. But, as is the case with most tools for hunting, it takes more than a little skill to operate a quad safely. For most hunters, a good dose of common sense goes a long way, but even experienced riders can find themselves in precarious situations. If you go too fast over rough terrain or ask the machine to do something it wasn't designed to do, you're asking for trouble—and it will find you. Learn these five ATV driving skills, and you'll always be in control of your rig whether you're encountering unexpected obstacles or scaling the heights. —P.B.M.

LOAD UP Put oversize cargo—such as a field-dressed deer—on your rear rack, as close to the vehicle's center as possible. Setting a heavy load outside the frame can seriously compromise your ATV's maneuverability.

Once the load is centered, strap it firmly in place; rough ground can cause cargo to shift and impair handling. Use adjustable cargo straps rather than rope. Pick the least aggressive trail for the return trip and take your time getting back to base camp.

If your trophy is heavy enough to lift your quad's front end, forget about carrying it. Your only option is to drag it back to camp behind the machine.

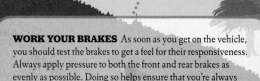

WORK YOUR BRAKES As soon as you get on the vehicle, you should test the brakes to get a feel for their responsiveness. Always apply pressure to both the front and rear brakes as evenly as possible. Doing so helps ensure that you're always able to bring the ATV to a controlled stop.

If you cross through water deep enough to get the brakes wet, proceed with caution. The pads' performance will degrade until they dry. To speed this process, ride your brakes lightly to heat them up.

Fine gravel, mud, and the like can be very hard on your brake components. Rinse your ATV off after long rides to guard against mechanical failures.

RIDE OVER AN OBSTACLE Engage four-wheel drive and put your quad into a low gear. Approach the obstacle at a perpendicular angle and take it slow. Bear in mind that rocks and logs can move as you drive your ATV over them. The idea is to keep the rig balanced so it doesn't tip over. You may need to stand and shift your weight forward or rearward (or to the left or right) to maintain balance and see what's ahead of you as you're passing over the obstacle.

CLIMB A STEEP HILL Newer quads are climbing marvels, but that doesn't mean you can forget common sense. When a steep hill looms, engage the lowest gear in four-wheel drive that's still capable of generating steady forward momentum.

Approach the hill straight on, stand, and move your weight as far forward as you possibly can without losing contact with the handlebar and foot controls. Cresting a sharp incline requires momentum, and that means speed. At the same time, you don't want to goose the throttle halfway up. This can cause the wheels to spin, leading to a loss of control. If you can't make it up the hill safely, hit your brakes and set the parking brake. Carefully get off your quad and walk the rest of the way up the hill.

Anytime you sense that your ATV wants to take a tumble—whether heading up- or downhill—simply get off and let it go. It's not fun watching your machine roll down a slope, but it sure beats the alternative—you rolling with it.

DESCEND A STEEP HILL Steep declines demand extreme caution. If a hill is both steep and muddy, you should just find an alternate route.

Downshift to your lowest gear in four-wheel drive. This way, the engine and transmission will help slow the ATV as you travel. You want to avoid stomping on the brakes, to avoid the risk of locking them up. If the brakes lock up, that can cause a slide and loss of control. The idea is to feather your brakes intermittently—just enough to keep the descent safe and under your control.

Approach the drop head on. Lean as far back as you can while remaining in reach of your brakes; this weight shift helps keep rear wheels on the ground. Point your quad directly downhill. Turning off to the side could cause a rollover.

16 RATION AND REUSE FISH-FRYING OIL

You can reuse fish-frying oil several times during the same camping trip if you carefully strain it after cooking. Just carry an empty container the same size as the original oil bottle. After you fry the day's catch, let the oil cool, then strain it through a coffee filter into the empty container. After the next night's fish fry, filter the oil again by pouring it through another clean coffee filter into the original bottle. You can repeat the process several times. —T.E.N.

17 TIE A BOWLINE KNOT

Forced to limit themselves to a single knot, most experts would choose the bowline (pronounced BOH-luhn), which is often called the King of Knots. The bowline has several magical properties. It is jam proof—meaning it unties easily no matter what kind of load it has been subjected to—and it is very secure. It also can be tied one-handed, making it the knot of choice should you find yourself adrift in the water with an unconscious buddy to rescue. A running bowline (a bowline in which you simply pull the standing end of the line back through the finished knot) creates a noose suitable for snaring game. Still, the real reason to learn it is that to seamen, fire and rescue personnel, and others who live and die by the rope, all humanity can be divided into those who know how to tie a bowline and those who don't. And it's always better to be on the side that's in the know.

STEP 1 Remember the phrase: *"The rabbit comes out of the hole, runs around the tree, and goes back in the hole."* Make an overhead loop in your rope (the rabbit hole) and pull the working end (the rabbit) through the loop from the underside.

STEP 2 Circle that working end behind the rope above the loop (the tree), and then back through it.

STEP 3 Pull to tighten. —B.H.

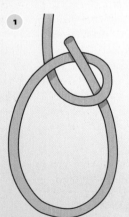

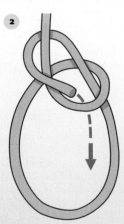

18 SEASON A DUTCH OVEN

Dutch ovens can be hung over an open fire, buried in a pit of coals, and perched atop a gas grill or electric range. In the same Dutch oven you can fry fish, cook bacon, bake biscuits, and turn out the best apple fritters in the world. And absolutely nothing surpasses a Dutch oven for a lot of game cooking.

The secret is in the famous black pot patina. The surface of cast iron is rough and porous and will rust quickly. Seasoning a Dutch oven gives it a rust-proofing, nonstick, and flavor-enhancing coating that works better the more you use the pot.

DRIVE THE WATER OUT Preheat a kitchen oven to 450 degrees F. Wash the Dutch oven with soapy, hot water, and rinse well. Put it in the oven for ten minutes.

BAKE THE FINISH ON Remove the Dutch oven and let it cool. Turn your kitchen oven down to 300 degrees F. Now, grease the entire Dutch oven inside and out, including any and all lids and handles, with a light coating of cooking oil. Place it back in the oven for an hour. Crack a few kitchen windows and turn all smoke detectors off. It's going to smoke and smell like burned metal. Don't worry.

FINISHING TOUCH Remove the Dutch oven and let it cool. Wipe away excess grease. Store with a paper towel inside. A newly seasoned Dutch oven will sport a shiny caramel color that turns black with use, especially if you cook bacon in it the first few times. —T.E.N.

19 CRAP LIKE A CAT

Only a pure jackass leaves toilet paper on the ground. Dealing with human waste in the woods is easy. Do it right every time by burying your poop in a cathole.

STEP 1 Select a spot at least 70 paces from the nearest water source. Open sun is best because it speeds decomposition. Use the heel of your boot to kick out a hole 6 to 8 inches deep and 4 to 6 inches in diameter.

STEP 2 No need for details about this step.

STEP 3 Use a stick to mix your output with soil to give decomposing bacteria a jump start.

STEP 4 Deal with the toilet paper. According to the organization Leave No Trace, "burying toilet paper in a cathole is not generally recommended." That leaves three choices: Carry it out (can you say double-wrap?); burn it (with a stick, put all the used toilet paper in the cathole, ignite it, and then fill the cathole with water); or bury it anyway—just tamp it down in the bottom of the cathole.

STEP 5 Fill the hole with dirt and camouflage it with leaves and brush. It takes 30 seconds to render a cathole invisible. —T.E.N.

20 CUT PARACHUTE CORD WITH FRICTION

No knife? No problem. Tie the piece of parachute cord to be cut to two stout points—trees, truck bumpers, whatever. Leave plenty of slack. Take another few feet of cord (or the end of the line you're cutting if it's long enough) and place the middle of it over the piece of parachute cord to be cut. Grasp each end of this second piece firmly, and saw back and forth. Friction will melt the parachute cord right where you want it cut. —T.E.N.

21 TIE A BUTTERFLY LOOP

Tie this loop in the running part of a line and use it to hang gear, as a ladder step, or make a canoe bridle to tow a canoe behind a boat.

STEP 1 Hang a rope from your hand and coil it twice to form three coils (a). Move the right coil to the left, over the middle coil (b). The center coil now becomes the right coil.

STEP 2 Move this coil to the left over the top of the other two coils (c).

STEP 3 Take the coil you just moved to the left and pass it back to the right, under the remaining coils, to form a loop (d).

STEP 4 Pinch this loop against your palm, using your thumb to hold it. Slide your hand to the right, pulling this loop (e). Tighten the knot by pulling both ends of the rope (f). —T.E.N.

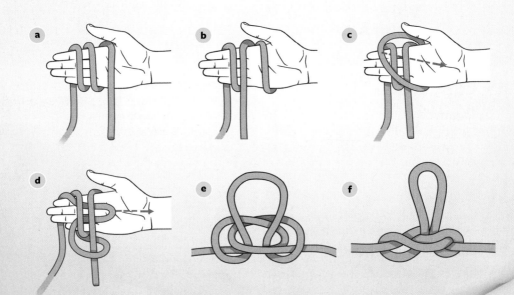

22 MAKE A WICKED SLINGSHOT

Slingshot aficionados turn out sturdy handmade models capable of firing heavy slugs at 225 feet per second—fast enough to take game from squirrels to wild turkeys to ducks on the wing. Here's the drill on crafting the world's most awesome slingshot.

THE FRAME Dogwood, hickory, and oak will make the best frames. You don't have to look for the perfect Y-shaped fork. The typical right-hander will hold the slingshot in the left hand, so look for a fork where the main branch crooks to the left at 30 degrees or so, but a fork goes off to the right at about a 45-degree angle. Cut the frame and let it dry for three weeks.

THE POWER A number of companies sell ready-made replacement bands for slingshots. The trick lies in a strong connection. An inch and a half from the top of each slingshot "arm," drill a hole slightly smaller in diameter than the replacement band. Bevel the end of the band with scissors and thread it through the hole—a pair of hemostat clamps will make this easier. Snip off the bevel. Next, take a dried stick slightly larger in diameter than the inside diameter of the tubing and carve two half-inch-long stoppers to a point. Plug each the end of the tubing with a stopper. —T.E.N.

Dutch oven   layer of dirt

hot coals   length of chain

FIELD & STREAM CRAZY-GOOD GRUB

23 DIG A BEAN HOLE

Digging a bean hole is a storied tradition in the North Woods, but there's no reason you can't do it anywhere. The wood smoke and molasses flavors in this bean dish can't be duplicated any other way.

INGREDIENTS

10 cups dried Great Northern or yellow-eyed beans
1 lb salt pork, cut into 2-inch strips
2 large onions, diced
2½ cups molasses
4 tsp. dry hot mustard
2 tsp. black pepper
½ cup butter

STEP 1 Dig a hole that's twice as deep as and one foot in diameter larger than the Dutch oven you're planning to use. Next, toss a few rocks or a length of chain into the bottom of the hole. Fill the hole with hardwood and then burn the wood down until the hole is three-quarters full of hot coals.

STEP 2 Over your open fire (or on a camp stove), precook the beans by slow-boiling them for about 30 minutes. Drain and set aside.

STEP 3 Place the salt pork in the Dutch oven, layer onions on top, and pour in the beans, molasses, mustard, and black pepper. Slice the butter and place on top. Add enough boiling water to cover the beans by ½ to 1 inch. Cover the pot with aluminum foil and then the lid.

STEP 4 Shovel out about a third of the coals and put the bean pot in the hole. Replace the coals around the sides and on top of the oven; fill the rest of the hole with dirt. Cooking time varies, but give it a good 8 hours.

—T.E.N.

24 SIPHON GAS THE SAFE WAY

This method relies on physics to work. You need 6 feet of clear tube, a clean container for the gas, and possibly something to stand on.

STEP 1 Run the hose into the gas tank until the end of it is submerged. Blow gently into the hose and listen for gurgling noises to know you've found the liquid.

STEP 2 Form a loop in the tubing with the bottom touching the ground and the end rising to a level higher than the gas in the tank. Here's where something to stand on helps.

STEP 3 As you gently suck on the hose, watch the gas move to the bottom of the loop and start to rise. Stop sucking at this point; the gas should now come to the level of gas in the tank on its own.

STEP 4 Stick the tube's free end into a container and then slowly lower it to the ground. When you have enough, raise the container to a level higher than the gas tank. Remove the hose from the container and straighten it so excess gas reenters the tank. —T.E.N.

---

25 TWIST UP A CONSTRICTOR KNOT

Easy to tie and extremely reliable, the constrictor knot is one of the most useful knots on earth. It exerts a ratchetlike grip on any curved surface, such as a post, rail, tree, or human appendage. You can use it to close the mouths of food bags and gear bags large and small; make a whipping in string around the end of a larger rope, preventing the latter from fraying; secure a rod tube to a backpack; and fashion a string leash for your eyeglasses. Tie it around the snout of a bear after placing a hardwood stick through the jaws behind the fangs, and, with a noose over the nose and around the ends of the stick, you can tote the critter without ruffling its fur. To hang camp tools, file a rough groove in each tool's handle, tie a constrictor hitch around it, and then knot together the ends of the cord. The constrictor's virtues are, alas, also its only vice: It is not easily untied. Then again, it won't come undone accidentally, either.

STEP 1 Make a simple loop, crossing the working end of the rope over the other.

STEP 2 Circle the working end behind the item you're tying up then pass it under the standing end and under your "X."

STEP 3 Pull both ends to constrict. —B.H.

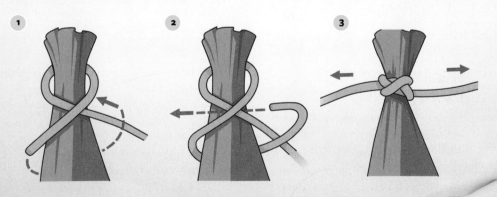

26
CLEAR A DOWNED TREE WITH A CHAIN SAW

Before attempting to buck a fallen tree, take time to figure out the binding pressures. Next, clear out any saplings or branches that the downed tree has fallen on; these can spring up forcefully when pressure is released. Stand on the uphill side of the tree and come prepared with a few plastic wedges to keep the chain-saw bar from binding.

TREE FLAT ON THE GROUND Cut from the top. Don't let the chain touch the ground, which dulls the blade and can send shrapnel flying. Cut partway through the log, then either roll it to continue or lever it up from the bottom and shim it with a piece of wood.

TREE SUPPORTED AT ONE END Make an initial cut from the bottom up, about one-third of the log's diameter. Finish with a second cut from the top down to meet the first.

TREE SUPPORTED AT BOTH ENDS Make the first cut from the top down. Watch for binding, use wedges if need be. Then cut from the bottom up. —T.E.N.

27
MAKE WATERPROOF MATCHES

To make your own waterproof matches, use clear nail polish instead of paraffin wax. Nail polish is more durable and won't gunk up the match striker.

STEP 1 Fill a soft-drink bottle cap with nail polish (a).

STEP 2 Dip each match head into the polish (b) and then lay the match on the tabletop with its head extending off the edge (c). Repeat.

STEP 3 Once the polish has dried, hold each match by the head and dip the entire remaining wooden portion of the match into the nail polish bottle (d).

STEP 4 Place matches on wax paper to dry. —T.E.N.

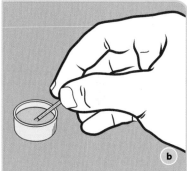
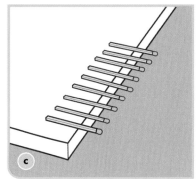
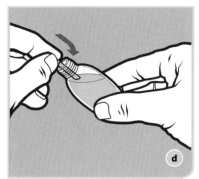

28
BREAK WIND LIKE A COMMANDO

The occasional bout of morning thunder is as much a part of deer camp as five-card stud. Foster a universally appreciated rip with a combination of nuance and nerve.

AMBUSH Approach your pals with detached nonchalance and let fly with a drive-by toot. Go easy on the volume and vacate the premises promptly.

CAMO JOB Get the wind moving. Ruffle papers, stand by a fan. Light a cigar.

BLAME GAME Don't draw attention to yourself. Try a slight turn of the head and a softly muttered oath, followed by a rhetorical "Someone need a little private time?"

JUST THE TWO OF US If you're stuck in a car or tent with just one pal, name it and claim it, buddy. Be loud. Be proud. —T.E.N.

29 STAY WARM ON A COLD NIGHT

Take care of your bag: Each morning, spread your sleeping bag out in the sun to dry accumulated moisture. At day's end, fluff it up to restore its full loft as soon as you put up the tent. A half hour before bedtime, toss a bottle of heated water into the foot of your bag.

IN THE SACK You'll regret that last mug of coffee during your 2 A.M. bladder dash. Eat a snack to generate body heat from digestion and warm up with a few jumping jacks. Pee right before you get into the tent. Zip your jacket around the foot of your sleeping bag. Sleep with your face exposed to reduce moisture accumulation from your breath.

IF YOU WAKE UP ANYWAY If you wake up cold, eat a small snack. If you have to go, go. Your body is wasting precious heat keeping all that liquid warm. Guys, you did remember the pee bottle, right? (Again, sorry, ladies.) —T.E.N.

F&S Field Report: HEAVEN ON EARTH

You've got to want to be here bad, to be here at all.

Since 1929, four generations of mostly Michigan hunters have trekked to Drummond Island's back-of-beyond Stevens Recreational Camp. First, they drive across the Mackinac Bridge, with Lake Huron to the right, Lake Michigan to the left. Then it's 60 miles to the eastern tip of the Upper Peninsula. Grab a ferry to Drummond Island and drive some more. Leave the hardtop maybe 8 miles west of the Canada border, then both hands on the wheel: Seven miles of logging road. One mile of rough trail through cedar thicket and birch woods, barely wide enough for a truck with the mirrors pulled in. For miles the woods are dark and deep. Then suddenly, an opening. There's a buck pole lashed to a pair of trees. Stacks of firewood. Kettle grills. A rough camp clinging to the edge of a cedar swamp. A welcoming curl of woodsmoke.

"It's agony to get here," says camp patriarch Ham Peltier. "But it's the Garden of Eden once you make it."

Peltier should know. He's hunted these big north woods for more than half of his 80 years. He knows all the places you'll never find on a map, but only in the memory of a Stevens Camp member. Pork Chop Hill and Slaughter Valley and the Cathedral. The Stone Pile, which is not to be confused with the Pile of Stones, which is not so far from the Stone in the Path. He knows every blind. Bear Den. The Office. The Boardroom. The Dumpster. And Ham's Perch, where Peltier has hunted for decades.

Peltier is the link to the deer camp's past. He remembers the sound of a sledgehammer banging an old tire rim that hung from a tree, a gong that brought home lost hunters. He remembers when you had to walk the last five miles in.

Things have changed a bit in recent years. These days, poker is played under propane lights. A small television and toaster run off car batteries. "Those old guys would turn over in their graves at all this newfangled stuff," says Chuck Decker, another steady hand at Stevens Camp. But this is hardly the Hilton. No showers. Brush your teeth with hot water heated in an old bean can. Ten bunks shoved into a bunkroom the width of a johnboat. A two-holer out back. "You love it or you hate it," Decker says. "There's no middle ground."

And they love it. To a man. Don Franklin is dressed in red and green wool plaid. He wears L.L. Bean boots. His belt holds an Old Timer sheath knife, 20 rounds of .30-06 ammo in a battered leather shell case, and an ancient Marble's No. 5 hatchet. He can show you the bones of the blind that his daddy hunted for 70 years.

"All year long," he says, small eyes misting, "a part of me never leaves this place." This is deer camp.

—T. Edward Nickens
Field & Stream, "Welcome to Deer Camp," October 2009

30 OPEN A BREW WITH A BLADE

With practice, you can open a beer bottle by slicing off the neck with a single blow from a cleaver, but there's an easier and much safer method. Hold the neck of the bottle tightly, with the top of your hand just under the bottom of the cap. Place the back of your knife blade across the top of the third knuckle of your index finger and wedge it under the edge of the cap. Pry up. —K.M.

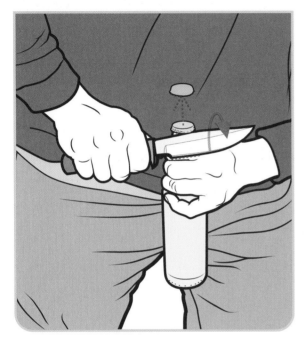

31 BUILD FOUR COOKING FIRES

In the same way that the proper ingredients make a recipe work, the right fire makes the cooking come together. The best backcountry camp cooks match the blaze to the dish. Here's how.

TEPEE FIRE If you need a steady, hot source of heat for a reflector oven or for roasting meat on a skewer, build a tepee fire of standing lengths of wood. Tall flames will produce the high-level heat required for even cooking. Keep plenty of small and medium-size pieces of wood ready to add to the fire for temperature regulation.

PINWHEEL FIRE To fry fish, you'll want a relatively small-diameter blaze closer to the ground, and one with precise temperature control. A pinwheel fire does the trick, with 1- to 2-inch-diameter sticks of firewood laid out in a starburst pattern. Build it inside a ring of rocks or logs to hold the frying pan and feed the fire with dry wood to keep the oil roiling.

LOG CABIN FIRE The log cabin fire is made of crosshatched logs. This arrangement provides lots of air circulation and plenty of wood surface for an even blaze. The result is a quick supply of cooking coals for a Dutch oven or foil-wrapped game.

KEYHOLE FIRE Multitask with a keyhole fire. Build a rock firepit in the shape of a keyhole. In the round part, build a tepee fire, whose tall flames provide both heat and light. In the narrow end, build a log cabin fire between the rock supports. The tepee will provide a constant source of coals once the log cabin fire burns down. —T.E.N.

32 WHITTLE A WHISTLE OUT OF A STICK

Cut and peel the bark from a finger-length section of any stick with a soft pith, such as elder. Next, use a thin twig to bore out this pith, leaving a hollow cylinder (a). Cut a notch near one end (b). Whittle a smaller piece of wood that will fit snugly into the notch end and then slice a little off the top of that plug to allow for the passage of air (c). Fit the plug into the cylinder, trimming the end to shape (d). Place your finger in the other end and blow into the mouthpiece to force the air over the notch in the top of the whistle. When you get a clear whistle, the plug is well fitted. Permanently plug the end with a short piece of wood (e). —K.M.

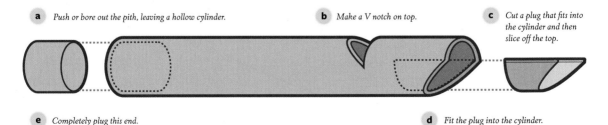

a Push or bore out the pith, leaving a hollow cylinder.

b Make a V notch on top.

c Cut a plug that fits into the cylinder and then slice off the top.

e Completely plug this end.

d Fit the plug into the cylinder.

33 CREATE SHELTER WITH A TARP

If you have two utility tarps with grommeted edges, you can create the Taj Mahal of shelters, complete with a handy campfire vent hole.

STEP 1 Look for four trees in a rectangle and a fifth located between two of the others on the short side.

STEP 2 Tie a tarp between the four trees. The back edge should be about 3 feet off the ground, with the forward edge as high as you can reach. Call this the lower tarp.

STEP 3 Now tie the upper tarp in place. Be sure that you position it so that it slides under the forward edge of the lower tarp by a couple of feet. Once it's in place, tie the side grommets together so that you create an open flap in the middle of the two tarps.

STEP 4 Tie a guyline from the middle of the back edge of the lower tarp to the fifth tree, cinching it tight. You now have a smoke vent.

STEP 5 Build a fire with a stacked-log back wall, and smoke will rise to the tarp roof and exit through the hole that you've created. —T.E.N.

34 BUILD A FIRE FOR MAXIMUM COOKING COALS

The perfect call, the perfect shot, your bull quarters are hanging like clean laundry, and it's time to eat. Don't blow it by rushing the fire. Building the perfect grilling fire takes about 45 minutes, but the results definitely make it worth the effort. Follow the steps below to be sure of success.

STEP 1 Look for woody debris in the form of dead lower limbs on standing lodgepole and whitebark pine trees. When choosing limbs to break off, look for those with plenty of brown needles still attached. Once you have enough, pile them up in the fire pit. The needles will serve as tinder, the twigs as kindling, and the branches are the beginning fuel to get your fire going.

STEP 2 You'll need 4 to 6 inches of glowing coals, so pile on the pine. Forgo the tepee-style fire for a crisscross log cabin setup that allows more air to circulate around larger pieces of wood. Burn pieces that are 4 to 6 inches in diameter and short enough so that each chunk of wood burns in its entirety at the same rate.

STEP 3 As the last of the pine flames die down to coals, it's time to pile on dead aspen limbs. These should be about 20 inches long and 3 to 4 inches in diameter. Once they burn down to coals, and no flames are visible, slap on the steaks. The aspen smoke turns a good elk steak into a meal to remember. —T.E.N.

35 BUTCHER A WET LOG

Forget searching for tinder fungus and belly-button lint to start your fire. With a hatchet, you can render fire-starting scrap from a wet log.

STEP 1 Find a solid log no more than 10 inches in diameter. A coniferous wood like pine or cedar works best due to its flammable resin. Cut a 12-inch section from the log.

STEP 2 Split the log into quarters. Lay one quarter on the ground, bark side down. Score the edge with two 1-inch-deep cuts, 4 inches apart (a). Shave thin 4-inch-long dry wood curls and splinters (b). Pound these curls with the back of the hatchet to break up the wood fibers and then rub some of these between your palms to separate the fibers further. This is your tinder; you'll need two handfuls.

STEP 3 Split pencil-size pieces from the wedge corners of a remaining quarter. Break these into 6-inch pieces for kindling.

STEP 4 Continue to split the quarters, utilizing the innermost and driest pieces. Use these as small and large pieces of fuel. —T.E.N.

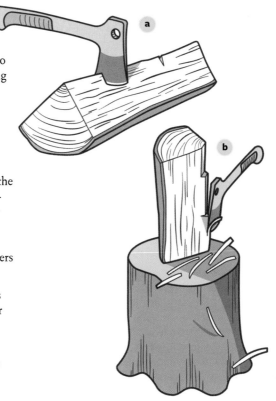

36 RECOVER A STUCK VEHICLE

Two difficult tasks await: summoning the courage to ask for help and getting your rig out of the soup without trashing the frame or maiming a bystander. You're on your own for getting help, but here's the step-by-step to follow once you do.

STEP 1 Clear the area around the wheels and differentials and then shovel out a trench in front of the wheels in the direction you need to move.

STEP 2 Shove floor mats, sticks, or sand under the wheels to give your vehicle traction.

STEP 3 Attach the tow strap to tow hooks, holes in the frame, or receiver hitches of your vehicle—and then to the other vehicle. Avoid attaching the strap to axles or anything else that moves. Don't use a trailer hitch ball as a recovery point. Share the tow load by using two tow points if possible.

STEP 4 Put both vehicles in four-wheel drive low, slowly pull out the slack in the strap, and bump up the RPMs in each vehicle. Pull in as straight a line as possible. If this doesn't work, have the tow vehicle back up a few feet and get a rolling start at 3 mph. —T.E.N.

37 CHOOSE THE RIGHT KNIFE

No other tool is called upon to perform as many tasks, in as many ways, under as many conditions, as the knife. It can take a life and save one. Cut cord, open the belly of an elk, help spark a fire, and skin a fish. A good knife is a tool, an icon, a symbol of its bearer's take on what it takes to live well in the woods. And the know-how to use a sharp blade never goes out of style. —T.E.N.

SPINE The back of the blade, most often unsharpened and unground. A thick spine gives a knife strength.

JIMPING Corrugated grooves in the blade spine, choil, or handle for increased grip and a no-slip feel.

THUMB RAMP An elevated hump on the spine of the blade near the handle. It provides increased control of the knife and reduced forearm fatigue during periods of extended use.

CHOIL The unsharpened edge of the blade between the end of the handle and the beginning of the edge bevel. Many knives have a finger indent at the choil to aid in choking up on the blade.

BELLY The curved arc as the sharpened edge nears the blade tip. A knife with a lot of belly will have a sagging, swooping profile, perfect for the sweeping cuts needed to skin big game.

RICASSO The shank of the blade between the handle and the beginning of the sharpened edge. The ricasso often carries the maker's identifying mark, or "tang stamp."

THUMB HOLE OR STUD A hole in the spine or a stud that protrudes from the blade of a folding knife near the handle and allows the user to open the knife one-handed.

GRIND The finished shape of the blade when viewed in cross section. There are two basic grinds. Hollow-grind blades have a concave shape and are easily sharpened, but tend to hang up in deep cuts. Flat-grind blades taper evenly from the spine to the cutting edge and hold an edge well.

FIXED BLADE KNIVES are inherently strong due to the tang, the extension of the blade that carries into the knife handle. Also called sheath knives, fixed blades are easy to clean and quick to put into action. They have no moving parts to break or gunk up with hair, blood, or grit. And the sleek lines of a fixed blade knife speak to the essence of outdoors competence—simple elegance and deadly efficiency.

FOLDING BLADE KNIVES can be smaller and easier to carry than fixed blade models. Larger folding blades with pocket clips and strong locking mechanisms are hugely popular. Many are designed to be opened with one hand through the use of a thumb stud or blade hole, and some are built with assisted-opening devices that propel the blade into a fixed position after the user opens it partway.

THE SHAPE OF THINGS THAT CUT

The shape of a blade determines how well that blade will perform specific tasks.

FILLET A thin, flexible blade allows the fillet knife to be worked over and around bones and fins.

CLIP POINT The classic general-use blade in which the spine of the blade drops in a concave curve to the tip (the "clip") to make a strong piercing point with a slightly upswept belly.

DROP POINT A downward convex curve along the blade spine forms a lowered point, which keeps the tip from cutting into an animal's organs during field dressing.

SKINNER The full curving knife belly is perfect for long, sweeping motions, such as skinning big game.

CAPER A short, pointed blade with a slightly downturned tip is easy to control in tight spots, such as removing the cape from an animal's head.

RECURVE The slight S-shaped belly forces the material being cut into the sharp edge. Recurves can be designed into most blade profiles.

CAMP WITHOUT A TENT

dern tent rain flies can double as tarps, but
othing wrong with a standard tarp as long
e-tie guy lines and follow this routine.

PREP AT HOME Attach two 18-inch guylines to each corner of the tarp. Attach 12-inch guylines to all other grommets. In the tarp's stuff sack, stash a 50-foot length of parachute cord for a ridgeline, another 10 sections of cord cut to 20-foot lengths for extra grommet ties, and 12 tent stakes in case there are no trees.

IN THE FIELD Once you're out in the woods, all your prep pays off. To create your lean-to-style shelter, start by tying a ridgeline to two trees. To attach the tarp, wrap one corner guyline clockwise a half-dozen times around the ridgeline and wind its mate counterclockwise a half-dozen times in the opposite direction. Connect them with a shoelace knot. Stretch the tarp out and repeat on the opposite corner. Tie the remaining guylines along this edge to the ridgeline. Stake out the back and sides. Erect a center pole to peak the tarp so the rain runs off. —T.E.N.

39 FELL A TREE WITH A KNIFE

A knife isn't as good as an axe in the backcountry. But when you're lost in the woods and it's your only friend, you can do a lot with a sturdy sheath knife—including felling a tree for a wickiup frame or firewood.

STEP 1 FROE AND MALLET Using a stout fixed-blade knife, hold the blade horizontally against the tree, with the cutting edge pointing slightly downward. With a heavy stick, pound the blade into the trunk. Remove the blade, and make another cut with the blade turned slightly upward to remove a wedge of wood.

STEP 2 ROUND AND ROUND You need to completely girdle the tree this way. Don't bend it over until the cuts go all the way around, or you'll splinter the wood, which makes it harder to cut.

STEP 3 PUSH AND SHOVE Once you've cut all the way around, give the trunk a shove. If it doesn't budge, remove more wedges. —T.E.N.

40 TRUCKER'S HITCH

It's far better to learn how to tie a few knots with (literally) your eyes closed than to kinda-sorta know a bunch. Here is one to add to the basics—the trucker's hitch. This knot will secure a canoe to a car, tighten a tarp, and truss a dozen rods into a tidy bundle. It's one of the best knots out there.

STEP 1 Tie a quick-release loop above any tie-down point, such as a canoe rack.

STEP 2 Run the end of the line around the tie-down and back up through the quick-release loop.

STEP 3 Cinch it down tight and finish with two half hitches.

STEP 4 Pull to tighten. —T.E.N.

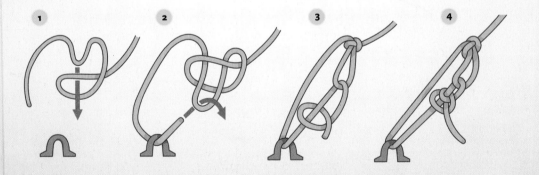

41 ANCHOR A TENT IN THE SAND

It's always been a challenge to anchor a tent or tarp on beaches, river sandbars, and other places where standard tent stakes won't hold. The solution: Bag it. Fill garbage bags or empty stuff sacks with sand, tie a knot in each bag's opening, and then tie the tent's stake loops and rain fly guylines to the bags. If you're expecting high winds, burying the bags will provide a rock-solid stake point. To help batten down the hatches, add a few small sandbags along the inside tent edges. —T.E.N.

42 ROCK THE PERFECT CAMP STORY

All good stories begin with a variation of "This is no bull," followed by "There we were..." It is essential that you cultivate an ally who will back up your stories in return for your supporting his. You may have no idea what the hell he's talking about, but if your ally says that the deer was 300 yards away when he took the shot and asks for confirmation, you say: "It was every inch of 300 yards. I'd say closer to 350." Your ally, in return, will help you push the deer that got away well into the Pope and Young Club category.

THE WEATHER SHOULD BE MISERABLE
For hunting, arctic is preferred: well below freezing, winds strong enough to bend trees nearly horizontal. For fishing, think equatorial: above 90 degrees F, merciless sun and oppressive humidity, without even a single breath of wind.

ACT RELUCTANT TO TELL YOUR BEST YARNS
Remember: Stories are what you tell about yourself; legends are the stories others tell when you're not around. When someone other than your ally says, "Tell these guys about the time you had to hang upside down from a limb to get a clear bow shot at that monster muley in Utah," you'll know you have achieved immortality. —B.H.

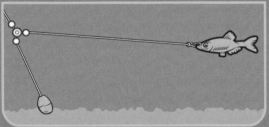

43 CATCH FISH AT YOUR CAMPSITE

In many parts of the country, bush hooking is a revered tradition. Using small boats and canoes, anglers rig a number of setlines to limbs overhanging the stream. For hunters and anglers camping on or near moving water, a bush hook is a fine way to fill a frying pan while attending to camp chores or chasing other fish and game. (Remember: You should check local regulations concerning unattended lines.)

Start by finding a stout sapling or limb that extends over the water a few feet upstream of a desired fishing location. Good bets are strong eddy lines, tributary outfalls, and deep holes beneath undercut banks. To set up the bush hook, attach a three-way swivel to 30- to 50-pound monofilament. Tie one dropper line to an egg sinker and another to the hook. Fasten the main line to the sapling or branch, load the hook with a bait that will hold up to strong current—cut bait, live shiners, shrimp—and drop it into the water. You'll want to check it every couple of hours. And be sure to remove it when you break camp. —T.E.N.

44 BE A BACKCOUNTRY BARISTA

Old-time cowboys wanted it thick enough to float a pistol and black as roofing tar. Here are three ways to brew the good stuff when you're miles (thank your lucky stars) from Starbucks.

RUGGED True cowboy coffee is as simple as you can get. To make it, bring 2 quarts of water to a slow boil in a coffee pot. Remove it from the heat and add two handfuls of coffee, ground medium fine. Steep for 4 minutes. Settle the grounds with a splash of cold water or hold the coffeepot handle with a serious grip and sling it once in an overhead circle. Some folks insist on adding crushed eggshells to settle the grounds.

REFINED A battered campfire percolator is a badge of honor, despite the fact that many coffee snobs snub the device because you have to boil the coffee. The secret is to use coarse-ground coffee and minimize boiling time. Use 1 to 1½ tablespoons of coffee for each 6-ounce cup and remove the percolator from the heat source as soon as the coffee color in the glass top meets your approval.

DANG-NEAR-FANCY Use a French press mug to brew seriously good backcountry joe the easy way. You can find 16-ounce presses that are perfect for camping. Pour 5 tablespoons of medium-ground coffee into the press, add 16 ounces of boiling water, and put on the top. Wait 3 to 4 minutes, slowly press the plunger to the bottom of the mug, and try not to smirk while you suck it down. —T.E.N.

45 SPEAK KNOT

Toss around some nifty rope-work lingo to assure bystanders that you're a knothead of the first order. The *bitter end*, *tag end*, or *working end* is the end of the line that is being used to tie the knot. The *standing end* is the other end. A *bight* is a doubled section of rope that doesn't cross over itself. A *loop* is a bend in the rope that does. And a knot is, alas, not always just a knot. A *bend* is a knot that joins two lines together. A *hitch* is a knot that attaches a line to a rail, post, or another line. —T.E.N.

46 SHARPEN A KNIFE WITH A WHETSTONE

Stroking a knife blade against a whetstone is the most traditional sharpening method. With a flat stone—medium grained (300 grit) on one side and fine grained (600 grit) on the other—you can maintain a fair edge on a knife using spit to grease the stone and eyeballing a 20- to 30-degree angle, just the way Grandpa did. You'll get a more even edge by using a good-quality honing oil instead of just water to wet the stone and by wedging a coin or two under the spine of the blade to help establish the proper angle for sharpening before you start.

GET THE ANGLE With the whetstone in a vise, place one or two coins under the blade to establish the angle. Then remove the coins and sharpen at that angle. You can easily damage your stone if you keep the coins under the blade while sharpening.

SWEEP THE STONE Slide the knife across the stone in an arc, using even pressure. Use the same number of strokes on both sides of the knife's edge.

To resharpen a dull blade, start with 30 strokes on the stone's medium-grit side, followed by 100 strokes on the fine-grit side. —K.M.

47 COOK THE CAMPER'S SUCKLING PIG

Cavemen cooked large hunks of meat on sticks—at least in cartoons—but what did they care if it took a couple hundred thousand years to char a mammoth leg? Too often, you're too beat to go into an *Iron Chef* smackdown gourmet extravaganza after a day of slogging through duck swamps. You want *hot meat now*. Sausages are perfect for roasting over a fire. The trick lies in cooking them sl-o-o-o-w, so they can cook all the way through without scorching on the outside.

Cut a green branch and sharpen the tip. Build a good bed of coals and hold the skewer 6 inches over the coals, rotating frequently. The sausage is done when the juices run clear.

If a kebab is what you're craving, slice the sausage into inch-thick chunks and rehydrate a few sun-dried tomatoes and dehydrated mushrooms. Skewer the goodies and cook them over a hot fire. Beats ramen noodles every time.

Mmmm...juicy. Skewered meat and fire is as basic as it gets. It's just about as delicious as it gets, too. —T.E.N.

48 PIPE WATER FROM A SPRING TO CAMP

Everyone wants a camp in the woods, but nobody wants to haul water. Locate your cabin or base camp downhill from a spring, and you can pipe water to where you need it.

Punch holes in the bottom of a jug and up one side (a). Wrap the jug with a filter of clean cloth and secure with cord (b). Cut a hole in the cap just large enough to insert tubing (c). Seal around the tubing with a silicone-based sealant. Place the jug in the spring with its mouth facing downhill (d). Anchor it with a log.

Run the tubing into a collecting bucket. Don't forget to purify water collected in the wild.

—T.E.N.

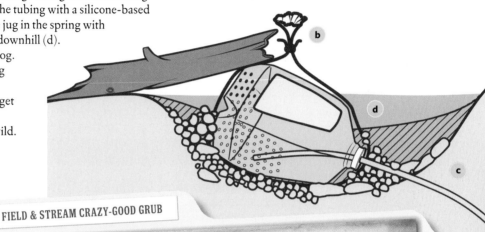

FIELD & STREAM CRAZY-GOOD GRUB

49 COOK A MEAN BANNOCK

Bannock is easy to make, infinitely customizable, and delicious. Some folks fry it, but if you bake it, it comes out suffused with wood smoke and history.

STEP 1 Put flour, baking powder, nonfat dry milk, oil, and salt into a bowl. Mix. Knead in enough water to make thick dough.

STEP 2 Toss in whatever goodies are handy, such as raisins, berries, jam, honey, cinnamon, or pemmican bits.

STEP 3 Make a pizzalike bannock cake no thicker than 1/2 inch. Heat a little oil in an iron skillet with straight sides. Fry the bannock on low heat for a few minutes until firm.

STEP 4 Prop the pan on a stick at a 45-degree angle beside the campfire. After 10 minutes, rotate the pan 180 degrees and bake 10 to 15 minutes more. Dig in. —T.E.N.

INGREDIENTS
2 cups flour
2 tsp. baking powder
1 tbsp. nonfat dry milk
5 tbsp. oil, melted butter, or lard
Pinch of salt
1 1/2 cups water (more or less as needed)
Raisins or other additives (optional)

50 DIG A BOOTY HOLE

So it's not exactly what you're thinking. For a more comfortable night in your sleeping bag, dig a "hip hollow" or "booty hole" before pitching the tent. Dig or tamp down a slight depression in the ground—a couple inches is plenty—where your pelvis will rest once you lie down. If you sleep on your back, the hole relieves painful pressure points at the small of your back. If you're a side sleeper, your hip will nestle into the hole, keeping your spine aligned for a more restful snooze.

—T.E.N.

51 WIELD A FIELD WRENCH

Can't get a rusty bolt loose? Wrap parachute cord tightly around the nut counterclockwise, leaving a tag end long enough to grasp firmly and pull.

—T.E.N.

FIELD & STREAM-APPROVED KNOT #5

52 TIE A KNUTE HITCH

Simplicity itself, the Knute hitch is perfect for tying a lanyard to the holes in knife handles and other essential tools.

STEP 1 Start by tying an overhand stopper knot in one end of the cord. Thread a loop through the lanyard hole, and push the stopper knot up through it.

STEP 2 Snug it tight, and you are done.

—T.E.N.

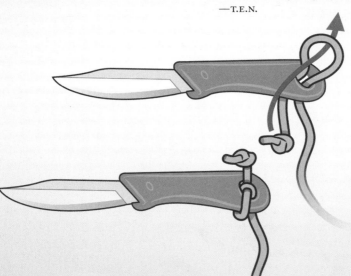

53 PACK FOR CAMPING IN 5 MINUTES

Plan your fun: Designate three large plastic storage bins and two large laundry bags for camping gear. Store the tent in one laundry bag and the sleeping bags in the other. In one bin, store air mattresses, pumps, pillows, and tarps. In another, pack up stoves, pots and pans, lanterns, hatchets, rope, saws, and other camp tools. Keep the third bin stocked with items that you'll need for camp and kitchen: a small bag of favorite spices, toilet paper, paper towels, camp soap, spare rope, the first aid kit, and the like. Resist the temptation to raid the bins when you're at home and down to your last paper towel. That way, when you're heading out for camp, all you have to do is load the bins and bags, and your work is half done. And once at camp the empty bins serve as great dirty laundry hampers and dry storage for firewood until it's time to pack up and head home. —T.E.N.

54 KEEP YOUR COOLER COLD TWICE AS LONG

Cut a piece of cardboard or minicell foam to fit inside the top of each of your coolers. These disposable gaskets will seal in the cold and make ice last much longer, especially in partially filled coolers. In a pinch, layers of newspaper work like a charm, too. —T.E.N.

55 FIX ANY TEAR, RIP, OR FRAY

Seam sealers are the best glues you've never heard of. Sure, the stuff waterproofs tent and tarp seams, but a urethane-based sealer also provides a flexible, waterproof, wear-resistant film that can save many a garment. Check out these uses.

WATERPROOF SYNTHETIC GUNSTOCKS Run a bed of seam sealer around butt pads and the threads of connecting screws. This will prevent water from leaking into hollow stocks.

REPAIR RAINCOAT RIPS Close the tear, using tape on the inside of the coat. Brush seam sealer on the outside, covering $1/8$ inch on each side of the rip. Let it cure according to manufacturer's directions and then repeat the sealing step on the inside.

KEEP ROPES FROM FRAYING Use seam sealer to permanently whip-finish the ends of ropes and cords. —T.E.N.

FIELD & STREAM CRAZY-GOOD GRUB

56 MAKE A TWO-STEP BACKPACKER'S MEAL

End of the trail, end of the day—the last thing you want to do is channel some television chef over a hot fire. This backpacking meal requires nothing but a single pot, a handful of lightweight ingredients, and minimum cleanup. If you and your buddy take turns digging a spoon into the mix, you can skip plates altogether.

INGREDIENTS
One 6-oz. package of instant stuffing mix
3 tbsp. olive oil
12 sun-dried tomatoes
Two 3.5-oz. tins smoked oysters
One 8-oz. can water chestnuts

STEP 1 To a 2-quart pot, add the stuffing's required amount of water, plus 3 tablespoons.

STEP 2 Follow box directions for stuffing with these exceptions: (1) Replace butter with olive oil. (2) Toss in the sun-dried tomatoes and simmer for five minutes before adding stuffing mix. (3) After stuffing is ready, stir in oysters and water chestnuts. Mix thoroughly. —T.E.N.

57 TEST GEAR IN THE STORE

What can 5 minutes of serious study tell you about the gear you're about to buy? Plenty, if you take advantage of these in-store gear tests. Just ignore the stares of other shoppers, and think twice about buying from a store that won't let you put its products through these paces.

SLEEPING BAG Take off your shoes, spread the bag on a cot or the store floor, and climb in. Sit up in the bag and try to touch your toes. If it binds you, opt for a longer size. Next, lie back down. Zip the bag open and closed three times from the inside, and three times from the outside. If the zipper hangs up on the zipper tape or draft tube, keep looking.

BOOTS Shop in the late afternoon when your feet will have swollen up as much as they're going to over the course of a day. Be sure to wear the sock combination you prefer in the field. Put them on, and then lean forward slightly. Slide your index finger between your heel and the inside of the boot. There shouldn't be much more than a half-inch gap. Next, kick the wall. If your toes rub or bump the front of the boot, tie the laces a bit tighter, and try again. Still bumping? Keep shopping.

DAYPACK Load the proposed pack with a volume similar to a typical day's worth of hunting or fishing gear, stuff one more spare vest inside, and sling it on. Raise your arms overhead to make sure the sternum strap doesn't cut across your throat. Hip belts should ride on the hips, not above the navel. Rock your shoulders back and forth—if loose webbing flies around, you can be sure it will catch on branches.

FLASHLIGHT First make sure you can manipulate all settings while wearing gloves. Headlamps, in particular, tend to have small switches. Next, tape a piece of unlined white paper to the wall of the store's changing room or bathroom, and turn off the light (if possible). Look for a bright central spot beam with enough spill—light around the edges—to illuminate the sides of a trail. Dark spots and circles show on the paper? Grab a different light. —T.E.N.

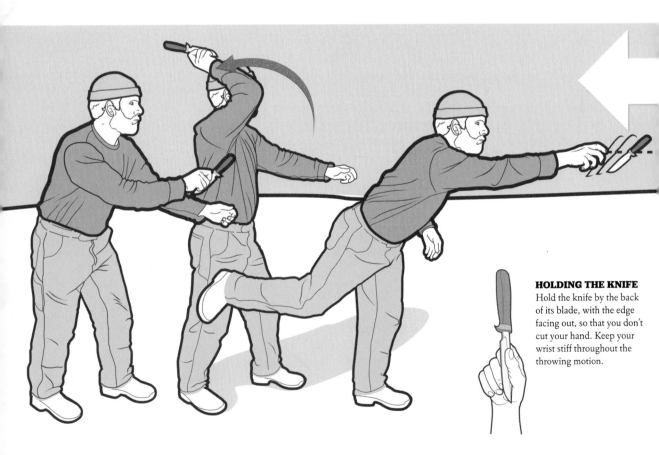

HOLDING THE KNIFE
Hold the knife by the back of its blade, with the edge facing out, so that you don't cut your hand. Keep your wrist stiff throughout the throwing motion.

58 SPLIT LOGS THE SMART WAY

Splitting firewood doesn't require the strength of an ogre. But whale away without a plan, and you will generate more body heat than campfire BTUs.

FORGET THE AXE Use a 6- to 8-pound maul, erring on the light side—velocity matters more than mass. Dulling the edge slightly prevents it from sticking in the wood. Set up a chopping block. Get a hard surface under the log. Otherwise the ground will absorb the blow.

THINK BEFORE YOU STRIKE Look for splits in the log that extend from the center outward, or other cracks in the end grain. Exploit these weaknesses first. Otherwise, aim your first blows toward the barked edge of the round. It's easier to extract the blade with a rocking motion if it's on the edge. Use your next blows to walk the split across the round.

AIM LOW Strike as if the first 3 or 4 inches of wood don't exist. Visualize the maul moving all the way through the wood. Make every swing count. —T.E.N.

FIND THE DISTANCE WHERE THE KNIFE STICKS IN THE TARGET

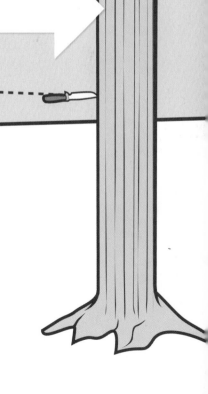

59 THROW A KNIFE

Throwing a knife isn't difficult once you learn how to gauge the speed of rotation. Special throwing knives are unsharpened and have metal handles, but with practice—and caution—you can throw a hunting knife. Three tips: Keep your wrist stiff, use the same speed and motion for each throw, and step toward or away from the target until you find the distance where the rotation turns the knife point-first. Experts can accurately gauge up to seven rotations, but start with one and a half. This will result in a point-first direction with about a 4-yard throw. —K.M.

60 ROAST THE PERFECT MARSHMALLOW

When you're roasting marshmallows, how often do you settle for a burned wad of ashy black marshmallow goo? Thought so. Achieving the perfect balance of golden smokiness and creamy gooliciosity (that's a real word—you don't have to look it up) is no small feat, so let's get serious.

ONLY JET-PUFFED OR CAMPFIRE BRANDS WILL DO
Many brands burn way too quickly. And only a chump uses a coat hanger as a skewer. Cut a straight roasting stick. No forked branches; no funky twigs. Keep it plain, straight, and simple. Hold the marshmallow level over embers, not flames. It's fine to have flames off to one side, but they shouldn't be directly under your precious glob of sugary wonderfulness. Rotate the marshmallow slowly, or go for a quarter turn at a time. (Here's where the straight stick comes into play: You don't have to change positions when you rotate it.)

WATCH FOR THE TELLTALE SAG As the marshmallow turns a tawny golden color, it will sag on the roasting skewer. When a vertical slit appears where the stick and marshmallow meet, you know the insides are approaching that desired state of gooliciosity. It is time. —T.E.N.

61 PERFECT THE DRUGSTORE WRAP

Many a campfire meal has been ruined with a fire-blackened version of this Boy Scout staple. It doesn't have to be that way. Start by learning the "drugstore wrap." Tear off a piece of heavy-duty aluminum foil approximately three times the size of your pile of food. Place it shiny side up on a flat surface. Put the food in the center of the foil (a). Bring up two opposite sides to form a tent, and roll over tightly three times (b). Press tightly along the fold to seal the seam. Seal the other two ends with three tight folds (c). Now add a second layer of foil, with looser folds. This layer protects the inner layer from punctures and keeps it clean so you can use it as a plate once opened.

What to put in a foil pouch? How about a Deer Hunter's Hobo Supper? —T.E.N.

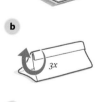
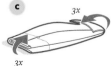

INGREDIENTS

10 oz. venison backstrap, cut into pieces
1 medium onion, quartered
1 potato, diced
½ red pepper, cut into 1-inch squares

20-oz. can pineapple chunks, drained
1 tbsp. pineapple juice
1 tbsp. soy sauce
Dash each coriander, ginger, cumin

Pile the venison, onion, potato, red pepper, pineapple chunks, pineapple juice, soy sauce, and spices onto the foil.

Fold the foil as shown at right and cook the pouches over hot coals for about 25 minutes. Unwrap, let cool, and enjoy.

62 TURN A CANOE INTO A CAMPSITE (ALMOST)

Sure, a canoe hauls mountains of gear, puts you in the fish, and floats out the biggest bucks with ease. But don't turn your back on this ancient craft once you get to shore. With a few tricks, that boat can make camp life a lot easier—and it could save your life.

CAMP TABLE AND KITCHEN COUNTER

Properly stabilized, a canoe makes a fine table for cooking and food preparation. Turn the boat upside down on level ground. Wedge rocks or logs under the bow and stern to prevent the canoe from tipping and wobbling. Now you have a rock-steady flat surface ready for a camp stove, wash bucket, and lantern. You can even fillet fish directly on the boat hull and let tomorrow's miles wash away the slime and guts.

WINDBREAK FOR FIRE
Canoe campsites are often exposed on sandbars, gravel flats, islands, and windy shorelines. Turn a boat on one edge and prop it up with a pair of sticks to blunt fire-sucking winds.

EMERGENCY SHELTER
A canoe can do double duty as a lifesaving shelter when the weather goes south. Turn the canoe upside down and prop one end on a low, sturdy tree branch, a boulder, or—in a pinch—a mound of gear. The high end of the canoe should be pointing away from the wind. Drape a tarp or emergency space blanket over the hull and stake down the edges. Crawl inside and wait out the weather. —T.E.N.

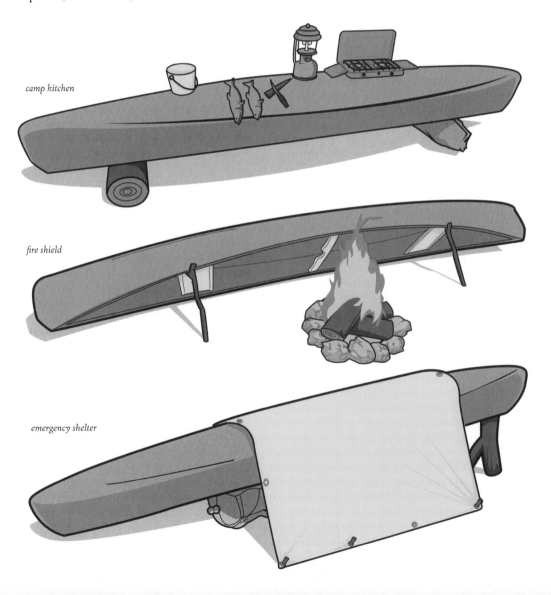

camp kitchen

fire shield

emergency shelter

63 CAMP LIKE A GHOST

GET IN Good campsites are found, not made. Don't clear brush for your tent or dig drainage ditches. Stick to existing fire circles in heavily used areas. Otherwise, plan to camouflage the fire pit by shoveling out a layer of soil and surface plants and setting it aside. And no surveyor's tape for flagging. Learn to use a map and compass or a GPS.

GET OUT Burn all wood completely. Saturate the ashes and then scatter them. Replace the sod and toss leaves and twigs over the spot. Scour the camp for tiny bits of micro-trash. Remove all cordage from trees, even if you didn't place it there. Naturalize the site before you leave. Rake matted grasses and leaves with a branch. Bring in rocks and sticks to hide your tent site. And the same rule applies no matter how near to or far from civilization you camp: Pack it in; pack it out. Yes, that means banana peels, apple cores, eggshells, and cigar butts. If it wasn't there when Columbus landed, remove it. —T.E.N.

F&S Field Report: RIVER ENDING

I'm not sure I could devise a more perfect ending to a week in the Ozark wilds. It's our last night on the Eleven Point River, and the tents are up, and as the light falls, black-crowned night herons wing overhead to roost. My arms are sore from paddling four rivers, loading and unloading canoes, hauling bags over gravel bars, and casting tube jigs, Czech nymph rigs, and even a shrimp-colored spoon fly I offered to the Eleven Point when the storms came and the bite went flat after yesterday's breakfast.

Just downstream of our two-acre gravel bar campsite a hard current seam cleaves the river, with tendrils of fog swirling off the water like cigar smoke. Colby Lysne cinches down his belt and waves a flyrod. "This is the sword," he declares, "with which I will rule my kingdom."

I wave him off with a spatula.

For the next half-hour I trade rainbow trout and smallmouth bass nearly cast for cast, running back and forth between the river and a frying pan. Cast, strip, run, flip. Then suddenly, as if turning off a switch, it's over for me. I'm done. Fished out, plain and simple, after seven hard days on the water.

I lean my rod against the canoe and sprawl out on the ground, firelight flickering on Ozark stones, gnats pelting my face like a hard rain. A symphony of crickets trills in a chorus almost as loud as the sizzling fish, which are almost as loud as Lysne's cackle as he stands in the dark water, two-handing a trout. It's almost dark, and I can barely make him out in the fog, disappearing like some figure in a photograph that's faded in the sun.

A few stars wink overhead, and for the first time in a week I think about the fish and the fishing of days past, instead of plotting and planning and fretting about the fishing to come. I lie on the gravel bar, deep in the Ozarks, listening to the water that had taken all I had to give.

—T. Edward Nickens
Field & Stream, *"Ozark Mountain Breakdown,"* June 2009

"If people concentrated on the really important things in life, there'd be no shortage of fishing poles."

—Doug Larson

Never Enough

Used to be, all I needed was a half day off work during the full moon of May. Drag my canoe 100 yards through the woods to the Carpenter Pond and whack bedding bluegills until it got so dark even the wood thrushes quit singing. No fish finder. No scent-impregnated plastics. Just a box of sinking black ants and popping bugs and a 4-weight fly rod that I made myself. Have I ever been happier with a rod in my hand? Probably not.

Back then, panfishing encapsulated all that was pure and simple and right in the world. These weren't fish whose shapes were embroidered on $85 shirts. These weren't fish you worshiped. These were fish you could catch with a worm or a cricket or a 49¢ lure. Fish you threaded onto a stringer and released into a frying pan. Not that I would give back a single day of chasing fish to the ends of the continent. I don't regret a moment of Arctic char fishing, for starters. Standing in the spray of a waterfall pouring over a lip of Yukon tundra, fighting a fish that had very likely never seen a lure or a man—that's an experience to keep in pristine mental condition.

The same goes for the memories of pig walleye transferred within minutes from the base of an

Ontario waterfall to a black fry pan popping with hot oil. Or trout from Maine, Montana, Alaska, Arkansas. I'm a lucky man.

But I still can't turn my back on the blissfulness of a bluegill whopping a popping bug the color of hard candy. Most fishermen have experienced similar moments, I think. For most of us there's a place that we never forget: a certain crook in the river, a cove along the pond edge, a deepwater drop-off that always produced big fish. Or big memories. When it comes to fishing, one's about as good as the other.

Of all the outdoor pursuits, fishing may be the most knowledge-intensive. Every day is different. Every hour can change everything. Every species— every single fish—requires a specific set of actions and decisions designed to put forth what seems to be the simplest of requests: "Eat this, please."

There is so much to know. Twitch retrieve or slow strip? Let the bass run with the worm, or strike with every bump? Mayfly emerger or spinner or nymph or dun? Maybe not a mayfly at all? Rapala knot? Six-turn San Diego Jam? Rotten chicken liver or fresh?

For a lot of people, it's a little overwhelming. Those non-anglers can't get their minds around the unimpeachable necessity of five rigged rods for a single fisherman. Or a tackle box the size of an antique chest of drawers. (And we still wish we'd sprung for the next size up.) Do you really need the side-scanning sonar? A micro-scale pattern on the side of a minnow lure no bigger than a peanut? Can't you just go wet a line, for the love of Izaak Walton, without all the yammering about benthic invertebrates?

Let's be clear: There's not a thing in this world wrong with a cane pole and a bucket of red wigglers. But many of us suck up anything that

smacks of a new cast or a new lure or a new way to rig a live shiner like carp rooting in the mud. We nurse a fetish for new knots. We will argue over the pros and cons of circle hooks until the bar closes and we are swept out with the dirt. We lie in bed at night with dark thoughts that would shock our mothers: *Maybe there's a better way to drop a weedless plastic frog into a black hole of lily pads, coontail, and who-knows-what. Maybe I should hold off on setting the hook for a count of three because fish in the salad get a mouthful of lettuce along with the lure. And maybe I'm not sticking the fish hard enough or holding the rod tip high enough to skitter the fish clear of the weeds. Maybe I can do better.*

That kind of knowledge doesn't exactly rank up there with that found in the Dead Sea Scrolls, but we want all of it we can get.

We're hooked.

So a lot has changed about fishing since my long afternoons on the Carpenter Pond. But here's what hasn't: You need fresh line on the reel. You'd better know how to tie a good knot. Keep your bait in cool water. Keep your shadow off the stream.

And you'd better get going. More than likely, someone else knows all about your honey-hole, and they just knocked off a half day of work.

—*T. Edward Nickens*

64 FLIP A LURE THE FLORIDA WAY

When most people flip for bass, they let the line go, it hits the water, and if a fish hits the lure on the way down and then releases it, the angler never feels the bite. It's especially problematic in heavy grass—unless you know how to tighten your line before the drop. Cast right into the middle of a weed mat and let the lure drive a hole into the hollow beneath. But the real key is this: As soon as the lure hits the water, apply slight thumb pressure to the spool to control the drop of the lure. Don't let it free-fall to the bottom. Set it on the mat and lower it with your thumb. That gives you the chance to feel even the slightest take on the drop.

—T.E.N.

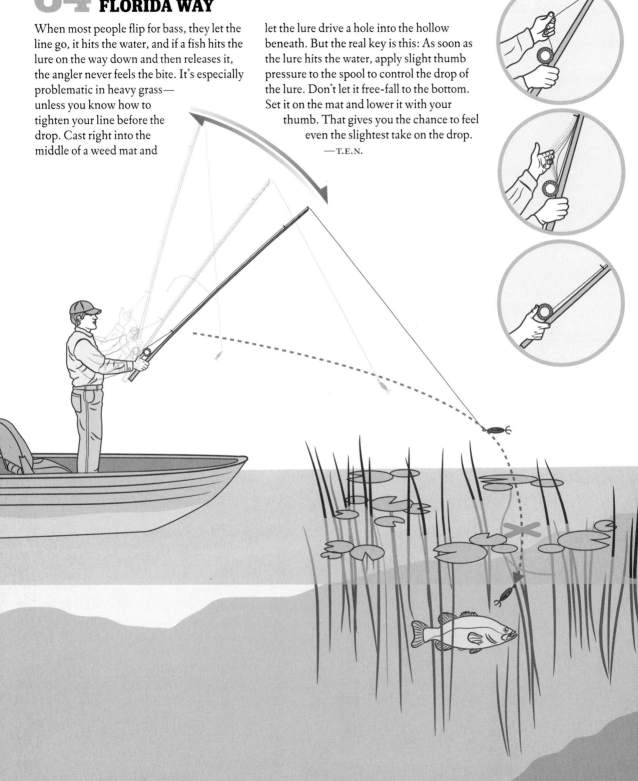

65 FISH WITH A SHINER

Florida is famous for its wild live shiner fishing. "The fish chase those shiners to the surface," says fishing guide Todd Kersey, "and, oh, man, the world blows up right in front of you. It's very exciting." Not in Florida? You can get in on the thrills wherever bass lurk.

GEAR UP Use a 4/0 live-bait hook and a standard egg bobber, and large baits—shiners between 6 and 10 inches. It's a handful, especially since the trick is to always keep the shiner right above the grass. Sometimes you need $1/8$ or $3/8$ ounce of lead to keep the shiners down, but if you use lead, make sure you've got a real kicker for bait. The minnow needs to spook and run because bass love to attack a moving target.

WORK IT The trick is in working the bite. A bass can eat a big shiner only headfirst—if it goes down tail first, the shiner's fins will get hung up in his throat. What happens is this: The bass blows out of the water, grabs that shiner, and starts buzzing drag off the reel. Your first instinct—to lock down and let him have it—is the worst thing to do. You have to let the fish run, and when he stops to turn that shiner around in his mouth, that's when you hit him. Sometimes it's 5 yards. Sometimes it's 35 yards. You never know.

—T.E.N.

FIELD & STREAM CRAZY-GOOD GRUB

66 TRY A BEER-POACHED FISH

A cold one is the 11th essential on a good fishing trip. Besides being the beverage of choice after a long day on the water, it also can be used to help you cook your catch. Any kind of beer is perfect for poaching fish, and the recipe is simple.

STEP 1 Build a good fire.

STEP 2 Lay out a sheet of heavy-duty aluminum foil that is two and a half times longer and deeper than your biggest fish. Drizzle the bottom of the foil with olive oil and then add a $1/2$-inch-thick layer of sliced green onions. Add a cleaned fish to the top of the pile and souse it with the first few ounces of a fresh beer. The rest of the can is for you. Roll up the foil, sealing the fish, onions, oil, and beer in a tight pouch.

STEP 3 Place the pouch near hot coals for about 15 minutes for a decent eating-size walleye. The onions will char. The beer will steam. The fish will flake with a fork. You will eat and drink like a king. —T.E.N.

67 FLY CAST TO FICKLE POND TROUT

When conditions are perfect, one of trout fishing's signature endeavors is fly casting to brook trout rising to surface flies in remote backcountry ponds. But when the stars haven't lined up over his favorite brookie water, Maine guide Kevin Tracewski has learned how to fool the pond squaretails. Here's how.

Anchor the boat fore and aft as far away from any structure, such as a suspended weedbed, as you can cast. Using a heavy sinking line, make a long cast. Strip out 10 feet of line and shake it through the tip-top guide. Drop your rod tip to the water—and then do nothing. The line will sink to form an underwater L, dropping straight from your rod tip and then extending out toward the structure. "Count down, say, 10 seconds before starting a retrieve," Tracewski says. "The belly of the line will pull the fly through the sweet spot until it is nearly to the boat." If you don't get a hit, cast again and count down 15 seconds before retrieving, then 20 and 25. —T.E.N.

68 LAND A BIG FISH BY KAYAK

The stakes are higher when you're fishing from a kayak. The craft's instability makes it tougher to manage how much pressure you put on the fish, not to mention the fact that landing a serious pike or muskie means you have to be wary of teeth in addition to hooks. Here's how to handle the heavyweights.

PREPARATION The key is letting the fish get tired enough to handle—but not so worn out as to prevent a healthy release. Straddling the kayak (1) will give you leverage and better balance. Make sure that all landing tools are within reach but out of the way (2). Because you're so low to the water, a net is rarely necessary. With the fish beside the boat, turn on the reel's clicker. Keep at least a rod's length of line out (3) since too much line tension loads up the rod and could result in you getting yourself impaled by a hook.

EXECUTION It's usually when you go to lift a pike or muskie that they are going to thrash about. Keep your eye on the lure at all times. Holding the rod in one hand, grab the back of the fish's head, just behind the gill plates (4). Pin especially big fish against the kayak. Once the fish is stabilized, pop the reel out of gear and set the rod in a rod holder (5). Use a fish gripper to lip the fish (6). Slide your hand below the belly to support the fish as you lift it out of the water. —T.T.

69 TRACK GRASSLINES WITH SONAR

Big Bass + Underwater Grass = Reel Bearings Shrieking in Pain. How to complete the equation in unfamiliar water? Follow what Texas guide John Tanner does:

STEP 1 "I look for coots hanging out in a cove or along the shoreline," Tanner says. "Ninety-nine percent of the time, they're over vegetation." Point the bow of your boat toward the birds and idle in. Keep a sharp eye on the console sonar. As the outer edge of the grassline begins to show on the bottom contour, cut the motor and turn the boat parallel to the grassline.

STEP 2 "Now I jump up front, drop the trolling motor down, and pick apart the grassline edge with the front sonar," Tanner says. You want to follow the very margin of the vegetation, so watch the bottom contour. If the sonar shows grass starting to get tall, steer away from it. If the grass gets sparse or disappears from the sonar, turn into it. Start fishing on the outside edge of the vegetation before working your way in. —T.E.N.

70 FISH LIKE A BIOLOGIST

Knowing the life cycle of a mayfly will hook you more trout. In 1496, Dame Juliana Berners described fly imitations for about a dozen mayflies in her *A Treatyse of Fysshynge wyth an Angle*. And so it began. There are more than 500 species of mayflies known to North America, and no telling how many mayfly patterns. Learn to match the fly to the mayfly life stage. —T.E.N.

PHASES

NYMPH The body shapes of mayfly larvae differ. As nymphs feed and molt, they move about the stream and become dislodged in the current. Trout whack them.

EMERGER Mayflies beginning to hatch rise to the surface, crawl to the water's edge, or shed skin underwater. Trout key in on this vulnerable stage.

DUN The first adult stage is also called the subimago. They drift on the surface until their wings dry. Still weak, they fly to a protected area to molt a final time.

SPINNER This is the fully formed, final adult breeding stage. A "spinner fall" occurs when the dying insects fall to the water, wings outstretched. Trout go nuts.

FLY TO MATCH

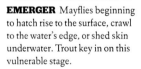

1 Pheasant Tail Nymph
2 Copper John

3 Klinkhammer
4 Emerging Para Dun

5 Sparkle Dun
6 Comparadun

7 Angel Wing Spinner
8 Krystal Spinner

TIP

This is when mending means the most. It will let you drift cleanly through riffles and runs.

Study the rise. If you see a trout head bulging out of the water, it's likely feeding on emergers.

If matching the hatch doesn't work, try an emerger. Trout will hit floating duns before they fly off.

Use a dropper rig with a larger fly as an indicator and a small submerged spinner as the trailer.

71 MIMIC THE TASTIEST CRUSTACEAN

Big trout can't resist the stop-and-drop flight path of a fleeing crayfish. Colorado guide Landon Mayer perfected this retrieve while targeting largemouth bass, and it's a coldwater killer as well. Use a weighted crayfish pattern for best results.

STEP 1 With the rod tip pointed at the surface of the water—or submerged as deep as 6 inches in the water—feel for tension on the fly. Then strip in 1 to 3 feet of line in a single, abrupt motion that lifts the fly off the stream bottom and into the water column, like a crayfish trying to escape a predator.

STEP 2 Pause long enough to feel tension from a strike or until you no longer feel the fly as it settles back on the bottom. The drop often puts up a little puff of sand, just like a crayfish hitting the dirt.

STEP 3 Repeat the abrupt strip. When a fish hits, set the hook with a pinch-lift strike: Pinch the fly line against the cork handle with your index finger and lift the rod hand sharply to a 45-degree angle.
—T.E.N.

72 READ TROUT LIKE AN UNDERWATER BOOK

Find glare-free viewing lanes of shade or darker colors reflecting on the water surface, such as shadows from streamside vegetation. These are windows of opportunity for sight-casting to trout. Got your viewing lane? Good. Here's what to look for.

WHITE "O" Analyze every speck of white on the stream bottom. An on-off glint of white is the inside of a trout's mouth. A broken pattern of white glints is a feeding trout (a).

MOVEMENT Look for a fish that moves slightly, then returns to the same location in the stream. That's a feeding fish (b).

SILHOUETTE Imagine a sketch of a fish with a heavy outline filled with color. Now remove the outline. That's the target: a ghostly underwater smear (c). —T.E.N.

73 CATCH THE COOLEST LIVE BAIT ON THE PLANET

Catching a tiger beetle larva is almost as much fun as using it to catch panfish. Look for a hole in the ground about as big around as a pencil. Likely spots are bare patches in a sunny backyard, a local park, a field, or just about anywhere you can find hard-packed soil or sand. Break off a tall reed, like broom sedge, about a foot long. Insert it gently into the hole, lifting and dropping until it finds the bottom—which isn't really the bottom, but the top of the larva's hard flat head. When the grub uses its pincers to move the offending stem, you'll see the reed start to jiggle. Quick as you can, snatch the grass straight out of the hole. If you're lucky, or just plain good, an inch or so of creamy grub will be yours for the taking. —T.E.N.

74 TIE A CLEAT HITCH

Quick and easy, the cleat hitch is one every angler should learn, whether you own a boat or not. Take a full turn around the cleat and then make two figure-eight loops around the cleat horns. Finish with a locking hitch: Twist the line so the free end passes under itself. Snug it tight and loop or coil remaining line out of the way. —T.E.N.

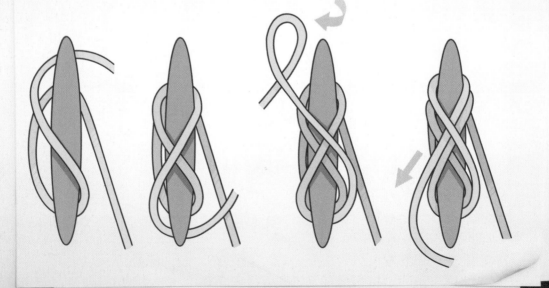

75 CHUM BREAM WITH A DEAD RACCOON

Old-timers did whatever they had to do to fill a stringer. Used to be, they'd nail a hunk of a dead cow to a tree over a farm pond, and sit back while the sun shined down and a thousand flies showed up at the party. These days using a roadkill raccoon is more common, but chumming with maggots still works. The process is pretty much the same as in days gone by—find an expired mammal of medium size, hang it over a pond, and come back in a few days. Bream that have swarmed to feed on the falling fly larvae will smack anything you cast. Just don't tell your dinner guests about your fishing partners. —T.E.N.

76 FISH EVERY SQUARE INCH OF A FARM POND

Farm ponds can be a fisherman's friend, coughing up big bass, bucketfuls of bream, and enough catfish for a church supper. How to get the most out of the experience? Sure, you could sit on a bucket and drown crickets for a few hours, but it's more fun—and often more effective—to target species with a plan in mind.

BASS A cane pole is perfect for stalking hog largemouths. Forgo the live bait for a stout 3-foot leader of 15-pound mono and a strip of pork rind on a bass hook. (An in-line spinner would work great, too.) Slipping stealthily along the pond, jig every stump, log, and patch of lily pads. Or go tandem in a canoe or johnboat, and trade off paddling and jigging duties each time one of you hooks a fish.

PANFISH Midsummer bream have moved off the spawning beds and into deeper water, so add larger split shot to the cane-pole line and go dredging. Start at the pond dam and dabble bait close to drain structures and any fallen trees, and work over any steep banks and the edges of weedlines. Look for places where shallows fall off into the abyss; submerged creek channels and long points are great targets as well. Use a slip bobber to figure out where the bluegills are hanging.

CATFISH Forget those honking huge flatheads grappled out of subterranean caverns. Younger, smaller cats make the best meals and are a snap to catch with a cane pole. About an hour before the fireworks start, toss chum along a stretch of pond shore—dog food will work, as will chunks of old hot dogs left over from lunch. Come back right after sundown, armed with the cane wand and a cooler of chicken livers or shrimp. Treble hooks will hold the liver better than a single hook. —T.E.N.

77

PIMP A RIDE FOR YOUR FLY

Dark, gnarly undercut banks often hold the biggest trout in the stream. But getting a fly under those banks, and getting it deep enough to prompt a strike from a monster trout, requires expert fly casting and a precise presentation. Or a leaf. Here's how to use fall foliage to float your fly into the perfect position.

STEP 1 Hook a weighted streamer or nymph fly, such as a Woolly Bugger, to the outer edge of a dry, buoyant tree leaf.

STEP 2 Carefully sneak upstream to a position above the undercut bank you're looking to target. Then strip off a few feet of line and ease the unconventional rig into the current.

STEP 3 Pay out line as the leaf drifts to the target area. As it approaches to within 2 to 3 feet of the hole, give the line a sharp snap back with your line hand to rip the fly from the leaf. Your weighted streamer will drop into the current, which will carry the fly under the bank and down to your target trout. —T.E.N.

78 FOOL THE WARIEST TROUT IN THE RIVER

Large brown trout don't behave like small ones. Here's what sets them apart: —K.D.

SMALL BROWN	VS	TROPHY BROWN
Juvenile brown trout eat frequently and typically focus on invertebrates like worms, aquatic nymphs, and smaller insects.	Forage	Large brown trout eat fewer, larger meals. They key on calorie-rich foods like baitfish, mice, leeches, and nightcrawlers.
Smaller brown trout are in tune with natural bait and fly presentations.	Attraction	Motion on a fly or lure often piques the interest of a large brown.
Smaller browns feed at various times, including midday.	Feeding Times	Large browns feed in low light, often in the dead of night.
Small browns cling to "ideal" trout habitat where insects are plentiful and easy to feed on. You will occasionally find these fish sharing the riffles with rainbow trout.	Location	Trophy browns travel to hunt for food, but they will defend the heart of the run. Large browns can survive and thrive in sections of the river with warmer water and fewer insects.
Small fish will forgive any casting faux pas. If you see a fish strike at your lure or fly and miss, and then come back, assume it's small. They are also sensitive to overhead shadows and motions but are forgiving of underwater vibrations.	Spookiness	You won't fool a monster brown trout if you make a bad cast. And if you rip that bad cast out of the run, that stretch is finished for the evening. Large browns will shut down entirely if they sense any of your movements.
Smaller brown trout are influenced by river currents as the battle ensues.	Fighting Ability	A hooked big brown isn't very affected by current and will head for cover.

79 HARVEST NATURE'S BAIT SHOP

If you have a shovel and a lawn, you've got all the worms you need. But that's not the only productive bait around. The creek you fish can supply its own—for free. (Just be sure to check bait-collection regulations in your area before heading out.) —J.C.

IN-SEINELY CHEAP
You probably have most of what you need to make your own seine at home. First, get a 6x9-foot piece of nylon mesh from a fabric shop. Find two old broom handles and position one at each end of the net. Staple the mesh to the handles, leaving a few inches of net hanging past the tips at the bottom. Finally, attach some ½-ounce fishing sinkers a foot apart across this bottom edge with zip ties. You're ready to drag.

Good bait shops carry some of these critters, but expect to pay a lot more for a dozen hellgrammites than you will for 12 shiners, or a pound of crayfish.

1 HELLGRAMMITES
Rare is the fish that won't devour one of these nasty aquatic larvae. Pick them off the bottom of submerged rocks by hand or stretch a seine across a fast-water section of the creek and flip rocks upstream. The current will then flush the bugs right into the net.

2 MINNOWS
Minnows are easier to catch off the main current. Approach from midstream with a seine and corral the school against the bank as the net closes. If the bait is thick and the water is fairly shallow, a quick swipe with a long-handled dip net will also work.

3 CRAYFISH
Choose a stretch of slow to moderate current; flip rocks and scoop the crayfish with a dip net. You can also stretch a seine across the creek and walk toward it from upstream while splashing and kicking rocks to spook crayfish down into the mesh.

4 SALAMANDERS
Often overlooked, this bait is like candy to bass and big trout. Look for them under larger rocks near the water's edge. The most productive rocks are dry on top but cool and moist underneath. Moss-covered rocks farther up the bank are prime spots, too.

5 GRUBS
Find some rotten wood near a creek bed. Peel away the bark to expose the soft, dead wood, or poke around in the dirt underneath, and you'll probably find some fat white grubs. Find a trout or crappie that won't eat them and you've done the impossible.

6 GRASSHOPPERS
The best way to catch all the hoppers you'll need is to walk through the tall grass that likely will be flanking almost any given stream. Use a butterfly net to skim across the tips of the blades and you'll have a dozen or more hoppers in a flash.

80 FISH A BREAM BED

For sheer action, few angling pursuits can touch spring-spawning bluegills. In ponds and lakes, look for sandy flats near deep water—they'll be Swiss-cheesed with beds. In rivers and streams, check out woody cover near hard bottoms and shallow water—a single dinner-plate-sized crater can hint at dozens more nearby. And no matter where you live, look for excuses to skip work on the full moons of spring and early summer, when bluegill spawning peaks and every cast can land a fish.

PRE-SPAWN 'Gills are suspended off shore of their spawning flats, so key in on creek channels near hard sloping ground and mid-lake humps. Back off into 5 to 15 feet of water and use small slip bobbers to suspend wax worms, wet spider patterns, and red wigglers in the water column. Retrieve a half-foot of line and then hold while the bait settles.

Fly anglers can trawl for pre-spawn bluegill with a weighted fly trailing a black ant.

SPAWN As water temperatures nudge 65 degrees F, the females move to the bream beds, followed by the bucks. Spawning will peak when the water reaches about 75 degrees F. You can't go wrong with crickets, worms, sponge spiders, hairy nymphs, tiny spinners, and crankbaits. The key is stealth. Stay as far from the beds as you can and still comfortably cast.

Cast to the outer edges of the spawning beds first and then work your way in.

POST-SPAWN Breeders need recovery time, and move into deeper water adjacent to the beds. Target tangles of roots, treetops, lily pads, and deep channels where the bottom falls steeply. Try weighted bobbers to detect the lightest bites. And don't give up when the bites go flat. Many bluegill spawn multiple times, so check bream beds as the next full moon nears.

One-pound trophy 'gills are not worried about bass predation, so you'll want to hunt for them on the outside edges of shady structure. —T.E.N.

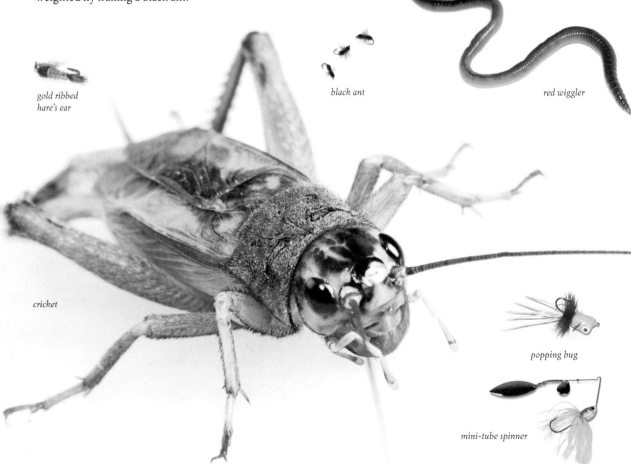

gold ribbed hare's ear

black ant

red wiggler

cricket

popping bug

mini-tube spinner

81 STORE BULK FISHING LINE

Most manufacturers will tell you that storing line for up to a year is no problem, but there are some significant caveats. First, long-term storage should always take place on bulk spools, not 1/4-pound—or less—spools. The larger diameter of bulk spools will cut down on the problem of line memory, in which the coiled line retains loops that will snarl your casts come spring. You should also be careful about storing lines in a garage. Garages are often full of chemical vapors that can degrade monofilament and fluorocarbon lines, so you don't want your spools anywhere near cleaning agents, solvents, automobile fluids—just the kinds of thing you typically keep in the garage.

Equally important to line stability is a stable environment without large temperature fluctuations, so unless your garage is heated, it's better suited for beer than for bass string. A simple solution: Stack bulk spools in a couple of shoeboxes and jam them up on the highest shelf in the hall closet. —T.E.N.

82 PATCH A KAYAK WITH DUCT TAPE

Launching kayaks off riprap landings and concrete boat ramps can be really hard on a boat. When this treatment leads to a cracked hull, here's how to fix that kayak and get back to chasing stripers in 30 minutes.

STEP 1 Stop the crack from enlarging by drilling a hole at each end of the split. Rub the cracked area with sandpaper, and clean it with a damp cloth. Let dry.

STEP 2 Heat the patch area with a hair dryer until it's nearly hot to the touch. Neatly place duct tape over the crack, overlapping it by 2 inches. Push out air bubbles. Now heat the patch with the hair dryer until small wrinkles form under the tape. Use a spoon to press as hard as you can, starting in the middle and working to the edges of the duct tape. Don't drag the spoon. Pick it up, press down, and roll toward the tape edge.

STEP 3 Repeat with three other layers, overlapping them by about 1/4 inch. —T.E.N.

FIELD & STREAM CRAZY-GOOD GRUB

83 FRY FISH STREAM-SIDE

You fish. You fry. This is the sacrament of the river trip, and here is how you get from a cooler full of fish to a riverbank communion.

At home, fill a break-resistant 1-quart plastic water bottle with peanut oil. Pour 2 cups of breading mix into a 1-gallon, zip-seal bag. Stuff it, along with a second empty bag, coffee filters, paper towels, and a baggie of Cajun spice mix, into a second plastic water bottle. Your fry kit is complete. At the campsite, it'll be quick and easy to put it all together. —T.E.N.

STEP 1 Pour enough peanut oil into a skillet to cover the fillets' sides but not spill over their tops. Place the pan on two long parallel logs and build a fire in between. You don't need coals. For precise flame control, keep smaller branches handy.

STEP 2 Season the fillets liberally with Cajun spice and toss them into the empty plastic bag. Shake well. Add bread crumbs and, using your fingers, work the breading into the cracks. Shake off the excess. Now get ready—here comes the magic.

STEP 3 The oil should be almost smoking hot. Ease in a small piece of test fish. You want a rolling, sputtering boil around the edges. Nothing less will do. Gently add the other pieces but don't crowd the pan.

STEP 4 Give the fillets 2 to 5 minutes per side. When the fish turns the color of caramel, turn carefully—and only once. It's done when you can flake the fillet all the way through. Drain fillets on paper towels. Let the excess oil cool and then strain it back into its bottle using a coffee filter to reuse.

84 UNHOOK YOURSELF

Depending on how deeply you've sunk the barb into your own flesh, your choices are good, bad, and worse. If the barb protrudes from your epidermal layer, removing the hook is a snap. Just cut the hook shank below the barb and back the hook out. If the barb is embedded but is still close to the skin surface, it's time to grin and (literally) bare it: Push the hook point the rest of the way out, cut it off behind the barb, and then put it in reverse. A deeply embedded hook point requires a nifty bit of macramé, line lashing, Newtonian action-reaction physics, and a quick, courageous yank. It's not so bad. Really.

Here's how. First, double a 2-foot length of fishing line (at least 10-pound test) and slip the loop around the midpoint of the bend in the hook. Hold the line ends between the thumb and forefinger of one hand and wrap the line around the opposite wrist, leaving a few inches of slack. With the free hand, press the hook eye down against the skin to keep the barb from snagging. Don't let the hook shank twist. Grasp the line sharply, line it all up nice and straight, breathe deep, and yank. Really.
—T.E.N.

85 FLY CAST UPSIDE-DOWN

Well, sort of. Learning to cast underhanded will soothe a number of tricky flyfishing situations. It's a good way to cast into a wind. It'll slip a fly under overhanging brush. And it's a go-to cast for a bow angler situated where a traditional cast might bang the fly against a tall console or pierce a friend's earlobe. The loop in the fly line actually travels under the tip of the rod. Here's the drill. —T.E.N.

86 DETECT LIGHT BITES

Even experienced anglers struggle with the light takes of walleye. It's especially tough with jigging. Nine times out of 10, a jig bite feels as if you're nudging weeds or about to get hung up on something. The rod just loads up a bit and feels a little heavy. That's likely to be a walleye, but people will end up pulling bait away from fish half the day. You're better off setting the hook. If it's a fish, you're a genius. If not, what did you lose?

To catch the bite, hold the rod at a 45-degree angle away from you, not straight out in front. Hop that jig as you bring the rod from the 45- to a 90-degree angle and then reel back to the original 45-degree angle again. This step is critical. Why? Because if you hold the rod straight out, you can't see the line hesitate or the rod tip bump. —T.E.N.

87 CAST INTO A TORNADO

Heavy lures require a rod at least 7 feet long, with action in the tip to help load the forward section. Here's how to launch into a gale.

STEP 1 Holding the rod with both hands, bring it all the way behind you and stop when it is parallel to the water surface. Keep the rod horizontally behind you, knuckles up, and chill. Now, let 'er rip.

STEP 2 Right-handed casters should have their weight on the right foot. Shift your weight to the left as you begin to power the rod tip overhead. Instead of carving an arc in the air, shift your right shoulder forward to flatten out the top of the stroke. Accelerate through the cast, arms extended out. Then hold the pose, Madonna. It'll take a while before the lure lands. —T.E.N.

KEEP TO THE BOW This is the go-to cast for a bow angler situated where a traditional cast might hook a friend's earlobe.

STEP 1 Start with a side cast, with the rod held nearly horizontal to the water surface. Turn the rod grip almost 90 degrees so the butt rests against your forearm. This gives you leverage.

forward

STEP 2 Begin your false casting. At the end of each forward and backward stroke, you need to lift the rod tip up slightly. This will form the essential upside-down loop.

backward

STEP 3 Deliver the fly with a strong forward cast. This should be powered with a strong flick-and-stop of the forearm; the motion is as if you were throwing a Frisbee™.

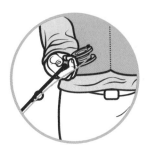

TROLL WITH SURGICAL PRECISION

Often, maintaining a precise speed is the key to successful trolling, and often it's best to go very, very slowly—sometimes less than a mile per hour. You always want to troll with the wind, but the problem comes when a stiff breeze pushes the boat too fast. Here are three ways to slow it down.

LOCK When using a trolling motor, put the main engine in gear to lock the propeller. This can slow your forward speed by 0.1 or 0.2 mph—which can make a critical difference when fishing for sluggish walleyes.

TURN Turn a bow-mounted trolling motor around and slip it into gear. Now it's pushing backward, and you can use the big engine as a rudder.

TRAIL Clip a drift sock to the bow eye and let it trail under the boat. Most people only use drift socks while drifting, but this trick can save the day. —T.E.N.

F&S Field Report: CATCH OF THE DAY

Throughout the trip we'd had moments of total fish chaos—multiple hookups, the Cane Pole hole, outrageous rainbow trout. But fishing remote Alaska isn't about the numbers, or the variety of species. It's about the way the fish are seasoned with fear, sweat, miscues, and the mishaps that make for an authentic trip in authentic wild country.

On the night before our scheduled pickup, we camped at the juncture of the Aniak river and a long, sweeping channel. After setting up the tents, Colby Lysne cooled his heels. His toes were swollen, chinook-red, and oozing pus from day after day of hard walking in waders. "I can't even think about wading right now," he stammered. "I'm just gonna lie here and fish in my mind."

The rest of us—Scott Wood, Edwin Aguilar, and I—divvied up the water. The others headed off to hunt rainbows down the side channel, while I hiked upstream to fish a wide pool on the main river.

Since I'd lost my rods and reels when our boat flipped, I fished a cobbled-together outfit of an 8-weight rod with a 9-weight line. It was a little light, but heavy enough for the fish we'd landed over the last few days. In an hour of nothing, I made 50 casts to an endless stream of oblong shapes. Then suddenly my hot-pink fly disappeared. Immediately I knew: This was my biggest king, by far. The salmon leapt, drenching my waders, then ripped off line and tore across the current.

The rod bent deep into the cork, thrumming with the fish's power. I'd have a hard time landing this one solo, so I yelled for help, but everyone was long gone.

So I stood there, alone and undergunned, and drank it all in. It no longer mattered if this was my first or fifteenth or thirtieth king salmon. What mattered was that wild Alaska flowed around my feet and pulled at the rod, and I could smell it in the sweet scent of pure water and spruce and in the putrid tang of the dying salmon. I felt it against my legs, an unyielding wildness. Part of what I felt was fear, part of it was respect, and part of it was gratitude that there yet remained places so wild that I wasn't so sure I ever wished to return.

Then the big king surfaced 5 feet away and glimpsed the source of his trouble. At once the far side of the river was where the salmon wanted to be, and for a long time there was little I could do but hang on.

—*T. Edward Nickens*, Field & Stream,
"*The Descent,*" June 2007

89 MISS A RAFT-EATING BOULDER

When you're dealing with long cumbersome oars and a craft that has all the maneuverability of a 14-foot-long wet pillow, oaring a raft doesn't come naturally. Here's how to manhandle these river monsters.

SETUP Sit just aft of center so the oars are centered in the middle of the raft for maximum pivot power. Adjust the length of the oars by starting with 4 inches of space between the handles.

COILED SPRING A proper oar stroke is part leg press, part upper-body row. Stay compact and don't overextend your body or arms. Reach too far with the oars and you lose control.

A GOOD DEFENSE A back-ferry stroke is the rafter's best move. [1] To skirt a rock or obstacle, use oars to swing the bow at a 45-degree angle to the obstacle and back-row. [2] Now fine-tune raft placement by pushing with one oar (a) and pulling on the other (b) to realign the boat, then slip by the rock in the current. —T.E.N.

90 CAST WITHOUT DRAG

There's a step-by-step process to master the short, accurate slack-line cast. First, choose the target, be it a rising fish or a rock. Too many people skip this part, and the game is over. Account for current speed and drag and guesstimate the exact spot where you want the fly to land. Second, as you cast, carry 2 to 3 feet of extra slack in your line hand. When you carry through that final forward stroke, aim precisely at your target spot. As the fly reaches the target, release the slack line, and, when the line straightens out, check the rod tip abruptly. That will cause the line to recoil and drop in a series of S-curves that will defeat drag. —T.E.N.

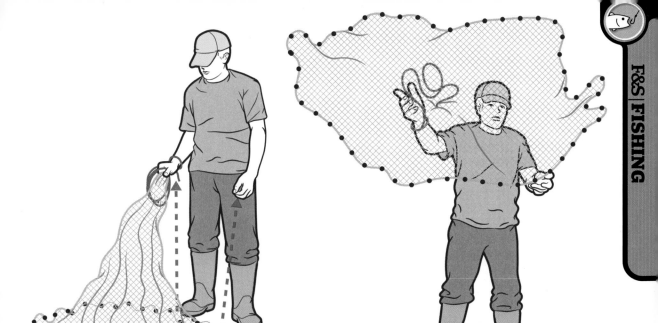

91 THROW A CAST NET

Despite its reputation, throwing a cast net requires neither voodoo nor the gyrations of a matador. These simple steps are the stripped-down basics, good for nets up to 6 feet wide, which should cover most freshwater needs.

STEP 1 Cinch the rope around your right wrist and coil all the rope in the palm of your right hand. Hold the top of the net with your right hand, with a few inches of gathered net sticking out from the bottom of your fist. Hold your right hand at waist height.

STEP 2 With your left hand, reach down and grab a lead weight; it should be the one that's hanging as close to directly below your right thumb as possible. Bring it up to your right hand and grasp it between your thumb and index finger. Pick up another weight that's an arm's length from the first. Hold this between your left thumb and index finger.

STEP 3 Next, point your feet toward the water; rotate your upper body to the right; and in one swift, smooth motion, swing your right arm out at a slightly upward angle. Release your right hand first and then your left. The net should open into a circular shape and drop.
—T.E.N.

92 SCALE FISH WITH BOTTLE CAPS

Do you drink beer from a bottle? Can you scrounge up a piece of wood about 6 inches long? Do you have two screws and a screwdriver? If so, you can assemble this handy-dandy fish scaler. —T.E.N.

93 STICK A SHORT-STRIKING SALMON

Short-striking fish can drive a fly angler batty, a situation well-known to landlocked salmon fishermen who must contend with conflicting currents in larger rivers. What to do when you don't have a fly with a trailing hook handy? This: Let the accidental back cast level out behind you and then forward cast to the same spot where the fish spat out your lure. Keep the line fairly taut but let the fly drift and sink naturally, as if it were mortally wounded by the original chomp. Give it 5 seconds and then give it a good twitch. That's often enough to entice a salmon to show up for a second helping. —T.E.N.

FIELD & STREAM-APPROVED KNOT #7

94 TIE A RAPALA KNOT

The Rapala knot is a winner because the wraps, which are ahead of the initial overhand knot, relieve stress where the standing line enters the rest of the knot. Also, line passes through the overhand knot three times, which serves to cushion the standing line.

STEP 1 Tie an overhand knot six inches above the tag end of your line. Thread the tag end through the lure eyelet and then through the overhand knot.

STEP 2 Next, take the tag end and wrap it three times around the standing line.

STEP 3 Pass the tag end through the back of the overhand knot.

STEP 4 Run the tag end through the new loop you formed in Step 3.

STEP 5 Lubricate and tighten by pulling on the tag end, main line, and lure. —J.M.

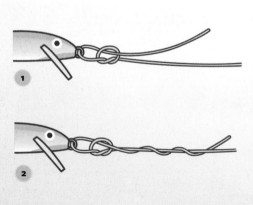

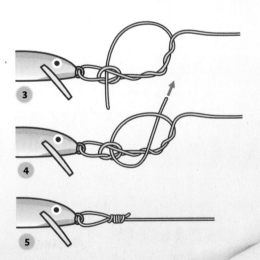

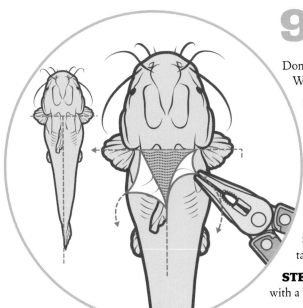

95 SKIN A CAT IN A JIFFY

Don't pout when a catfish pounces on your jig. Cleaning Mr. Whiskers is not as difficult as some people think.

STEP 1 Hold the catfish belly down and make two shallow slits through the skin: one should nearly girdle the fish's head from pectoral fin to pectoral fin, and the other should run from the top of this cut past the dorsal fin and down to the tail.

STEP 2 Grasp a corner of the skin flap firmly with pliers, and pull down and across the body all the way to the tail. Repeat on the other side.

STEP 3 Remove the head by bending it first toward the tail and then the stomach and then pulling it free of the body.

STEP 4 Remove the entrails by opening up the body cavity with a knife.

STEP 5 Fry and eat with a smile. —T.E.N.

96 DRAG FISH OUT OF A CAVE

They are deep and dark as Grendel's lair, which is why Grendel-size trout, snook, and redfish like to hole up in undercut banks. Follow these tips to foil a cave dweller.

Cast a plastic tube bait, lizard, or other light lure with an embedded hook point onto the bank a few feet upstream of the undercut. Jiggle it into the water and let the current carry it under the bank. Leave a bit of slack so the lure sinks, reel in quickly, and jerk the rod tip to impart action. Stop to let the lure slow down, enticing a strike. —T.E.N.

97 SKATE A FLY WITH A RIFFLE HITCH

A riffle hitch can be a very effective tactic. It is a knot that enables a fly to skim and skitter across the water surface, leaving a V-shaped wake that often results in a strike. That's called "skating a fly," or, as it is otherwise known, "Holy moley! Why haven't I tried this before?"

STEP 1 Your first line of action is to attach tippet to the fly with an improved clinch knot.

STEP 2 Next, you're going to want to add a half-hitch behind the eye of the hook, taking care to pull the tag end of the leader straight down. Add a second half-hitch in front of the first one. Pull the tag end of the leader straight down and snip. The half-hitches can be placed as far down the fly as the gape of the hook for a variety of actions on the water.

STEP 3 Cast down and across. The fly floats higher in the water column and will skate across the surface film. Spincasters can use this technique with the addition of a casting bubble. —T.E.N.

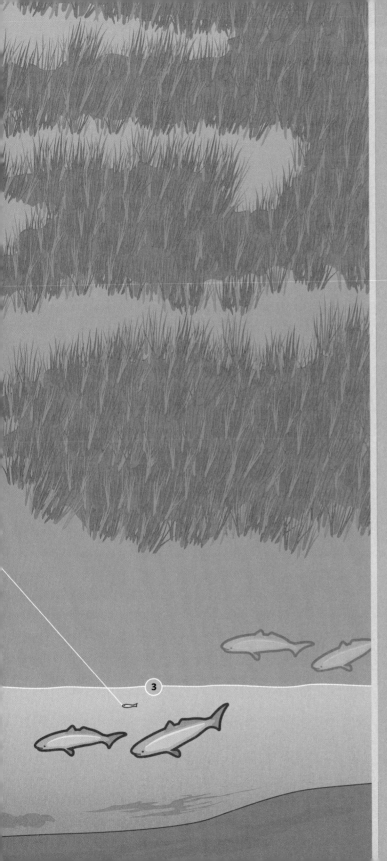

98

GET SALTY WITH YOUR BASS SKILLS

Your largemouth tactics can come in handy during a week at the beach. You can adapt them to fishing in a saltwater marsh—and you could be pulling trout, flounder, and redfish from the water instead of sulking at your 10th round of miniature golf.

GEAR UP Spool a medium-weight spinning reel with 8- to 10-pound monofilament line. Stay away from braided lines; the mouths of marsh fish such as trout and flounder are surprisingly soft, and you'll need some stretch to keep from tearing hooks out. For a basic tackle kit, carry a dozen leadhead jigs in white and red, and a handful of curly-tailed jig bodies in colors that imitate shrimp and in chartreuse (1).

POUND THE STRUCTURE Every dock piling, patch of oysters, bulkhead, rock pile, and abandoned crab pot is a potential reef full of fish. Target these areas just as you would fish around the tree stumps in the farm pond back home (2).

AMBUSH HOLDING FISH Analyze each stretch of tidal current as if it were a river and then fish accordingly. Marshy points, undercut banks, and deep water beside oyster beds and sandbars are great places to cast for fish holding in the lee of the tides (3).

BE THE BAIT In most cases, your lure will mimic shrimp or small baitfish. Lift and twitch your rod tip to allow the lure to rise and fall (4).

CHECK THE TIDES Tides affect fish movements and feeding times to a huge degree because moving tides sweep a buffet of prey—shrimp, small crabs, and baitfish—into the feeding lanes of holding fish. In most coastal regions, two high tides and two low tides come in and out of the marsh each day. Fish the hour or so before and after each change of tide. —T.E.N.

REEL FOOT
Slides into mounting slots of the rod's reel seat.

SPINNING REEL

Spinning reels have fixed spools that do not rotate—the line uncoils from the front of the spool, pulled by the weight of the lure. Since the cast lure doesn't need to have enough force to spin a rotating spool, spinning reels can utilize very light lures—ultralight spinning reels can handle lures as feathery as $1/32$ of an ounce—and backlash is rarely an issue. The downside to spinning reels: stopping a cast isn't a straightforward task. And spinning reels are notorious for twisting line. It's best to pump the rod up and reel on the way down to minimize twist.

BAIL Serves as a line pickup device to return the line evenly on the spool after the cast.

ANTI-REVERSE LEVER Prevents the reel handle from turning as line is playing out.

DRAG ADJUSTMENT KNOB The drag is a system of friction washers and discs. Front-mounted drags are typically stronger than rear-mounted drags.

SPOOL Holds the fishing line. A skirted spool covers the main reel shaft like a skirt to prevent line entanglement.

GEAR HOUSING Protects the internal gears that connect the handle to the spool.

HANDLE Activates the gears to retrieve line. Spinning reels come in a wide range of gear ratios, which is the number of spool revolutions to the number of gear handle revolutions. High-speed retrieve reels have gear ratios in the 4:1 class or higher. Lower gear ratios support more cranking power.

99 CHOOSE A REEL

At the most basic level, a fishing reel is simply a device used to store, deploy, and retrieve fishing line. But in the hands of a skilled angler, a strong, well-designed reel is a tool used at every step in the quest to catch a fish. It helps vary the speed and action of the lure, lets a light-biting fish take the bait without a hint of your presence, halts the strongest drag-screaming run, and controls the line when the fish is just about in hand. Here are the three most common reel types. To know them is to love to put them to hard use. —T.E.N.

SPOOL Holds the fishing line.

STAR DRAG Adjusts tension on a stacked series of washers and brake linings that make up the reel's internal drag.

LEVEL-WIND GUIDE Attached to a worm gear, this device moves the line back and forth across the face of the spool evenly to prevent line from getting trapped under itself.

SPOOL TENSIONER Is a braking device to reduce spool overrun and resultant "bird's nest" line snarls.

BAITCASTING REEL

The spool on a baitcasting reel revolves on an axle as it pays out line. By applying thumb pressure to the revolving spool, an angler can slow and stop a cast with pinpoint precision. Baitcasting reels require skill and practice and are a favorite of bass anglers, many of whom insist the reels afford more sensitive contact with the line than spinning reels. Baitcasters get the nod from trolling fishermen, too, for the revolving spool makes it easy to pay out and take up line behind a boat and also reduces line twist.

HANDLE The latest upgrades offer ergonomic grips with grooves for better control.

FREESPOOL BUTTON Allows the spool to turn freely for the cast.

DRAG KNOB Adjusts drag tension. Some smaller reels have a spring-and-pawl drag, while reels for larger fish sport strong cork and composite disc braking systems.

ARBOR The spindle around which the fly line is wrapped. Many modern reels have larger arbors that help recover line more quickly when a fish swims toward the angler.

FRAME Holds the spool. A weak frame will warp, causing friction as the spool revolves.

FLY REEL

Flyfishing reels don't revolve during a cast, since fly anglers strip line from the reel and let it pay out during the back-and-forth motion called "false casting." In the past, fly reels have served largely as line-storage devices with simple mechanical drags. Advancing technology and an increase in interest in flyfishing for big, strong-fighting fish have led to strong drag systems that can stop fish as large as tarpon. Other recent developments include warp- and corrosion-resistant materials and finishes and larger arbors—the spindles around which the line is wrapped—that reduce line coils and help maintain consistent drag pressure.

SPOOL Many reels are fitted with removable spools. Having different fly lines ready on a number of spools allows an angler to switch tactics more quickly.

HANDLE Unlike spinning and baitcasting reels, rotating the handle of a fly reel typically turns the spool a single revolution.

100 CARRY A TACKLE BOX AROUND YOUR NECK

Trout anglers figured this out ages ago: Why weigh yourself down when all you want to do is blitz a local creek? Bass busters can do the same. Turbocharge a flyfishing lanyard with the items listed below, and you can work your way around a pond unencumbered.

Start with a neck lanyard with at least five disconnects. If your lanyard comes preloaded with floatant holder, small nippers, or other trout-specific tools, remove them. Then load it up with the following essentials.

PLIERS Look for the lightest fishing pliers you can find. Some models even float (1).

FILE A short hook file. Yes, you need one (2).

SPINNERS AND JIGS Stuff a small fly box with a few spinners and jigs and whatever else you might need once you're on the pond (3).

SCISSORS Super braid scissors will cut heavy gel-spun and superbraid lines (4).

MULTITOOL Look for a small multitool that can do business as a mono clipper, a screwdriver, and a bird's-nest detangling aid (5). —T.E.N.

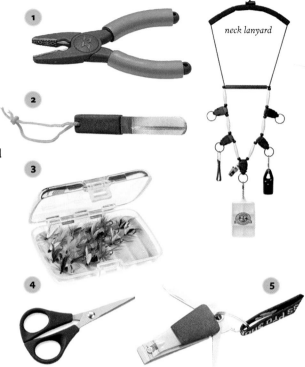

neck lanyard

101 FINE-TUNE A WACKY WORM FOR PENNIES

Rigging a wacky worm the traditional way—driving the hook through the middle—results in a lot of expensive baits flying off the hook or hanging up in brush. Here's how to solve two sticky wacky-worm problems at once.

SHOP IT Take your favorite wacky-worm baits to a hardware store and start shopping: You need black rubber O-ring washers like you'd use on a leaky kitchen sink, and they need to fit snugly on the body of your worm. While you're there, pick up a few small black panel nails or brads.

RIG IT Snip off the nail head with wire cutters and insert the long part of the nail into the head of the worm. Slip the O-ring down to the midpoint of the worm. Thread your hook through this O-ring, so that the hook point is in line with the worm.

FISH IT Cast into the salad with confidence. The rubber O-ring absorbs the force of the cast, preserving the bait. And the weight will make the worm fall slightly headfirst, carrying the hook with the point facing up. You'll snag less often—and catch more fish. —T.E.N.

102 FISH UNFISHABLE WEEDS

Pulling hog bass from heavy slop requires the right gear. Long, stiff rods have the muscle to horse them out of weeds. Baitcasting reels have the winching authority. Braided superlines cut through heavy vegetation and have near-zero stretch, which makes hooksetting much easier.

Drop a weedless plastic frog right into the mess. Wiggle, skitter, pause, and pause it some more. Watch for a bulge of water behind the frog, created by a stalking bass waiting for open water, but be ready for an out-of-nowhere explosion. When the fish hits, hold off on the hookset for a count of two or three. Then stick it hard and keep your rod tip high. Try to get the fish's head up and pull it out of the very hole it made when it surfaced. Keep up the pressure to skitter the fish across the slop and turn back all attempts to head for the bottom. —T.E.N.

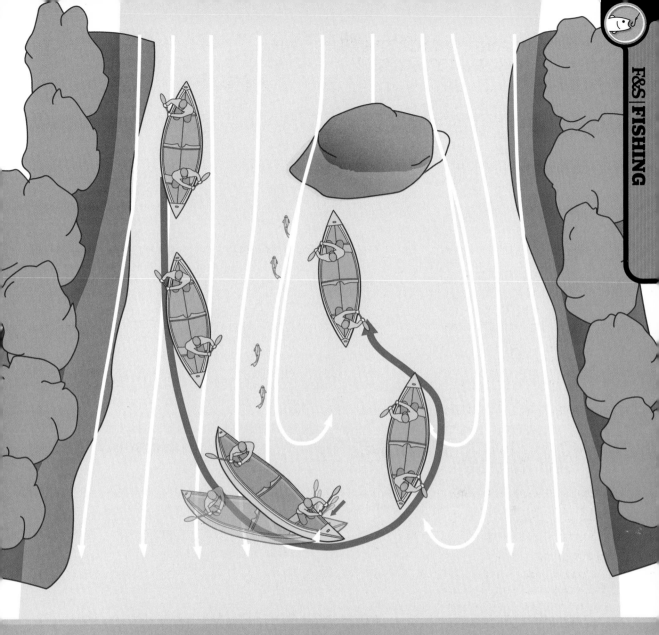

103 CROSS AN EDDY LINE FOR STACKED-UP FISH

It's a fact that strong eddy lines below rapids and boulders hold fish, but it's also true that it takes a good eddy turn to place a boat in casting position. Remember the word PAT: *power, angle,* and *tilt.*

POWER The canoe has to be moving forward in relation to the current speed. You need enough momentum to cross the eddy line.

ANGLE Position the canoe at a 45-degree angle to the eddy line. Aim high in the eddy—higher than you want to go because the current will carry you downstream. Maintain angle and speed until the center of the boat crosses the line; then the bow paddler should draw to turn the boat into the eddy.

TILT Two guys in a loaded boat sitting on the seats risk a quick flip as the eddy pushes on the hull. You have to lean and bank the boat into the turn; the stronger the eddy, the harder the lean. —T.E.N.

104 TUNE LURES

Test each crankbait or spinnerbait by making a short, 20-foot cast. Hold your rod tip straight up, and reel. A lure that runs more than 5 or 6 inches off to one side needs tuning. To tune a crankbait, replace bent split rings. Straighten out hook hangers with needle-nose pliers. If all appears fine, hold it so that the lip faces you and use light pressure to bend the line tie in the direction you want the lure to run.

Retest. Repeat until you're satisfied. For a spinnerbait, hold it with the line tie pointing at you. Look straight down the top wire; it should be situated directly over the hook and aligned with the shank. If not, bend it into place. If the spinnerbait rolls left or right during the retrieve, bend the top wire in the opposite direction. —T.E.N.

105 TIE A BLOOD KNOT

Join the tippet to the leader with this classic flyfishing knot.

STEP 1 Cross the tag ends of the lines, and leave 6 to 8 inches overlapping. Hold where the lines cross, and wrap one tag end around the other standing line four to six times.

STEP 2 Repeat with the other line, and bring the tag ends through the gap between the wraps, making sure to go in opposite directions.

STEP 3 Pull the lines, moisten, and draw the knot tight. —T.E.N.

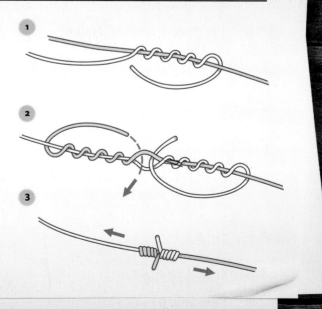

106 CATCH A CAT WITH PANTYHOSE

Dough balls are notoriously difficult to keep on a hook. Here's a way to solve this problem. Make dough balls by mixing bloody hamburger and flour, liver and dough, or hot water and cornmeal mixed with licorice and sugar. Toss one into the toe of a pantyhose leg and tie it off with a piece of dental floss snugged next to the dough ball. Now tie another piece of dental floss next to the first knot; snip the hose between the knots. Turn the remainder inside out. You'll have an encased hunk of catfish bait, and the pantyhose is ready for you to make some more. —T.E.N.

107 STICK IT TO SHORT-STRIKING FISH

Steelhead regularly short-strike, one of the many reasons these fish drive anglers crazy. Teach nimble-lipped steelies a lesson with a trailer-hook streamer pattern, tied with bunny strips, Flashabou, and other materials. Easy to tie, it's a great fly for largemouth and striped bass, pike, and other fish with a big appetite. (Check local laws for multiple-hook regulations.)

STEP 1 Make a loop with approximately 5 inches of 20-pound Dacron backing. When the fly is completed, the tail materials should not extend past the trailer hook, so decide now how long the fly will be. Thread the loop through the eye of an octopus hook for drop-shot rigs, with an upturned eye.

STEP 2 Lay the two tag ends of the Dacron loop along opposite sides of the shank of the fly-pattern hook. Next, rotate the loop so the dropper hook point rides up. Apply drops of a super glue or epoxy to secure the loop to the hook shank. Wrap very tightly with thread.

STEP 3 Build up the body of the fly in whatever pattern you choose. —T.E.N.

108 AVOID SINKING YOUR BOAT IN HEAVY WATER

Some lakes dish up big, nasty rollers day after day, but just about any lake can throw up bruising water in the right—or wrong—wind.

You don't want to pound through endless 4-footers in an 18-foot boat, so tack across the rollers as long as they're not breaking. As the roller approaches, run down the trough parallel to the crest, as far as you can or need to, and slide over the crest into the trough behind it. Then turn the bow straight into the swell and ride up and down the rough spots until you need a break. It's slower going, but it's better than getting beat up for miles. —T.E.N.

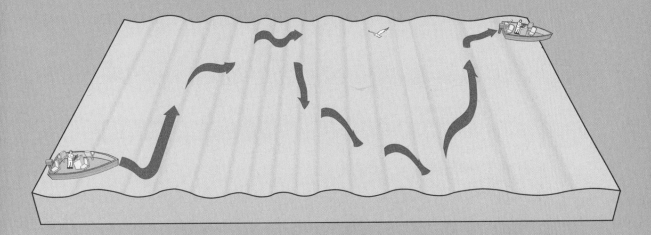

109 STEER BIG TROUT AWAY FROM DOWNED TIMBER

CHECK THE RUN Apply pressure above the trout by lifting the rod from the butt section—not the tip. This will have the effect of forcing the fish into a head-shaking posture and blunts the surge.

STILL GOING? Don't lift the rod tip. Sweep the rod in the same direction the fish is moving so that the momentum of your rod and line movement guides the fish away from the obstruction.

KICKING YOUR BUTT? Stick your rod tip into the water and free some slack line. You want the tip to carry the fly line and leader low enough to clear the sunken timber. The current will keep enough tension on the

belly of the slack line. Once the fish clears the trees, bring the rod tip up and to the side to apply more side pressure and guide the fish out. —T.E.N.

110 TIE A SIX-TURN SAN DIEGO JAM

Because the San Diego jam uses wraps around both the tag end and standing line, the knot has a better cushion and is stronger than clinch knots, which wrap around only one strand. The improved clinch owes its popularity to its old age: It was one of the first knots that worked well with monofilament line, a WWII-era invention. Knots have since advanced—it's time to learn to tie the San Diego.

STEP 1 Thread the line through the hook eye and double it back 10 inches.

STEP 2 Wrap the tag end over itself and the standing line six times, moving toward the hook.

STEP 3 Pass the tag end through the first open loop at the hook eye.

STEP 4 Thread the tag end through the open loop at the top of the knot.

STEP 5 Lubricate and tighten by pulling the tag end and standing line, making sure the coils stay in a spiral and don't overlap. —J.M.

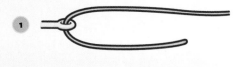

111 TURN A RATTY DUCK MOUNT INTO A NATTY FLY LINE RACK

The problem: A rat's nest of floating, sinking, and intermediate fly lines in weights from wispy double-taper 3s to double digits. Wind them on reels for storage and line memory sets in, setting you up for coil-snared casts in the spring. Dump them in a shoebox and they end up as tangled as Medusa's tresses on a bad hair day. You need a way to keep them orderly and stored in long coils.

The solution: A few Sharpie waterproof markers and a ratty old duck mount. Clean each line according to manufacturer's suggestions, let them dry, and then mark each line at the butt end where it will attach to backing. Come up with a system: Long ago, Lefty Kreh advocated using one long dash to represent a 5 weight, with slashes in front or behind that are added or subtracted to delineate line weight. (For example, a mark in front of the long dash would be subtracted from 5 to delineate a 4-weight line). Use different-colored markers for various tapers and sink rates.

Now coil each line in nice long 2-foot loops and hang it from your duck. Your newly repurposed bird will hold no less than eight lines: one from each foot, two from each wing, and a couple more draped over the neck. Make sure you hang the duck in a cool, dry place away from direct sunlight. No spare ducks in your trophy room? You can also tack up a set of middling-size antlers.

—T.E.N.

112 MASTER THE CANOE PADDLE

The much-lauded J-stroke kills a canoe's forward momentum. Try this: Finish off a traditional forward stroke by rolling both wrists over and away from the boat. This turns the paddle blade perpendicular to the water surface, like a rudder. Here's how:

STEP 1 This is a must: Rotate the upper body away from your paddle side. Your shaft hand grips the paddle above the blade, and that arm is nearly straight. Your grip hand is pulled back toward your nose. Get it right, and you should be able to see under your grip-hand arm.

STEP 2 As the paddle catches the water, unwind the upper body and pull the paddle back. Use the entire upper body, not just your arms. This power stroke stops when the paddle blade reaches your hips. After that, you're just pushing water up and wasting energy.

STEP 3 A powerful forward stroke turns the canoe, so now it's time to correct course. As the paddle reaches your hips, the thumb on your grip hand should be pointing away from you. Now rotate your wrist so that your thumb points straight down. This turns the paddle blade perpendicular to the water surface, like a rudder. Now give a slight push away from the gunwale as you bring the blade out of the water for the next stroke, and the bow tracks back in line. You can correct course and make all but the sharpest turns without losing forward speed.

—T.E.N.

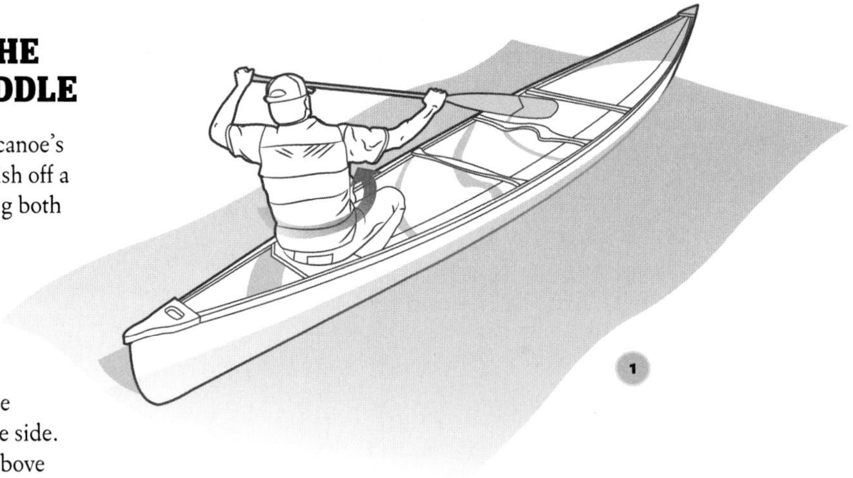

113 CATCH A MUSKIE AT BOAT SIDE BY DRAWING A FIGURE EIGHT

Wisconsin muskie guide and pro angler Jim Saric puts the finishing touch on muskies following a lure to the boat with an aggressive sweep of the rod tip in the shape of a figure eight. "Muskies, like pike, will follow a lure, but they're not nearly as aggressive," Saric says. The figure eight is a final enticement performed by the angler just before lifting the lure out of the water for another cast. To visualize the concept, think of a roller coaster. As you move the lure from side to side, it also moves up and down. That 3-D action can really turn on a fish.

"You don't want a lot of line out because you'll lose control of the lure," Saric says. "Also, be sure to maintain lure speed throughout the maneuver. If you slow down as you make a turn, the blade will stop turning and a fish will lose interest." Saric emphasizes that you should perform the figure eight on each cast. It needs to become routine so you do it properly every time.

"I've seen fish wiggle their tails and flare their gills near the boat, and you can't help but think, Here it comes!" he says. "And what happens is an angler may stop to look at the fish." That's a big mistake, as the loss of lure action is going to cause the muskie to turn away.

Try to set the hook across the face of the fish so that it rests securely in the jaw. "The basic idea is to initiate the fight close to the boat to maintain more control over the fish." But, Saric notes, "Big muskies will do what they do." Which is why we're there in the first place.

GET HIS NUMBER Cast and retrieve as usual, until there's 18 inches of line between the lure and the rod tip (1). Dip the rod tip 6 inches into the water (2). Draw a complete figure eight (3). The directional change can incite a reluctant muskie to strike. Keep in mind that a monster muskie can come from behind you. You won't see the fish until it strikes (4).

THE TACKLE Saric recommends 7- to 8-foot fast-action casting rods. The longer length lets you cover more water and helps reduce erratic upper-body movements that can spook fish. Spool a baitcasting reel with 80- to 100-pound-test braided line. "You have the opportunity to hook a 50-pound fish," Saric says. "This is no time for light line." —s.l.w.

114 TURN POOL NOODLES INTO CATFISH JUGS

Your little tykes have finally outgrown swim noodles. Good. That means they're at the perfect age for jugging catfish. Here's a way to recycle those foam noodles into a simple new twist on this time-honored summer pastime. Just remember to keep a noodle or two intact—you'll need something to grab should you sink your boat with whiskerfish.

NOODLE NINJA Cut one 5-foot pool noodle into five 1-foot sections. (You'll be able to store five noodle-jugs upright in a 5-gallon bucket—enough to keep you plenty busy.) Wrap one end of each with three wraps of duct tape; this will protect against line cuts. Use a large darning needle or crochet hook to string a 4-foot length of stout mono (60- to 100-pound) or trotline cord through the tape wrap. Tie off one end to a washer or bead, pull it snug, and tie a three-way swivel to the other end.

RIGGED AND READY To the swivel's lower ring, attach a length of 20- to 40-pound mono that's long enough to reach the bottom. To the third ring, tie in a 4-foot dropper line of 20-pound fluorocarbon and a circle hook. Anchor the rig with sufficient weight for the current—any old chunk of iron or half a brick will do. To reduce line twist while wrapping line around the noodle for storage, use a barrel swivel near the weight.

CAT FOOD A small live bluegill, large wads of nightcrawler, or cut bait will catch just about any catfish.

GLOWING RESULTS

If you fish at night, run a strip of reflective tape around the noodle on the opposite end from the line. It'll show up in a flashlight beam.

CATFISH RODEO

For a complete blast, use a 4-ounce weight on the bottom and free-float all the noodles as you monitor the action from the boat. Nothing says summer like chasing down a bunch of catfish noodles gone wild.

—T.E.N.

115 FLY FISH FROM A MOVING BOAT

This skill is not just about firing off the quick cast. Fly-fishing from a moving boat is both a mental and a physical game. You have to see things coming and process the future, and you have to simultaneously perform very well and adapt to what's happening right now and right in front of you. It's not something that you can just jump into a boat and do well the first time you do it, but the angler who can put together the right strategy will catch 25 percent more fish than the guy who can't.

The first step is to be acutely aware of what's happening on the river for the next 50 yards downstream. You need to be watching two places at once: your strike indicator or your fly, and the river coming up. Your mind and your vision must be constantly monitoring them both. Acquiring this ability is like learning to drive, but it's flip-flopped; with driving, you constantly watch the road but monitor the mirrors to have a sense of what's behind and beside you.

After all of that comes the really hard part: devising a kind of choreography of upcoming casts to take advantage of the lies—those are the little foam lines, pockets of still water, current seams—that are in that next 50 yards. And the next and the next.

And you have to keep that diagrammed in your head while you work the water at the boat. The trick to casting from a drift boat is throwing a bit more slack into each cast to compensate for the fact that the line slack doesn't last very long when you're moving, the boat is moving, and the river is moving. To do this, carry a little extra line in your line hand, and, right at the end of the power stroke, you actually feed that loop of slack line into the cast. Shake it through the guides at the end of the stroke, and you'll gain an extra second or two of drag-free float—critical in drift boat fishing.

—T.E.N.

116 SHARPEN A CIRCLE HOOK

The same qualities that enable a circle hook to embed its point into a fish's mouth also prevent the angler from easily sharpening the cutting edge of the hook. Place the bend of the hook in a small bench vise. Make light strokes from the point of the tip toward the barb with a high-grade diamond file (a rotary tool will overheat the metal). Don't oversharpen. The point of a circle hook is to let geometry do the work. —T.E.N.

117 STEER LIVE BAIT TOWARD A HIDDEN LUNKER

Savvy anglers fine-tune hook locations on live shiners to guide the bait into different kinds of structure. Hooked through the lips, a shiner tends to swim back to the boat or stay in one place. A hook at the base of the dorsal fin creates bait action as the minnow tries to swim away, and it will splash on the surface. Hook the minnow near the anal fin—close to the spine—to make it dive. To get the bait under floating mats of vegetation, hook it just above the anal fin. The shiner will swim away from the boat, and by gently lifting and dropping the rod tip, you can get the bait to swim deeper. —T.E.N.

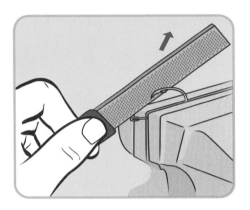

118 MAKE FISH FRIED RICE

Fish fried rice is everything most other fish dishes aren't. It requires a single pan, one spoon, and less time than you need to land a 10-pound striper. Go low-tech with this recipe as is or dress it up with slivered carrots, oyster mushrooms, or a tablespoon or two of Thai fish sauce. And it's a snap for shore dinners: Mix the soy sauce, ginger, and spices in a small bottle at home and complete in the field.

INGREDIENTS

1/4 tsp. minced ginger
4 tbsp. soy sauce
1/2 tbsp. Chinese five-spice powder
2 tbsp. peanut or sesame oil, divided
1 1/2 pounds fresh fish fillets,
    cut into bite-size pieces
1 cup green peas (rehydrate if using dried peas)
1/4 cup sliced green onions
2 cups rice, cooked and chilled
2 tbsp. fresh parsley, chopped
3 eggs

Mix ginger and five-spice powder with soy sauce. Set aside. Heat 1 tablespoon of oil in a wok or large skillet, and stir-fry fish fillets 1 minute. Add peas and onions, stir-fry 2 minutes. Add soy sauce and spice mixture; stir well and remove from pan. Heat remaining tablespoon of oil and add rice and parsley. Stir-fry one minute. Scrape rice mixture to sides of skillet, leaving a doughnut-shaped hole in the middle. Add eggs, scramble, and cook for one minute. Add fish and vegetable mixture, mix thoroughly, and continue stir-frying until eggs are cooked, about 2 to 3 minutes.

—T.E.N.

119 CONTROL YOUR WAKE

Many boaters believe that just slowing a boat down decreases its wake at a rate equal to the loss of speed. But there's more to it than that. Here's the right way.

STEP 1 Decelerate 50 yards ahead of the no-wake zone. Move all of the passengers to the bow to pull more of the stern out of the water.

STEP 2 Cut the power gradually and completely and then bump the throttle to maintain steering speed. The most common wake mistake is simply slowing down to a transition speed in which the bow is up and the stern is still plowing through the water.

STEP 3 You're going to want to go as slow as possible whenever you're in narrow channels. Waves rebounding off the shoreline are damaging to underwater structure.

—T.E.N.

120 TROLL FOUR WAYS

FLAT-LINING

In this least complicated trolling method, your line is attached directly to a lure without any secondary weight or device added. Usually seen as a near-surface technique, flat-lining allows you to reach moderate depths by trolling jigs or diving crankbaits.

BEST FOR Crappies, trout, salmon, walleyes, northern pike

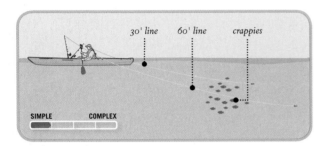

HOW IT'S DONE FOR CRAPPIES

Crappies are common targets for summer flat-line trollers. In many lakes, crappie schools suspend 10 to 15 feet deep, sometimes near structure but just as often in the open waters of the main lake. Here's one of many possible crappie-trolling tactics.

Spool 4- or 6-pound monofilament on common midweight spinning outfits. It's important to remember that crappies are soft-mouthed; a flexible rod tip keeps hooks from tearing out. Two-inch-long, $1/16$- and $1/8$-ounce crappie jigs are basic. If you're trolling with two or more rods, rig with jigs of differing weights or colors.

Slow-troll at 1 mph (best measured by a GPS unit) with one jig 30 feet behind the boat and the second jig 60 feet back. The more line you have out, the deeper a jig will run. This can be as deep as 10 or 12 feet, depending also on jig weight. Keep experimenting with line length, jig size, and color until you start hitting fish. When you do, throw out a marker buoy as a target for your next trolling pass, then match your other trolling rod to the line length and jig that took the first fish.

TIP For flat-line trolling with diving plugs, fine-diameter superline such as 10-pound-test Berkley FireLine will give you as much as 20 percent greater trolling depth compared with 10-pound nylon monofilament. That's because thinner superlines have less water resistance. You'll get better hooksets, too, because superlines have less stretch.

DOWNRIGGING

Trolling with one or more downriggers can run your lures deeper than any other method. In extreme cases, depths can be as much as several hundred feet, but 30 to 60 feet is most common. It's a great light-tackle method, too, because when a fish strikes, the line pops out of a release clip next to the trolling weight so the battle proceeds unencumbered by heavy gear.

BEST FOR Trout, salmon, walleyes

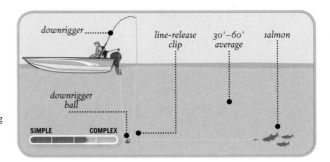

HOW IT'S DONE FOR TROUT AND SALMON A downrigger consists of a large reel holding a thin wire cable that passes through a pulley at the end of a short boom. The cable end is fastened to a 4- to 12-pound ball that usually has a fin or vane to keep it tracking straight. The whole assembly is permanently mounted on a boat's rear deck corner. Some small portable units are designed as clamp-ons.

With the ball at the surface and the boat moving at about 2 mph, let your lure out 30 to 60 feet behind the boat. Then fasten the line to the release clip and put the rod in the adjacent rod holder. Make sure the reel drag is set extremely light so line will pay out as you lower the trolling ball. Once the ball is at the desired depth, tighten the reel drag back to a normal setting and reel in enough line so your flexible rod tip is bowed down slightly. When a fish strikes, the tip will pop up and pick up the slack.

In most summer trout and salmon fishing, your sonar will show larger fish and schools of baitfish at or near the thermocline—that narrow band 30 to 70 feet deep where water temperatures drop radically. It's very simple to run your downrigger weights and lures at that depth all day long.

CONTROL YOUR WEIGHT Downrigger weights are heavy and can swing wildly in the air when you're trying to rig a lure in a wave-tossed boat. The ball can damage your boat's hull unless you control it. When rigging, keep the weight just under the water's surface, where it'll remain stable.

PLANER BOARDS

Planer boards can be the most effective trolling devices of all, but they are a bit complicated to use. These 7- to 12-inch floating "boards" hold your line 50 to 100 feet off to the side of the boat. Setting a pair of planers, one on each side, means you're covering a swath of water up to 200 feet wide and are thus more likely to encounter fish. And because the lines and lures are far away from your droning outboard, you're less likely to spook fish.

BEST FOR Walleyes, salmon, trout

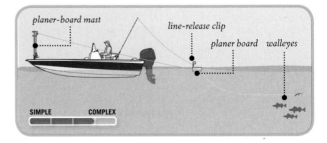

HOW IT'S DONE FOR WALLEYES The most common setup includes a 6-foot-high mast mounted in the boat's bow. This mast holds two large take-up reels with cord that attaches to left- and right-side planers. The planer boards are tapered or ballasted to run at the surface.

As the boat slowly moves ahead, pay out a board on its cord until the desired distance away from the boat is reached. As soon as you're there, release line from your reel so your lure is running about 60 feet behind the boat. At that point, attach a release clip to your line and also to a "quick clip" that you slip onto the planer-board cord. Line tension from the trolled lure makes the clip slide along the cord all the way out to the planer board. Reel up slightly so there's a little line tension between your rod and the board and put the rod in a rod holder.

TIP For what might be the ultimate in walleye trolling, you can run two planer-board lines out on the sides and run downriggers or flat-lines straight off the back of the boat. You'll be presenting a range of lures at a variety of depths and places, and you'll be so busy keeping track of it all that there won't even be time for lunch.

LEAD-CORE LINE

Lead-core line is the easiest, least expensive way to run lures deep. Lead-core is just that: a single-strand lead wire inside a braided nylon covering. Pound-tests range from 12 up to 45. The line is marked by a color change every 10 yards, which makes it easy to tell roughly how much line is extended. In general, each color in the water adds 5 to 8 feet of trolling depth (depending on speed). A 100-yard spool of lead-core line costs about $11. Most wide-spool baitcasting reels hold five or six lead-core colors plus some monofilament backing.

BEST FOR Walleyes, salmon, trout

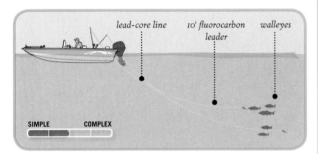

lead-core line   10' fluorocarbon leader   walleyes

SIMPLE   COMPLEX

HOW IT'S DONE FOR WALLEYES In summer, lake walleyes either hold near deep structure or cruise as scattered schools across deep flats and basins while following baitfish. To get these fish, use a loop-to-loop connection to add about 10 feet of 10-pound-test clear mono or fluorocarbon as a leader. Then tie on a swimming-minnow plug, crankbait, or trolling spoon. Running the boat at about 1.5 to 2 mph, pay out enough line to reach your desired trolling depth. If your sonar is marking fish at 25 feet, for example, let out about 3.5 colors. Put your rods in holders so the rods extend out from the sides of the boat and low to the water. That way, rod flex will cushion the shock of a strike.

TIP A trolled crankbait vibrates a rod tip very distinctly. Any slight variation in that rod-tip vibration means the lure has been fouled and needs to be reeled in and cleared. Several quick dips usually indicate that you're hitting bottom, so reel up a few feet and check the depth on your sonar. —J.M.

121 LAND A FISH WITH VELVET GLOVES

Always land fish in very clean water. Think about it: You're on a mud bank, and you're stomping around fighting a fish. The last thing you want to do is drag a tired fish through a bunch of crud. —T.E.N.

122 MAKE YOUR OWN CANE POLE

You could use one of those fancy side-scan sonar depthfinders with the new underwater fish-eye orthographic readouts. Or you could go cut a switch of bamboo and do a little cane poling.

If you choose the latter, a decent cane pole is as close as the nearest stand of bamboo. Everyday, ordinary, backyard bamboo works just fine for bream and the occasional small catfish. Make a cane pole our way, with the line anchored to the pole along its entire length, and you'll be able to land anything that doesn't pull you into the pond first.

So there. Drop your line right beside that stump. Sit on a bucket. Doesn't that mud feel squishy between your toes? Hey, where's your bobber?

STEP 1 Cut a straight piece of cane about 10 feet long. Trim the leaf stems as close as possible. Saw through the fat end at the bottom of a joint so the butt end will have a closed cap. Smooth the rough edges with sandpaper.

STEP 2 Tie a string to the slender tip and suspend the cane as it dries to a tan color. (This could take a month or longer.) You can weight it with a brick to help straighten out a curved pole.

STEP 3 With an arbor knot, attach a 20-pound Dacron line a few inches above the place where you hold the rod. Lay the line along the length of the pole and whip-finish the running line to the rod with old fly line at two spots in the middle of the rod—a few feet apart—and at the tip. (If the rod tip breaks, the line will remain attached to the pole.) Attach a 2-foot monofilament leader. Total length of the line from the tip of the rod should be about 14 to 16 feet. Finish with a slip bobber, a split shot, and a long-shank Aberdeen hook for easy removal. —T.E.N.

123 STICK A FISH WITH A FLY FROM A MILE AWAY

Flyfishermen moving from freshwater trout to quarry such as river stripers, migrating shad, and most saltwater fish need to learn how to strip-strike. Raising the rod tip on armor-mouthed or deep-running fish won't set your hook. Nor will it do the trick when you're dredging striper holes with weighted lines or battling currents and tidal rips with long lengths of fly line. Here's what to do once you feel a fish on the line.

STEP 1 Keep the rod tip pointed at your fly at all times.

STEP 2 Release the pressure on the line with the same rod-hand finger you use to control stripping.

STEP 3 Strip line in with a hard, quick, jabbing motion—from a foot to your full reach, depending on how much line is in the water. If there's a lot of slack in your fly line—a deep belly from fishing weighted lines, or swooping curves caused by river or tidal rips—then strip-strike while lifting the rod tip in several short pumping motions. Or follow up a strip-strike with a so-called body strike by holding the line taut and rotating your body to sweep the rod to one side. You can also pull the line and rod in opposite directions—a strip-strike offspring known as a scissors strike.
—T.E.N.

124 MASTER THE TUBE JIG

Stream-bred smallmouths are pigs for crayfish, and nothing imitates a craw like a tube jig.

SCENT CONTROL Jam a small piece of sponge soaked with scent into the tube.

DEPTH PERCEPTION In still water, use a $3/4$-ounce jighead for water less than 10 feet deep; $1/4$-ounce for water 10 to 20 feet deep; and $3/8$-ounce for water deeper than 20 feet. Add weight in moving water.

CRAW CRAWL Let the jig fall to the bottom. Reel up the slack and count to 10. Bass will often strike right away. Start a series of rod-tip lifts. The jig should swim a foot off the bottom and then flutter down. —T.E.N.

Nothing imitates crayfish like a crayfish-colored tube jig.

125
CAST LIKE A CHURCH STEEPLE

A steeple cast solves some of the roll cast's deficiencies. It's easier to use with weighted flies or lines, and you can change the direction of your cast midstroke.

But it's not easy. Practice first to prevent unholy language.

STEP 1 Start with the rod tip almost touching the water, and the rod hand rotated away from the body so the reel faces up. Begin with a sidearm backstroke, but rotate at the elbow and then raise the casting arm swiftly vertical. This is an outward and upward motion. With the rod tip directly overhead, the upper arm is at a right angle with your forearm, which is vertical.

STEP 2 Stop the rod abruptly at the 12 o'clock position. The line should be tight and straight overhead.

STEP 3 Make a brisk forward cast, stopping abruptly at the 2 or 3 o'clock position. —T.E.N.

126 KILL A FISH HUMANELY

The American Veterinary Medical Association's guidelines on euthanasia propose "cranial concussion [stunning] followed by decapitation or pithing [severing or destroying the spinal cord]." It's just five seconds, and you're done— and a better person for it.

STUN The brain of most fish is located behind and slightly above the eye, at about a 10 o'clock position relative to the pupil. Strike there using a short, heavy baton or a rock.

PITH Insert a knife blade into the skull and twist. Or slice just behind the brain to completely sever the spinal cord. —T.E.N.

127 WINTERIZE AN OUTBOARD ENGINE

Make sure your outboard motor starts with the first pull come spring.

STEP 1 Add fuel stabilizer to gas, following the manufacturer's directions. Run the motor for 5 to 10 minutes and then disengage the fuel line until the engine dies.

STEP 2 Remove spark plugs and spray fogging oil into each cylinder. Replace spark plugs. Crank the engine to spread the oil.

STEP 3 Change the lower-unit oil. This removes all water that might freeze and expand over the winter.

STEP 4 Pull the propeller off and grease the shaft splines. Replace the propeller.

STEP 5 Clear the lower-unit water inlets and speedometer pitot tube of any junk with a pipe cleaner. —T.E.N.

128 READ A TROUT'S TABLE MANNERS

When trying to figure out which fly to cast to a rising trout, most of us will take any help we can get. And in fact, there's help to be had right in front of you: A close look at how a trout is surfacing—its rise form—can speak volumes about what it's eating. Here's a guide to five common rise forms. It's not foolproof, but it will help you catch more fish. —T.E.N.

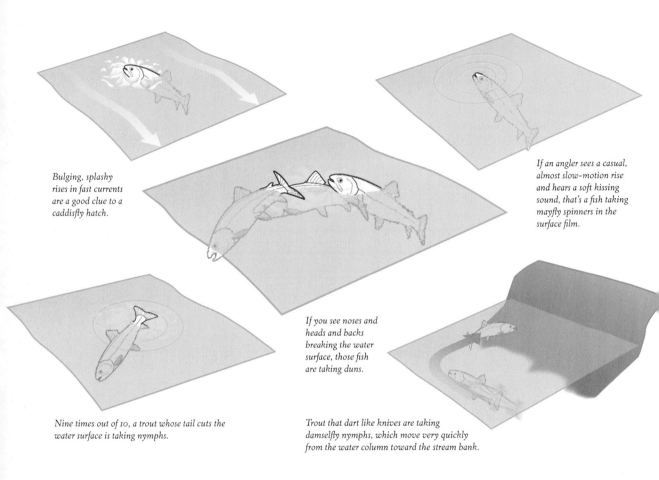

Bulging, splashy rises in fast currents are a good clue to a caddisfly hatch.

If an angler sees a casual, almost slow-motion rise and hears a soft kissing sound, that's a fish taking mayfly spinners in the surface film.

If you see noses and heads and backs breaking the water surface, those fish are taking duns.

Nine times out of 10, a trout whose tail cuts the water surface is taking nymphs.

Trout that dart like knives are taking damselfly nymphs, which move very quickly from the water column toward the stream bank.

129 MAKE A QUICK-SINKING FLY LINE

Fast-sinking fly lines are the bomb for catching shad surging up spring-swollen rivers, and they're deadly on striped bass, too. They're a cinch to build out of a few inexpensive materials and the leftover fly line that lies snarled on your workbench. For this, use LC-13, a lead-core line that weighs 13 grains per foot.

START SNIPPING (These are directions for a 9-wt line; experiment with lengths of lead-core for other line weights): Cut off the running line section of an old fly line. Cut a 28-foot section of LC-13. Cut a 6-inch length of 30-pound braided monofilament running line.

BRING ON THE KNOTS Attach backing to one end of the running line with a nail knot. Then insert the free tip of the running line into one end of the braided mono. Next, work the running line into the braided mono almost halfway by grasping the braided mono between thumb and forefinger of one hand and pushing toward it with the thumb and forefinger of the other hand, creating a bellows-like accordion.

FINISH Repeat above with one end of the LC-13. Tie a whip finish to the two ends of the braided mono sleeve and apply a few drops of pliable glue. Finally, tie in a loop—commercial or homemade with 40-pound mono—directly to the end of the sinking line. You're ready to dredge. —T.E.N.

130

CRIPPLE A FLY FOR AN IRRESISTIBLE TREAT

Heavily fished trout often require triggers in your fly pattern to prompt a strike. Many fish will key on malformed or wingless duns or crippled flies—put a fly out there with beautiful tails or upright wings, and they won't even look at it. That means you need to go with a pattern of trailing shucks. And get creative. Cut the wings off flies. Trim them so they fall over on one side. Most anglers can't bring themselves to take scissors to a perfectly good fly, but not every fish is a perfectionist. —T.E.N.

131

PULL OFF THE INVISIBLE CAST

You can perfect an arm-roll cast to deliver the fly upstream of the fish and to prevent false-casting over your target. Here's how it's done.

START Begin with the rod tip at the surface and pointing downstream. Load the rod with the tension of the line dragging on the water (1). Be sure to keep your forearm and wrist straight while you bring your arm up in a rolling motion (2).

FINISH Roll your arm down to the water, pointing the rod tip upstream (3). Allow the line to unroll in front while reaching out (4) before the rod tip stops at the water's surface. —T.E.N.

132

BACK A BOAT WITH STYLE

Had their captains backed the *Dartmouth*, *Beaver*, and *Eleanor* into their respective slips, the Brits might have been able to goose the engines and leave the Boston Tea Party rebels flatfooted on the dock. Moral of the story: There are lots of reasons to know how to back a boat into a slip. (Practice in a quiet cove to learn which way your bow turns when you attempt to back in a straight line—a phenomenon known as "propeller walk.")

STEP 1 Idle to your target slip. As your bow reaches the slip just before yours, stop forward motion by bumping into reverse. Shift into neutral and turn the wheel away from your slip as far as it will turn.

STEP 2 Bump the throttle into forward to start a pivot turn. Shift to neutral, turn the steering wheel in the opposite direction, and then bump into reverse. This will stop the pivot.

STEP 3 Align the transom with the slip, and back in slowly. Remember which direction your bow wants to "walk" when moving in reverse. Adjust course by bumping the drive into and out of gear. —T.E.N.

133 RIG A STINGER HOOK

Catch light-biting walleyes with a second hook rigged toward the tail of a live minnow. (This trick puts bait-stealing perch and crappies in the frying pan, too.) Using limp monofilament, tie one end of the stinger line to the bend in the primary hook with an improved clinch knot. Attach the stinger hook—a slightly smaller single hook or a treble—with another improved clinch knot, and embed it either behind the dorsal fin or into the muscle just ahead of the tail. Leave enough line between the two hooks so that the rig will work with baitfish of slightly varying sizes. —T.E.N.

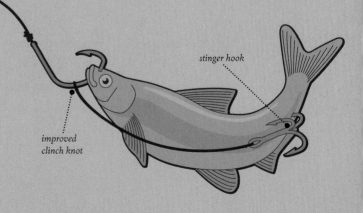

stinger hook

improved clinch knot

134

TIE THIS FLY IF IT'S THE LAST THING YOU DO

The Clouser Minnow has joined the likes of Woolly Buggers and Muddlers as a global standard among fly patterns. Unlike the others, though, Clousers are easily made by novice fly-tying fishermen. The fly's jigging action works great for everything from crappies and brown trout to striped bass and redfish (Lefty Kreh has landed 86 different species on it). Vary the fly size and color to suit your quarry.

For this example, you'll need a medium-shank-length streamer hook, some nylon or polyester size 3/0 thread, some dumbbell-style eyes, natural white plus dyed chartreuse bucktail, and some Flashabou or similar material. Use clear nail polish as a fly-tying cement. Here's how to put it all together. —J.M.

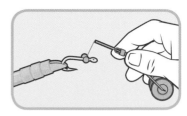

STEP 1 With the hook in a tying vise, secure the thread one-third of the shank length back from the hook eye. Tie dumbbell eyes securely on top of the shank with figure-eight thread wraps. Add a small dab of cement to the wraps.

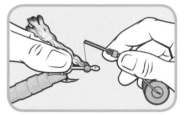

STEP 2 Tie in a sparse bunch of white bucktail behind the hook eye and in front of the eyes. Wind the thread to a position right behind the eyes. Pull the white bucktail firmly into the groove between the eyes, and tie it down again right behind the eyes.

STEP 3 Turn the hook over in the vise so that the hook point is up. Add about six strands of Flashabou or a similar material.

STEP 4 Tie in a bunch of chartreuse bucktail, and build a neat conical head with thread wraps, finishing with two half hitches. Coat the finished fly head with nail polish (two coats). —J.M.

135 PADDLE A CANOE INTO A GALE

The right way seems wrong: Trim the canoe slightly bow heavy to keep it heading into the wind. Kneel in the bottom of the boat and use short, quick strokes. Feather the paddle on your return stroke, turning the blade parallel to the water surface so it won't catch the wind. Keep the boat pointed into the waves and use every bit of windbreak possible—even distant land points can provide relief from wind and swell. —T.E.N.

136 SET ANY ANCHOR, ANYTIME

Head upwind or upcurrent and then lower the anchor all the way to the bottom. Anchors grab best when they first lie down. Reverse the engine and slowly back away to a distance of 7 to 10 times the depth of the water. —T.E.N.

fluke hooks for sandy coastal waters   *mushrooms for lakes*   *river anchors for moving water*

137 DRESS A FLY CORRECTLY

It's easy to destroy a fly's profile by smashing and grinding in floatant. Here's the lowdown on the correct way to make your fly float.

Grasp the hook point between your thumb and index finger. Place one drop of floatant directly on the top of the hackle fibers. Instead of applying the floatant to your fingers and then working it into the fly, use a finger on your other hand to flick the floatant into the fly materials. —T.E.N.

138 FILLET THE BONIEST FISH THAT SWIMS

The Y-bones embedded in the dorsal flesh of a northern pike prevent many anglers from dining on one of the tastiest fish around. Learn to remove them, and you will never curse when a 3-pound pike bashes your walleye rig.

STEP 1 Fillet the fish, removing flesh from the ribs as you would with any other fish.

STEP 2 Find the row of white dots visible midway between the spine and the top of the fillet. These are the tips of the Y-bones. Slice along the top of these dots, nearly through the fillet, following the curve of the bones.

STEP 3 Next, you'll want to slice along the bottom of the Y-bones, following their shape, while aiming the knife tip toward the first incision.

STEP 4 Connect the two cuts above the fish's anus. Remove the bony strip. Get the grease popping. —T.E.N.

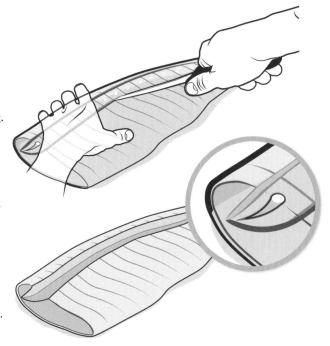

139 TAKE THE FIGHT TO THE FISH IN SMALL WATER

Big fish are so strong and tough in tight quarters. Two things are crucial to landing monster fish in small rivers. First, as soon as you know the fish is hooked well, go to the head of the pool. Put some distance between the rod and whatever rapids and logs and rocks are jumbled up in the tailout. Second, once you have some room, it's critical to make the fish go through at least two runs against the drag. Don't be afraid to wave your arms above the water if you have to. You simply must get the fish to work and tire out.

Instead of fighting with the rod held straight up and down, turn it at a 45-degree angle, and sweep the tip to the left or right to lead the fish into the current or into deep runs. You may need to steer a big fish into shallow water so it will get nervous and make a break for the current. If it just sits in the stream, holding, do something to get it moving again. Take control of the action. —T.E.N.

140

FLY CAST IN CIRCLES

When brush or high ground limits your back cast, break the rules with a lob cast.

STEP 1 Strip the line in so you have the leader and about 10 feet of line in the water. Point the rod at the fly and then pick it all up, right out of the water at once, and make a big, fast, clockwise, circular pass overhead. The reel should actually move in a half-circle above your head.

STEP 2 Stop the rod behind at the position where you would stop a traditional back cast, feel it load, and then fire all the line out with one forward shot. You can seriously launch a heavy fly or sink-tip line this way.
—T.E.N.

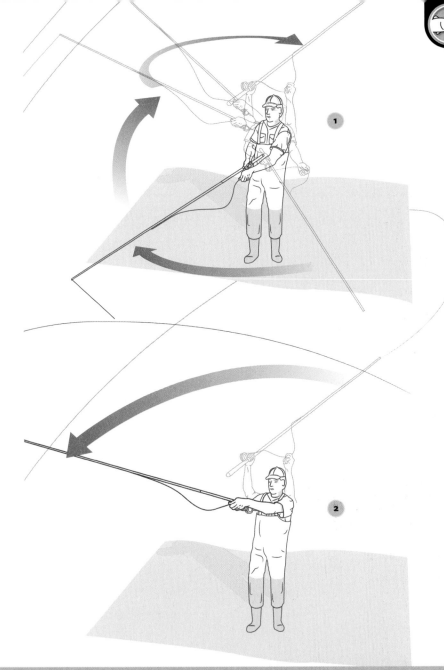

141 CATCH BAIT WITH A SABIKI RIG

Sabiki rigs are ready-to-fish dropper lines festooned with small hooks trimmed with reflective materials and sometimes bucktail. These rigs are great for catching marine baitfish, but freshwater baits like white perch and small bream will suck in the hooks too. (Check local regulations before using.)

In freshwater, you're going to want to go for the smallest hooks you can find. Attach a 1- or 2-ounce weight, and jig slowly up and down with a long rod over likely structure. Don't make the mistake of bringing it in with the first strike. A hooked fish will move the hooks around and attract other fish.

To store your sabiki rig, wrap the rig around a wine cork, sticking each hook into the cork as you wrap.
—T.E.N.

142 LAND BIG TROUT SOLO

A 20-inch trout on the line and no one to marvel at your fishing skills? First things first. You can't gloat until you get the fish in, so here's how to land a brag-worthy trout all by your lonesome.

STEP 1 Start with your rod overhead, and with 10 feet of line out. Next, rotate your rod arm to move the rod to a horizontal plane, being sure it's pointing upstream, keeping the pressure on the fish.

STEP 2 Back up toward the bank, steering the fish toward shore.

STEP 3 Raise the rod back overhead to vertical. Drop your net and scoop the fish under its chin. —T.E.N.

143 HAUL-CAST A FLY 60 FEET OR MORE

If you can tug on a fly line, you can learn to do the single and double haul. The trick is timing. The key is practice.

Grab the fly line close to the rod with your line hand. Start your back cast. Just as you begin your backward power stroke, pull the line (in your line hand) toward your hip pocket. Don't jerk—just make a smooth, fast motion of a foot and a half or so and release. Your back cast should shoot rearward with added zip. That's a single haul—and often all you need for a little extra distance.

To complete the double haul, start by easing your line hand back toward the reel as your back cast unfurls.

Then, just as you begin your forward power stroke, pull downward again as before. Finish the cast and let the slack line shoot through your hand. —K.M.

144 RUN A RAPID

Learning to negotiate a straight-on ledge drop or chute of water between two rocks are a couple of Whitewater Canoeing 101 basic skills.

SCOUT IT OUT First, get a good look at what you're getting into. It's best to scout from shore because looking at a piece of moving water from the side gives you an entirely different perspective.

Make sure it's what you expect—no rocks or drops you won't be able to see from the water. Find the V of water that flushes through the rapid cleanly, with a series of standing waves at the bottom that are a sign of clear deep water. Be sure that you plan how to avoid curling waves formed by underwater rocks and souse holes.

PREPARE TO PROCEED Next, move into position slowly. That way, you can escape if you have a last-second change of mind. Set up the approach without a lot of power until you establish your line.

COMMIT YOURSELF Once you've done all of your preparation, it's commitment time. Get yourself correctly lined up, and just start powering forward. Be aware that the forward stroke is the simplest means of bracing a canoe in turbulent water, so the best thing to do is to keep paddling. That will also prevent you from committing the worst rapids-running mistake: grabbing the gunwale. —T.E.N.

145 RIG LEAD-CORE LINES FOR THE DEEPEST LUNKERS

Knowing how to troll with metered lead-core lines is indispensable for many big-lake fisheries, where the majority of anglers pull lead-core lines from fall to ice-up. These lines are metered in colors, and each color is 30 feet long. Use 18-pound lead core in a splice-in rig to get lures down deep and defeat the lack of sensitivity that comes with heavy sinkers. Here's how:

STEP 1 Spool up 200 to 300 feet of 14- or 20-pound monofilament backing. Tie on a No. 18 barrel swivel with an improved clinch knot.

STEP 2 Peel back the Dacron sheath from the last 4 to 5 inches of lead-core line and pinch off the lead. This leaves a length of sheath that you can tie onto the barrel swivel with an improved clinch knot.

Wind three colors of lead onto the reel. Peel back another length of sheath, pinch off the lead, and tie on another No. 18 barrel swivel.

STEP 3 Attach to the barrel swivel 50 feet of 10-pound-test fluorocarbon line, then a ball-bearing snap-swivel or plain plug snap, and then the crankbait. —T.E.N.

146 REPLACE TRAILER BEARINGS ON THE SIDE OF THE ROAD

Burn out boat trailer wheel bearings while on the road and you'll face lost fishing or hunting opportunities, long hours hitching rides to nearby towns, longer nights in fleabag motels, and painful repair bills. That is unless you're prepared with a bearing fix-it kit and the know-how to use it.

ASSEMBLE A FIRST-AID KIT In a surplus ammo can, place spare bearings, races or "cups," seals, a seal puller, marine-grade bearing grease, a small notepad and pencil, and these instructions. Stow it in your boat.

DISASSEMBLE Remove the grease cover or Bearing Buddy–type cap. Remove cotter pin from spindle nut, remove the nut, and the entire hub should slip off the axle. There are two sets of bearings: one on the inside and one on the outside. Remove them. Tap out the grease seal. If you're unfamiliar with the process, sketch out which parts come off in which order.

CLEAN Clean all the old grease from the bearings, hub, and axle spindle. Wipe away what you can with paper towels and then use mineral spirits or kerosene. Inspect the parts carefully: Look for rust spots, cracks, or bluish staining that indicates overheating. Replace if necessary.

REPACK Hold the bearing with the fingers of one hand, and place a glob of marine bearing grease in the palm of the other hand. Now work the grease into the

bearing cage, turning the cage to lubricate each bearing. Put a thin coating of grease onto the spindle and inside of the hub.

REASSEMBLE To replace the grease seal without bending it, position it in the grease bore, place a piece of wood across it, and tap the wood lightly with a hammer. Now reverse the disassembly process, replacing all items in the opposite order.

GO PROFESSIONAL Unless you're 100 percent confident of your ability to get it right, have a mechanic look at your handiwork once you're home. —T.E.N.

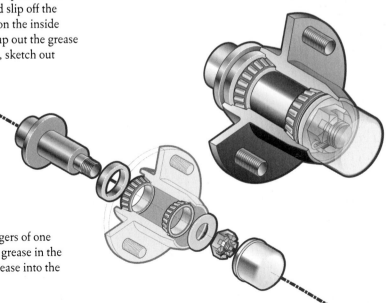

147 SUPERCHARGE SALMON EGG BEADS

Beads resembling eggs are the fly patterns of choice wherever trout, char, and steelhead follow spawning salmon. Unaltered beads will draw strikes right out of the package, but you can make them more effective by applying a realistic finish and softer texture, so the fish won't spit them out before you can set the hook.

STEP 1 Stick one end of a toothpick through the hole in the bead to use as a handle. Paint the entire bead with fingernail polish (something sheer or clear). Stick the toothpick upright into a block of Styrofoam and let dry one hour.

STEP 2 Pour some soft epoxy into a bowl and roll the bead in it, coating all sides. Stick the toothpick back into the Styrofoam in a horizontal position. The epoxy will gather more heavily on the bottom side, so the bead will be slightly out of round after drying. Dry overnight.

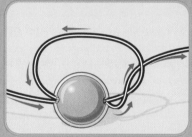

STEP 3 To rig, slip a bead onto your tippet, and then pass the end of the tippet back around and through the bead again, forming a loop. Pass the end of the tippet through the loop and cinch tight to secure the bead. Tie on a hook with an upturned eye to the tippet 1 to 3 inches from the bead. With the bead secured above the hook, it will look and drift more naturally, and the fish you catch will be hooked on the outside of the jaw. Fish this under a strike indicator.

NOTE It is against regulations to use a bare-bead, bare-hook combination in some fly-only waters. Check before you try this tip.

Match the beads you use to the size of eggs drifting in the river: 6mm for sockeye salmon, 8mm for coho, 10mm for kings. Fish may choose older-looking eggs over "fresh" ones, so stock up on a variety of colors. —K.M.

148 TURN A KID ON TO FLYFISHING

Schooling your kids on flyfishing doesn't have to be as trying as helping them with their math homework. Start by limiting the time on the pond to a half-hour chunk. That prevents the kid from getting frustrated and the teacher from blowing a fuse.

Here's how to optimize those minutes.

KNOW YOUR STUDENTS Tailor your comments to your kids' age levels. A 14-year-old might understand what you mean by "feel the rod load," but an 8-year-old won't. Remember to bring your own rod so you don't take the rod from the kid; that feels like punishment. Don't wait for perfection. Instead, introduce new concepts quickly to battle boredom.

TEACH TIMING Start off with sidearm casts so that the kids can watch the fly line and better understand the physics of casting. Emphasize that fly casting is about timing, not strength.

MAKE A CASTING CALL Tell your kids to treat the rod like a ringing telephone: Bring the rod up close to their ear, say, "Hello, this is Drew Smith," and then set the "phone" down. That's the basic fly-casting movement: Sweep the rod back, stop it, let the rod load, and then make a forward cast.

KEEP THINGS ROLLING If the kids struggle with the basics, switch to roll casting for the time being. It's easier to learn, and with a bit of success, they'll be ready to tackle a standard cast.

TIME TO FISH Find a likely spot: Choose a time and place where the fish are willing. Bream beds are perfect.

GO PRO Do your kids bristle at every suggestion you make? Sign up for a casting school, or hire a guide for a half day and outsource the tricky parts.

CHOOSE A ROD A soft action helps kids feel the rod flex and load. Be wary of supershort rods, which can be difficult to cast. Go for an 8-foot, 6-weight, two-piece outfit.

CONSIDER LINE WEIGHT Overline the rod by one line weight for easier turnover.

GO EASY WITH FLIES Get a barbed fly stuck in your child's forehead and you can forget about him or her as a future fishing buddy. Only use flies with barbless hooks. For practice, tie orange egg yarn next to the fly to make it visible. On the water, cast big high-floating flies like Stimulators.
—T.E.N.

149 TRAILER A BOAT IN A HEAVY WIND

If you have to load your boat in a vicious crosswind, follow these steps for success.

STEP 1 Don't back your trailer too deeply into the water. You need firm contact between the hull and the bottom bunks.

STEP 2 Steer into the wind for control.

STEP 3 Approach the trailer at as close to a 90-degree angle as you can get, given ramp design. As you near the imaginary line that extends backward from the trailer, turn slightly toward the trailer.

The wind will catch the bow and move it toward a centered line with the trailer. Bump up the throttle so the bow enters the back of the trailer at an angle pointing slightly into the wind. Momentum will carry the boat into a straight line.

STEP 4 Apply enough power to push the bow eye to within 6 to 8 inches of the bow stop. Check your centering. Take a bow.
—T.E.N.

150 CHOOSE THE RIGHT BASS LURE

Bass lures can be divided into five broad categories depending on the lure's design and how the angler manipulates the bait. Pack a tackle box with a few lures from each of these categories, and you'll catch bass in any weather, from any water. —T.E.N.

SOFT PLASTIC Few baits have changed the fishing world as much as soft plastics. Introduced as a large worm imitation in 1951, the realistic, lifelike baits now come in a dizzying array of shapes—worms, salamanders, baitfish, crayfish, snakes, slugs, frogs, lizards, mice, and more. Fishing tactics for soft plastics are just as varied. Many are threaded on to a lead jig. Others are rigged with no weight on a weedless, wide-gap hook. And some of the most popular soft plastics are among the most pungent—many of these baits are manufactured with natural or artificial scents and oils that prompt bass to chow down. If you ever feel overwhelmed by soft-plastic selections, it's hard to go wrong with a purple or black worm slow-twitched across the bottom.

SURFACE LURE Otherwise known as topwater lures, these hard-bodied baits kick up a fuss. They gurgle, pop, jerk, waddle, and dart across the water surface and can draw explosive strikes from hungry bass. Surface lures with a cupped face are known as "poppers," and pop and spray water as the angler snaps the rod tip. Poppers can imitate anything from dying baitfish to frantic frogs. Thin, lightweight "pencil poppers" skitter like a minnow on its last legs—and few bass will turn down such an easy meal. One of the best retrieves for cigar-shaped surface lures is called "walking the dog," in which the lure glides back and forth with a zigzag action as the angler twitches the rod tip low to the water.

CRANK BAIT These hard-bodied diving lures imitate a wide range of tantalizing fish foods, most often baitfish such as shad or bluegill, but they can also imitate crayfish when worked right off the bottom. Made of wood or plastic and clad in realistic paints and holographic finishes, most crankbaits sport a hard plastic lip that forces them to dive and wobble when "cranked" through bass water. Crankbaits come in shallow, medium, and deep-diving versions, depending on the size of the plastic diving bill.

STICKBAIT Imitating everything from long, slender minnows to full-grown trout, stickbaits are most often fished with a twitching, stop-and-start motion that looks like prey species darting in and out of cover, or an injured and crippled baitfish struggling to stay alive. That herky-jerky death dance action spawns vicious strikes by feeding bass and can coax even the most close-mouthed largemouth to open wide. Many stickbaits come in a jointed version for even more emphatic action.

SPINNERBAIT Safety-pin style spinnerbaits look nothing like a natural food—but they catch bass like crazy. Built on a V-shaped wire frame, the baits have one or more revolving blades threaded to one wire shaft, while the other is tipped with a weighted hook dressed with an often garish skirt of brightly colored rubber or silicone. The spinning blades produce flash and vibration, while the wild, undulating rubber skirts—often glittering with metal flakes—give bass a temptation they often can't resist. Depending on the rate of retrieve, spinnerbaits can be skittered across the water's surface, helicoptered straight down through the water column, or bumped along the bottom. Many anglers consider spinners "search baits," because they allow you to cover lots of water fast and help you figure out where bass are holding in short order.

THE ONE LURE YOU NEED FOR ...

WALLEYE *grub lure*

PIKE *spoon lure*

SMALLMOUTH *grub lure*

PANFISH *mini-tube*

TROUT *in-line spinner*

STRIPER *stickbait*

151 FIX A FUSSY MOTOR

Our outboard motors take us to fish and game-rich waters and woods. And sometimes they leave us there. Modern motors don't give broken-down boaters a whole lot of options, but these five first-aid tips might get you back to the dock when your motor doesn't want to take you there.

TERMINAL BREAKDOWN Loose battery connections lead to corrosion buildup and arcing—which means you're going nowhere. Finger tight isn't tight enough. Scrape the battery terminals clean with a knife blade and tighten the wing nuts with pliers so they bite into the terminal (1).

BACKWOODS NITRO Starter fluid isn't an everyday solution, but sometimes it's the only way to get home when a carburetor-equipped motor seems to have given up the ghost. It's not hard to jerry-rig some with an empty plastic soda or water bottle: Pour gas in, prick a small hole in the top, and screw it back on. Now you can shoot atomized fuel into the carburetor (2).

HOSE WOES Fuel-line hoses are notorious for kinks, dry-rot patches, and collapsed sections. Rebuild them by cutting out the bad part and reusing the hose clamps to reattach the pieces—or use zip ties or fishing line to tie them tightly (3).

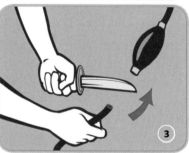

SCRUB THE PLUGS To clean fouled spark plugs, remove the plugs and rinse any goop you find from the firing end with gas. Scrape off burned carbon deposits with whatever's handy: a swatch of sandpaper, small knife blade, a hook sharpener, or even a fingernail file (4).

FUEL-PUMP BYPASS If the outboard quits with its primer bulb full of fuel, the problem could be a fuel pump. Bypass it by pumping the primer bulb continuously (5). You'll limp, but better that than a bivvy in the bottom of the boat. —T.E.N.

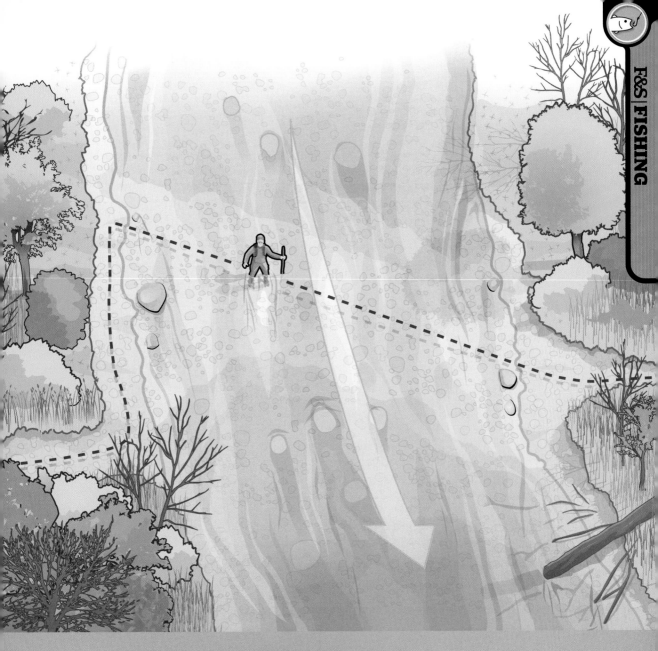

152   CROSS A SWOLLEN CREEK OR (SLIGHTLY) RAGING RIVER

Look before you leap. Current moves most swiftly where a stream narrows, so try crossing at a wider, shallower spot. Scout the far shore to make sure you can clamber to safety—no slick mudbanks or bluffs. Unhook hip belts and loosen shoulder straps on packs in case you need to jettison your load before going into the drink. Cut a shoulder-high staff or break out the trekking poles and remove your socks and insoles. Wet shoes are easier to tolerate than wet everything. Lace your boots firmly and then cross the stream diagonally, moving sideways like a crab and slightly downstream, yielding to the current. Nice and easy keeps you upright. Move only one point of contact at a time: Plant your staff, take a step, plant your staff, take another. —K.M.

153
CATCH KILLER BROWNS

Just about every trout stream has them—huge, predatory brown trout that fishermen rarely see and hardly ever catch. Few fishermen are as dialed in to the nuances of catching large brown trout as Michigan guide Ray Schmidt. For 45 years, Schmidt has been chasing browns in the waters where the species was initially introduced to the United States. Schmidt's biggest Michigan brown is a 26-incher, taken on a streamer at night next to a logjam. Schmidt says that most anglers have no clue what really lurks below the surface of their favorite trout stream. At the right time—usually night—that gentle, meandering river can radically transform into a veritable "killing field" for predatory browns. "These large browns sometimes go on the hunt for food, traveling a mile or two each night in search of prey," says Schmidt. "This is a predator that eats mice, baby ducks, and other creatures in, on, or around the water." In other words, if you want to catch large, you have to fish large, and usually in low-light conditions.

Summer is a particularly opportune time to fish for big nighttime browns. The warm water increases trout metabolism, meaning they must eat more. And these big predators will go on the hunt when the waters cool down at night. —K.D.

1 SHUN THE RIFFLE

Sure, riffles typically hold trout—rainbows. When you're stalking big browns, you want to avoid the water where smaller fish will seize the opportunity to take your bait or fly. If you're looking for a trophy brown, they're distractions.

2 SCOUT AND LISTEN

Some of your most productive time may be spent on a high bank. Learn to recognize the sound that a brown trout makes as it gulps something from the surface. And watch for subtle disturbances in current lines.

3 FIND THE LION'S DEN

Large brown trout thrive in river runs with three ingredients: depth, cover, and slow and steady current. Find the spot in the river where currents and obstructions have scoured a deep hole.

4 FOLLOW THE BUBBLES

Look for seams where fast currents meet slow or where deep water meets shallow currents. Cast into the bubble line created on the surface. Memorize these locations and fish them at night.

5 CASE THE BANK

Big browns will often lurk in the shadows of undercut banks, where they are protected from their predators but can easily dart out and inhale a baitfish or a grasshopper. Fish tight to the bank to catch them.

6 TARGET THE CUSHION

Large browns frequently ride the hydraulics in front of a large rock or tree stump in the river. You want to cast both in front of that rock or stump and into the deep scour behind it.

7 FISH MARGINAL WATER

The biggest browns are hardy fish that can thrive in waters often overlooked by most trout anglers. Don't hesitate to fish downstream from the "prime" section of your favorite trout river.

154 WIN THE TOUGHEST FISH FIGHT

Occasionally, when it all comes together, a true behemoth will suck in your lure. What you do next is the difference between glory and another "almost" story.

KNOW YOUR KNOT WILL HOLD Most big fish are lost due to failed knots. Wet each knot with saliva before cinching it tight, and make sure you seat it properly. If you are less than 100 percent confident in the knot you just tied, take the time to retie it. Every time.

CLEAR THE COVER Bruiser fish will quickly burrow into weeds or head for a snag, so establish authority as soon as you set the hook. Resist the temptation to hoot, holler, and point. Put pressure on immediately and keep your rod tip up. Don't force the action but steer the fish into the clear.

TURN AND BURN Once the fish is in open water, let it wear down. As the fish moves, bend the rod away from the direction in which it's swimming and lower the rod to tighten the angle. Don't winch it; you simply want to turn the head and guide the fish in a different direction, burning energy all the way.

DON'T CHOKE The few seconds after your first boat-side glimpse of a bona fide monster are critical. If you can see him, he can see you. Prepare for a last-ditch escape maneuver. Be ready to jab the rod tip into the water if the fish dives under the boat. Don't grab the line. Stay focused on keeping the fish off-balance until he's in the boat. If you're using a net, make sure you lead the fish in headfirst. —T.E.N.

155 TIE A CLOVE HITCH

The clove hitch is Boating 101—good for a temporary stay to dock or piling.

It's also the foundational knot for many pole-lashing techniques, which may be useful if you don't tie it correctly the first time, your boat drifts away, and you have to lash a long pole together to snag it back. —T.E.N.

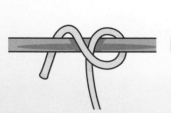

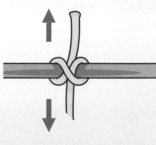

156 LAY YOUR HANDS ON A RIVER MONSTER

There are a number of ways to get your hands on a really big catfish. Noodling expert Gerald Moore places casket-shaped catfish boxes—with a hole the size of a football in one end—in chest-deep water.

On the other hand, some hand-grabbers seed their favorite waters with old water heaters modified for fish. After a few months, a three-person team returns to the box and takes the following steps.

STEP 1 The "checker" blocks the hole with his feet and checks for a fish with a 7-foot pole.

STEP 2 A "helper" stands on the box and helps to steady the checker. Meanwhile, the "grabber" goes underwater and sticks his right arm in the box, up to the elbow to grab the fish.

STEP 3 If the fish bites, he will get all four fingers in the pocket behind its teeth, with his thumb on the outside, then pull it out and wrap it with his left arm. —T.E.N.

157 FLY CAST FROM A KAYAK

Casting from a kayak will test the skills of even the best fly angler. Here's how to modify your style for the confines of a sit-on-top.

MIND YOUR LINE The tall sides of a traditional stripping basket don't cut it when you're casting from a seated position, but you need something to keep your fly line from tangling. A cheap 9 x 11-inch baking pan works as a makeshift stripping basket.

OVERLINE YOUR ROD Using a line weight one step up from the weight of a fly rod will add distance and cut down on false casts.

CUSTOMIZE YOUR CAST Keep your back cast out of the water. To begin, hold your rod arm farther in front of your body than normal to move the power stroke forward of the stopping position on the back cast. Start with the rod tip low and with zero slack in the line, accelerate smoothly, and stop the back cast a bit higher than normal. —T.E.N.

158 PLANT A CRAPPIE TREE

Crappies crave structure, and a PVC tree will attract slabs to the most barren lake bottom. The slick pipes keep hangups to a minimum, and the PVC will last.

THE TRUNK Drill a small hole through one end of a 4-inch-diameter PVC pipe. (The pipe length depends somewhat on the depth of its final destination. A 4- to 5-foot tree works well.) Next, drill three ¾-inch holes along each side of the pipe "trunk" at angles so the "branches" will angle upward and shed hooks easily. Insert a long nail into the small hole you drilled at the bottom of the trunk and anchor it in a 3-gallon flowerpot with concrete.

THE BRANCHES Cut six 3-foot lengths of ¾-inch PVC pipe for your branches. Drill a small hole through the end of two of these. Insert the PVC branches into the holes in the trunk, securing them with PVC glue. —T.E.N.

To attract crappies, fill two empty 20-ounce water bottles—punched with small holes—with dry dog food and cap the bottles tightly. Tie these to the branches that have the small holes.

PVC may not register on many fish finders, so mark your tree's location on your GPS.

159 CATCH TROUT AND BASS WITH YOUR ELK

The hide of one bull elk will produce enough hair for 984,376 flies—give or take. So follow these simple steps, and don't let it go wasted.

STEP 1 Cut 6-inch squares of hide. Flesh with a knife blade by removing as much fat and meat as possible without slicing through the roots of the hair.

STEP 2 Salt each square with 1/4 cup of salt, rubbing the salt into the flesh side of the hide with your fingers. Let it sit for eight hours, shake off the wet salt, and repeat.

STEP 3 Hang the squares from the game pole and air-dry until it's time to break camp. To get them home, store in an air-permeable bag, such as a pillowcase.

STEP 4 Think outside the caddis box. Sure, elk hair is perfect for caddis imitations. But use your hide for other dry flies such as Humpys and Stimulators; for nymphs such as little yellow stoneflies; and for terrestrials like the Henry's Fork Hopper. Elk hair, because it is a little coarser than deer hair, floats higher, so you can even use it for poppers and bass bugs. —T.E.N.

160 TARGET DEEP WATER FOR PIG BASS

Underwater points, submerged roads, old pond dams— deep-water structure holds bass, but many anglers aren't used to probing 30 and 40 feet down. Here's how.

SCHOOL DAZE Once you locate fish, analyze the fish finder to figure out whether they are hanging on top of the hump, to the left or right of the ridge, or off the face of the point as it plunges. A lot of anglers see fish on the fish finder and turn off their brains and pick up a rod. Figure out exactly how the fish are using the structure.

MARK THE FISH Idle 50 feet past the school (75 feet in a headwind) and drop a marker buoy (a).

ANCHOR AWEIGH Circle around to the right or left, always staying about two-thirds of your maximum casting distance away from the school.

In calm conditions, drop anchor (b) when you are even with the marker buoy and then back down until you are even with the school. In a wind, continue past the marker buoy before dropping anchor (c) and drift down until you are even with the school.

MAKE THE CAST Think before you cast. Don't throw right at the fish; by the time your lure reaches the target depth, it will be halfway back to the boat. Instead, throw your bait beyond the fish (d) as far as you can and let the lure sink. Now you're placing the bait right in the strike zone. As for gear, go no lighter than a 7-foot heavy-action rod. Deep water means dealing with serious line stretch, and a long stiff rod results in better hooksets. —T.E.N.

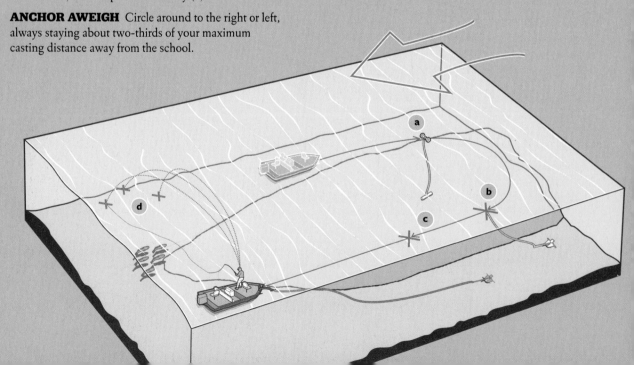

161 DOCUMENT A TROPHY FOR A RIGHTEOUS REPLICA

When you catch a memorable fish, you'll want to preserve the memory. Here's how to record the details for a wall-worthy replica.

MEASURE Always carry a measuring board at least 25 inches long—larger than many standard bass boards. (Saltwater fishing boards work great.) Dunk it in the water before laying out the fish. Measure from the tip of the mouth to the tip of the compressed tail. Gently lift the midsection and measure girth at the widest point. Weigh with a digital scale.

PHOTOGRAPH Take photos of each side, the top of the fish, and the belly. Then switch the camera to "macro" mode and take close-ups of the cheeks, top of the head, and lateral stripe patterns. Capture any distinctive markings.

RECORD Make notes about where you caught the fish. Fish that spend a lot of time in deeper water tend to have light colors; the reverse is true for shallow-water bass. Your detailed notes will help the taxidermist work up the right palette. —T.E.N.

FIELD & STREAM CRAZY-GOOD GRUB

162 TRY A PLANKED FISH

Here's a method that won't result in half your freshly caught dinner falling into the fire like a roasted marshmallow.

PREP THE PLANK Soak a 3/4- to 1-inch-thick plank of aromatic wood—you can use cedar, oak, or hickory—in water for one to two hours. The plank should be slightly wider than the fish and long enough so that you can prop it up beside the fire in a near-vertical position. Preheat the plank by placing it upright near the fire until it is very hot.

PREP THE FISH Season the fish to taste and secure it to the plank with a couple of nails—drive one into the head and place the second one near the tail.

PROP IT UP Stand the plank up in front of the fire, with the fish tail down. Never flip the fish; monitor the fire to provide a slow cook until flesh flakes in the thickest part of the body. —T.E.N.

163 PADDLE A TANDEM CANOE SOLO

Do it wrong and you look like the single biggest goofball on the lake. But do it right and bystanders will swoon at your power and grace.

GO BACKWARD Turn a tandem canoe around and paddle from behind the center thwart.

GET LOW AND LEAN Kneeling slightly off-center keeps your center of gravity low and puts your paddle closer to the water than if you sit upright. A slight lean gives the boat a long, keel-like profile, which makes a huge difference.

CHOP CHOP Get started with short, powerful strokes right at your hip. Once the canoe is under way, lengthen the strokes for a steady cadence. —T.E.N.

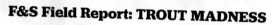

F&S Field Report: TROUT MADNESS

I wake to the sound of a tent door zipper. Scott Wood is ready to roar at 5:15 a.m., the Rocky Tangle's torture seemingly forgotten. But I feel like 40 miles of bad road. I pull the sleeping bag over my head and curl my body around knobs of rock and tussocks of blueberries.

In just five minutes, though, I'm climbing into cold waders. As the sun winks through spruce trees, we pick our way across a ledge drop at the bottom of the Rocky Tangle. Fog rises from a slot of water maybe 20 feet by 40 feet.

It's the swiftest, deepest run we've seen in three days. My hands are shaking, but I'm not sure if it's from the cold or from nervous anticipation. Months of planning and logistical troubles have led us here. If this river holds scads of big fish, this is exactly the kind of place they'll be—stacked up in pools as they nose upstream during prespawn runs.

It doesn't take long.

David Falkowski drops a fly into the water first, rips it cross-current, and hangs on as his rod bends double, like a diviner's stick pointing the way to the mother lode. "Three pounds, maybe. Not bad," he hollers as the fish comes to hand.

"Of course," he adds, "it's the largest brook trout I've ever seen in my life!"

In less than 60 seconds, each of us is into a brookie. We catch fish with 60-foot casts and we catch them six feet from the canoe. Hooked trout run between our legs. One takes Bill Mulvey's fly as he merely dabbles it into the water at his feet, wetting the marabou before making a real cast. Twice I catch a bragging-sized brookie while walking from pool to pool, dragging my fly behind me.

They are cookie-cutter characters, four-pounder after five-pounder after four-pounder again, and none of us complain. The females are hammered from verdigris and brass, swollen with roe. And the gaudy, prespawn males have the appearance of a brook trout with its tail stuck in an electric socket. Many are slashed with scars from close calls with toothy pike.

In an hour and a half, we catch 32 brook trout, two and a half to six pounds apiece. They hit the traditional northern speckle fare—Mickey Finns and Woolly Buggers, Stimulators and Sofa Pillows, streamers up to six inches long. They knock deerhair mice out of the water. But that's not all. One of my most effective flies is a chartreuse surf candy I tied for saltwater false albacore. We catch them on bass bugs, bream poppers, and silverside streamers. It's the fishing we came for, but not a one of us really thought we'd find.

In fact, none of us could have dreamed of the amazing, improbable day about to unfold. Twice more we haul the canoes and gear over shallow, rocky outlets, and twice more we pound swiftwater outfall pools that seem to boast a 50-50 water-to-fish ratio. That night we collapse on the rocky shore of an unnamed lake and watch northern lights arc overhead like a lava lamp stretched from horizon to horizon. Mars is up, and Bill swears he hears wolves howling. Scott and David stick their heads out the tent door to catch the sound, but I crawl to my sleeping bag to count the blue-haloed dots on the shimmering flanks of the brook trout that swim through my dreams.

—T. Edward Nickens, Field & Stream,
"Quest for the Mother Lode," April 2004

164 TOTE YOUR OWN BOAT (LIKE A MAN WITH A TITANIUM SPINE)

It doesn't take Herculean strength to hoist an 80-pound canoe onto your shoulders for a solo carry. The trick is to roll the canoe up your thighs first, then perform a bit of carefully timed clean and jerk to use momentum to lift the boat above your head. It's easy once you know how to do it—and incredibly impressive to perform in front of a crowd. —T.E.N.

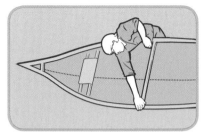

STEP 1 Face the canoe amidships and turn it so that it stands on the gunwale, the bottom resting against your knees. Bend your knees and roll the canoe up on your thighs, with your right hand grasping the far gunwale right at the center thwart and the left hand gripping the near gunwale. Stop and take a breath.

STEP 2 Rock slightly backward two or three times and, on the last rocking motion, push the canoe up and over your head, using both your thighs and your arms.

As your right elbow crosses your face, push with your left arm, straighten your bent legs, and lean back slightly to balance the weight.

STEP 3 When the outside gunwale rises above eye level, lower your head slightly and twist your body to the right. At the same time, push the outside gunwale upward. Now lower the canoe gently with the center thwart resting on the back of your neck. Move your hands slightly forward on the gunwales to fine-tune balance.

165 SHOOT A FLY

If it's hunting season, then it must be time to start thinking about fishing—especially if you like to tie your own flies or bucktail jigs. Many commonly (and not so commonly) hunted birds and animals can and will provide prime fly-tying materials, as long as you know what to clip, pluck, or cut, and how to store and maintain the stuff. To preserve hides, you simply need to salt the patch of fur you wish to keep. If you're saving bird feathers, store them in a zippered plastic bag or screw-top jar. To keep matched feathers from curling or getting smashed, tape the quills together, and you'll have a perfect pair for streamer tails.

The most common natural material for lures is the tail of a whitetail deer. Here's the 4-1-1 on preparation.

STEP 1 Before you convert a whitetail's white tail into jigs or streamers, there's some prep work you'll need to do. Start by skinning the tail. First, split the underside with a fillet knife to within a few inches of the tip. Then peel back the skin, wrap the tailbone with burlap, grasp it firmly, and pull the bone free. Continue the incision to the tip of the tail and scrape away all flesh and fat. Rub with salt or borax and freeze.

STEP 2 To dye the hairs, soak the tail overnight in water and dishwashing detergent, rinse, and dry completely. Mix a solution of sugar-free powdered drink mix (such as Kool-Aid™), water, and vinegar at a ratio of 2 ounces vinegar to 1 cup water. Pour this into a glass jar and submerge the tail. Place the jar in a larger pot of gently boiling water for 20 minutes to an hour or more. Check often for color. Remove the tail, blot, and tack to a piece of plywood to dry. —T.E.N.

ANIMAL	FLY MATERIAL	FLY PATTERN
Elk	Bull body hair	*Elk Hair Caddis and parachute wings*
Whitetail deer	Bucktail, natural or dyed	*Body and wings for Clouser and Deceiver patterns; tails for bucktail jigs*
Rabbit	Fur strips	*Leech, Rabbit Candy patterns; guard hairs for white streamer throats*
Gray squirrel	Tail hairs	*Dry-fly tails and wings, crayfish legs*
Red squirrel	Red, black, and gray tail fur	*Collar on tarpon streamers*
Wild turkey	Secondary wing quills	*Wings for caddis, hopper, and Atlantic salmon patterns*
Wood duck	Barred body feathers	*Classic streamer patterns, tails on dry emergers*
Ringneck pheasant	Rooster tails	*Knotted grasshopper legs*
Sharptail grouse	Body feathers	*Pheasant Tail Nymph tails*
Ruffed grouse	Neck feathers	*Patterned body on tarpon flies*
Hungarian partridge	Neck and body feathers	*Hackles for wet flies*

166 BUMP BAITS OFF AN UNDERWATER CLIFF

Contour trolling is deadly. Walleyes herd baitfish against sharp dropoffs and walls and then cruise the breaks for targets. Approach these sharp breaks with your boat. As soon as the bottom starts coming up, turn away at a 30- to 45-degree angle. Your baits will still be swinging into the breaks as you turn, and they'll actually dig right into the wall, drag for a few seconds, and then drop out of the sand or rock and dart away. Wham! Many times that erratic action will trigger a bite you'd never get otherwise. —T.E.N.

167 SURF CAST A COUNTRY MILE

Make a good "off-the-beach" cast, and the stripers beyond the breakers will learn to fear your truck. You'll need a shock leader of three times the test of your fishing line—as well as plenty of beach.

STEP 1 Face the water, with your left foot forward. Twist your upper body 90 degrees to the right, and look away from the water. Drift your rod tip back and let the sinker or lure drop to the ground at the 3 o'clock position. Move the rod to about the 1 o'clock position. Drop the rod tip down until your left arm is higher than your right. Reel in the slack.

STEP 2 Start with your right arm straight. With the sinker or lure on the beach, rotate your body at the hips, rod still behind you but moving in a smooth circular pattern, trending upward. Rotational energy fires the cast.

STEP 3 As your body straightens, shift your weight to the left foot, pull your left arm sharply down and in, and push with your right arm. Practice the timing of the release to straighten out a curve in the cast. —T.E.N.

168 TOW A CANOE WITH A BOAT

Towing a canoe behind a motorboat is a neat trick, giving anglers a way to haul gear and have a boat ready to portage into remote waters. But a towed canoe can flip almost without warning. Make things go smoothly by towing with a harness that provides the pull from beneath the canoe's keel line.

STEP 1 Turn the canoe so that it will be traveling stern-first. This helps by putting the seat closer to the towing vessel. Use water jugs to provide 40 to 50 pounds of ballast behind the center thwart.

STEP 2 Attach a towline bridle to create a towing point at the canoe's keel. Tie a large butterfly loop in the rope; this is one end of the bridle. Wrap the bridle under the canoe and fasten the loop and one tag end to the seat thwarts. The knot itself should remain under the keel.

STEP 3 Connect the towing end of the rope to the midpoint of a Y-harness attached to the corners of the tow boat's transom. Retain about 30 feet of line between the tow vessel and canoe—enough slack so that you can fine-tune the length if needed.

STEP 4 Watch the canoe carefully, make gradual turns, and do not cross strong wakes. —T.E.N.

169 CATCH EVERY FISH THAT BITES

Fish the first cast with as much focus as the sixth or seventh. People walk up to a pool and throw the line in. They're not ready. Make that first cast count, and when you're that close, treat all line tension as fish. Don't hesitate and think, "Oh, that's not a fish. Maybe next time." That was next time. —T.E.N.

170 FISH FROM A CANOE

Working a river from a canoe, especially one loaded with gear, requires different skills than shore fishing. These tactics will help you succeed.

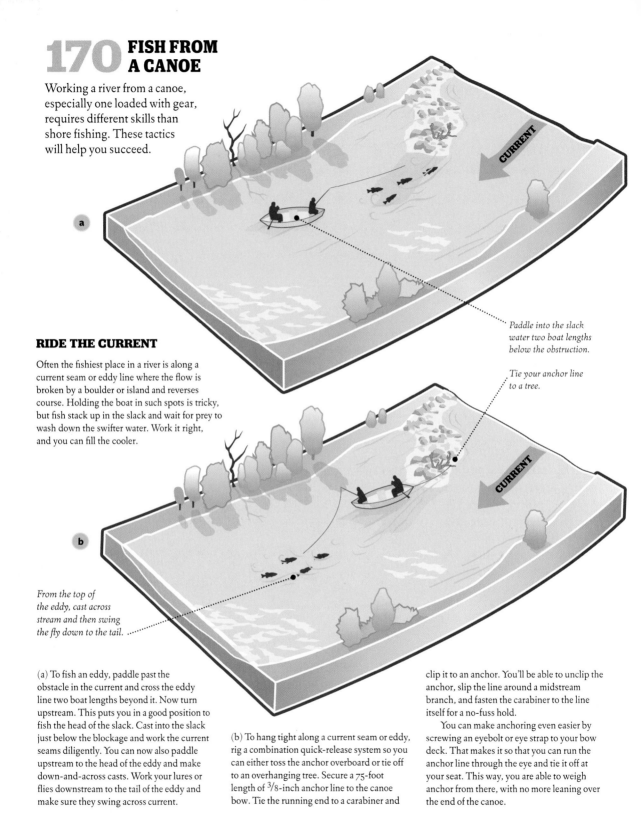

Paddle into the slack water two boat lengths below the obstruction.

Tie your anchor line to a tree.

From the top of the eddy, cast across stream and then swing the fly down to the tail.

RIDE THE CURRENT

Often the fishiest place in a river is along a current seam or eddy line where the flow is broken by a boulder or island and reverses course. Holding the boat in such spots is tricky, but fish stack up in the slack and wait for prey to wash down the swifter water. Work it right, and you can fill the cooler.

(a) To fish an eddy, paddle past the obstacle in the current and cross the eddy line two boat lengths beyond it. Now turn upstream. This puts you in a good position to fish the head of the slack. Cast into the slack just below the blockage and work the current seams diligently. You can now also paddle upstream to the head of the eddy and make down-and-across casts. Work your lures or flies downstream to the tail of the eddy and make sure they swing across current.

(b) To hang tight along a current seam or eddy, rig a combination quick-release system so you can either toss the anchor overboard or tie off to an overhanging tree. Secure a 75-foot length of 3/8-inch anchor line to the canoe bow. Tie the running end to a carabiner and clip it to an anchor. You'll be able to unclip the anchor, slip the line around a midstream branch, and fasten the carabiner to the line itself for a no-fuss hold.

You can make anchoring even easier by screwing an eyebolt or eye strap to your bow deck. That makes it so that you can run the anchor line through the eye and tie it off at your seat. This way, you are able to weigh anchor from there, with no more leaning over the end of the canoe.

DRIFT AND DREDGE

A drifting canoe is a superb platform from which to dredge deep water. You're covering fresh structure constantly and moving at the same speed as the river lets your lures—especially sinking flies—probe deeper down in the water column. Cast straight across the current for the deepest drifts, or slightly downstream so the lure swings across the current and then turns toward the boat. Fish often strike right when the lure changes direction.

To slow your drift, turn the canoe around and float backward. You and your buddy should take turns fishing because the stern paddler has to control the speed with occasional paddle strokes. This is a great way to fish long pools. Another option is to rig a "drag chain." Attach a length of heavy chain to your anchor rope—remove the anchor first, of course—and drag it behind the boat. Covering the chain with a bicycle-tire inner tube dampens the noise from any contact with the hull and bottom.

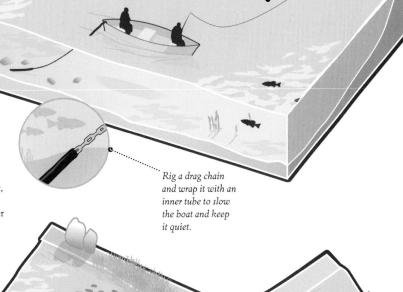

Cast just downstream, working the lure across the current.

CURRENT

Rig a drag chain and wrap it with an inner tube to slow the boat and keep it quiet.

Troll in zigzags, bringing lures past weedbeds and deep runs.

PADDLE TROLL

Why waste all that paddle power simply getting from point A to point B? You can load up on pike, lake trout, walleyes, largemouth and smallmouth bass, and panfish by trolling streamers and plugs behind canoes. A canoe's typical pace seems designed for imitating baitfish, and the inconsistent rate of speed keeps your lure moving up and down in the water column—a strike-inducing action.

To troll a floating or floater-diver plug, attach a few split shot to the line 2 feet ahead of the plug. Or work a shallow-running crankbait over beds of submerged vegetation. Run 100 to 150 feet of line behind the canoe and vary your paddle strokes to lend a stop-and-start action to the plug.

Trolling streamers and wet flies for rainbow and brook trout is a classic lake tactic, but you can also effectively apply the same set of steps to rivers. Use an intermediate or sinking fly line to put a Muddler Minnow or Woolly Bugger down deep. Trolling through long, apparently unproductive stretches will ensure that you leave no structure unfished. Paddle from bank to bank and back again to find where fish are holding. No, it's not really flyfishing. But the fish sure taste good even so.
—T.E.N.

171 TAKE A JAW-DROPPING FISH PHOTO

No matter where you land your fish of a lifetime, here's a fool-proof way to capture the moment. Talk your partner through these steps and then smile for the camera:

SET THE SCENE Move away from water muddied by the fight, and keep the fish in the water as much as possible, moving it gently back and forth to keep fresh water washing through its gills. Position the lure in the fish's mouth the way you want it to appear, or remove it. And clear the scene of clutter—drink cans, extra rods and reels, anything bright that will draw the viewer's attention away from the fish.

MODEL BEHAVIOR Have the angler remove sunglasses and hat, or, at least, tip the hat up a bit to prevent a dark shadow on the face. A shirt with color will add pop to any photo, but avoid muted greens and blues that might blend in to foliage or a big sky.

FIRE AWAY Have the angler kneel in the water, supporting the fish with both hands. Meter off of the fish and then have the angler dip the fish into the water. Take a shot as the fish comes up out of the water, streaming droplets of water. Try it again with the flash dialed in to the fill-flash setting. —T.E.N.

willow leaf blade

Colorado blade   *Indiana blade*   *willow leaf blade*

172 CHOOSE THE RIGHT BLADE

The configuration of spinnerbait blades dictates how the lure moves through the water. And that, of course, dictates in large measure whether a bass will ignore your lure or suck half the pond into its gullet during a boat-swamping strike (which would be a good thing).

There are three basic configuration styles. Round Colorado blades are akin to pimping your spinnerbait ride: They pump out tons of vibration, which makes them a go-to choice for stained water, and they impart the most lift to the lure, so they'll run more shallow than others. Willow-leaf blades create more flash than vibrating fuss, so you'll want to use them for clearer conditions. Willow blades also spin on a tighter axis, so they'll clear weeds more cleanly than others. Indiana blades are a compromise; they look like an elongated Colorado blade. Or a roundish willow-leaf. Nothing simple when it comes to bass fishing. —T.E.N.

173 BACK A TRAILER WITHOUT LOOKING LIKE AN IDIOT

Backing a boat trailer down a ramp isn't all that hard, but like establishing proper lead in wingshooting, it takes practice. The key fact to bear in mind is that the trailer will always go in the direction opposite the tow vehicle. This causes a great deal of confusion and is one of the main reasons you see guys jockeying up and down the ramp with a trailer that seems to have a mind of its own. Here's an easy way to master the maneuver.

STEP 1 Find a big empty parking lot where you can learn to gain control over your trailer without worrying about a long line of irate fishermen behind you. After you shift into reverse, place your left hand on the bottom of the steering wheel (remove fly-tying vise first!). When you move your hand to the right (which turns the steering wheel and front tires to the left), the trailer will move to the right (a). And when you move your hand to the left (which turns the steering wheel and front tires to the right), then the trailer will move to the left (b).

STEP 2 Move slowly. Most beginners back up too fast. If the trailer starts to move in the wrong direction, stop. Pull up, straighten the trailer, and start again. Trying to correct a wayward trailer will only make matters worse. Once you master the parking lot, you're ready for the ramp.

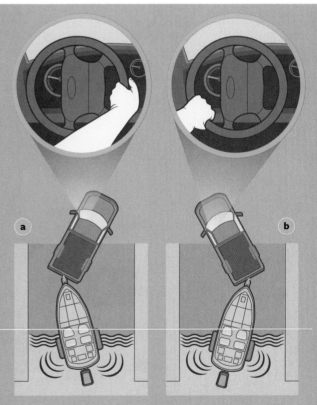

It takes a little getting used to (and your brain will fight you at first), but it works. —S.L.W.

"A man may not care for golf and still be human, but the man who does not like to see, hunt, photograph, or otherwise outwit birds or animals is hardly normal. He is supercivilized, and I for one do not know how to deal with him."

—Aldo Leopold

Born in a Tree Stand

We were bird-dogging the tundra like wolves, stalking through blueberries, bearberries, and cranberries with bows in hand. Deep in Alaska's Brooks Range foothills, somewhere north of the Yukon River, my buddy and I were road-weary and grimy with sweat from a freakish heat wave. And we were hungry.

Suddenly, two ptarmigan silhouettes popped up in the tundra, unmoving. I drew a judo-pointed arrow and settled the 25-yard pin on the near bird. A stiff breeze sent tufts of cotton grass tumbling in the air, so I shifted the sight three inches to the left and released. The bird crumpled, and four more appeared out of nowhere.

With the thwack of each shot, ptarmigan popped up like prairie dogs. We drew, aimed . . . and suddenly the target took off running. I took three steps and tripped, two steps and drew. Within minutes, seven birds were down and scattered across a half acre of tundra, and arrows lay everywhere. Across a shallow gully, my buddy Scott Wood held up a pair of ptarmigan by their feathered feet. "Finally," he hollered, "the red gods smile!"

We knelt down to study each ptarmigan, mottled brown feathers going to winter white, cradled in tundra grasses just beginning to turn with autumn's reds and golds. We gutted them on the spot, stuffed them into our vests, and headed back to camp.

There is something elemental about hunting, something deep-seated and hard-wired that links us to the land. There's a direct line that can be drawn from finger to trigger to stomach to soul.

Even when wild game isn't required to fuel our day-to-day needs, the pursuit itself is a sinew that ties us to a favorite clearing in the woods, a particular bend in a river.

All hunters have felt this. Ojibwa and Shawnee. Seminole and Creek. The Georgia swamper and the Midwestern farm boy and the weekend warriors who flee the city for weekends in the woods.

The great beauty about hunting is that it takes so many shapes and so many forms that you can spend all of your life trying to do everything just once. Ducks or deer, squirrels or moose—rifle, shotgun, muzzleloader, bow. Is there any other pastime that opens the door to more of the world? Is there anything more American than a man or woman in the woods with a gun, free to roam, his or her purpose to take a life in order to sustain life?

I don't think so.

But let's not overdo all of the spiritual mumbo-jumbo. We might hunt to put food on the table and stay in tune with earth, wind, and sky, but we also choose to go after deer and ducks and rabbits because it's just plain fun.

Following bird dogs through skin-shredding briars? Fun.

Going in over your waders to pick up a duck that fell across the creek channel? Fun.

Packing an elk out of the dark timber, two miles in and two miles out and three trips to get it all? We're the only ones who understand this, but, yes, even that's fun. At least, it will start to seem that way a few months later.

For many of us, hunting defines who we are in ways that defy explanation. We may not remember the first time we caught a football or even our first kiss, but we remember the first time we pulled a trigger. We remember those first hunts, when we were glowing iron on the anvil ready to be shaped by stories and places and people and sleepless mornings. We know when we became hunters.

The first time I went deer hunting, I was 13 years old. A friend of my dad's had been taking me squirrel hunting for a couple of years, and after he

listened to me whine about deer hunting for months on end, off we went. I remember following his footsteps through dark woods, and then he stopped and pointed his flashlight toward a tree. When he walked off, I was as scared to death as I'd ever been. I'd hunted with Keith many times, but never away from his side. Never alone.

That old climbing stand was a handmade job, and back then few folks thought to make a separate climbing seat so you could sit and stand your way up an oak. Instead, you bear-hugged the tree with your arms, hooked your boots into the metal frame of the climber, pressed your face into the bark and hung on with all your strength. Pulled your knees to your chest. Repeat. By the time you reached a decent height, your clothes were soaked with sweat, your hair was matted with sap, and you barely had enough arm strength left to lift a bow or gun.

After about 15 minutes of this torture, I figured I was so high I might soon run out of tree, so I stopped, my chest heaving, and settled in to hunt. As the sun rose and the woods lightened, I looked around and realized that the only way I was going to kill a deer that morning was if it ran through the woods so fast that when it hit its head on the climber it would break its neck. I was only a few feet off the ground.

But I remember clinging to that tree, a piece of rope knotted around my scrawny belly, forearms swollen and bloody, and telling myself that it didn't matter if I killed a deer or not. Because I was on my own, in the woods with a gun. No longer was I just a kid tagging along. From that day to this, I was a hunter.

—*T. Edward Nickens*

174 KNOW WHAT YOUR BULLET IS DOING

Dime-size groups fired on the range are one thing, but hitting game under hunting conditions is quite another. What you see here are some of the practical problems involved in the latter. The cartridge involved is one of the most effective long-range rounds available, the Federal version of the .270 WSM, loaded with 140-grain Nosler AccuBonds—real-world velocity in a 24-inch barrel, about 3,100 feet per second, or fps. —D.E.P.

GETTING OUT THERE
Here is where things get interesting. You have no worries about elevation, but the wind can move the bullet measurably. The greatest problem you face, however, is overcompensating for drift. And any twitches or faults in form will count far more than they did at closer ranges.

MOA = minute of angle

MEDIUM DISTANCE What applies to 100 yards applies here. The problem is one of appearances. Two hundred yards looks much farther than 100 yards and causes people to compensate for range and wind when they don't need to.

IN CLOSE At 100 yards, you don't need to think about ballistics. The trajectory is flat, and even a strong crosswind is not going to move the bullet enough to matter. All you have to do is pick an aiming point and not aim the rifle at the whole deer in general.

THE SHOOTER Offhand shots are sometimes a necessity, but always try for a rest or a more stable position. Only a fool shoots offhand past 100 yards.

Sighting and Aiming The best system of all, for those without range-compensating reticles, is to sight in 3 inches high at 100 yards. With the .270 WSM, that will give you an effective point-blank range of 300 yards, or a bit more. If you want to shoot at 400 yards, you had better get a reticle with mil dots that will allow you to avoid the horrors of holding off target.

*bullet drift 2.2 inches

MOA 2-inch group

*bullet drift 0.6 inch

MOA 1-inch group

200 yd.

100 yd.

Seeing the Target A deer-size animal looks very small at 400 yards; that is why variable-power scopes that magnify up to 10X were invented. Here is what the typical whitetail looks like with the scope cranked to 9X.

More magnification means more reticle movement with each twitch.

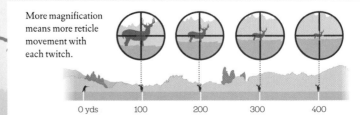

0 yds   100   200   300   400

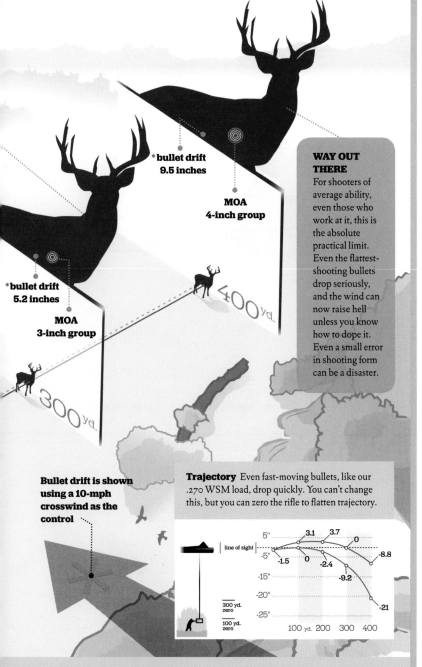

bullet drift 9.5 inches

MOA 4-inch group

bullet drift 5.2 inches

MOA 3-inch group

400 yd.

300 yd.

WAY OUT THERE
For shooters of average ability, even those who work at it, this is the absolute practical limit. Even the flattest-shooting bullets drop seriously, and the wind can now raise hell unless you know how to dope it. Even a small error in shooting form can be a disaster.

Bullet drift is shown using a 10-mph crosswind as the control

Trajectory Even fast-moving bullets, like our .270 WSM load, drop quickly. You can't change this, but you can zero the rifle to flatten trajectory.

line of sight

5"
-5"
-15"
-20"
-25"

3.1   3.7   0
-1.5   0   -2.4   -8.8
-9.2
-21

300 yd. zero
100 yd. zero

100 yd. 200 300 400

175
PLANT A MICRO FOOD PLOT

Farm and beaver ponds are perfect for seeding with Japanese millet strips, which ducks relish. It's easy and cheap and very effective. Here's how.

SCHEDULE IT Summer heat will often draw pond levels down, or you can lower the pool with flashboard risers. Millet matures in about 60 days. Plan with opening day in mind. Stagger the planting over a few weeks; plant deeper areas first and then move up the bank. That will keep the feed coming for a month.

RAKE IT If you're seeding mud, simply broadcast on the surface. For drier soils, use a steel rake or an ATV rake to score.

SEED IT Plant Japanese millet at the rate of 20 pounds per acre. You want to plant the seeds about an inch and a half apart. Plant it too densely and you'll stunt the growth of the new stems.

FEED IT Use one bag of 13-13-13 fertilizer per bag of seed and fertilize when the millet is 12 to 18 inches tall. —T.E.N.

The Flinch Factor We used trigonometry to calculate how far off your shot will be if you move the muzzle just 1/16 inch. The results are eye-opening. To see how we figured this out, go to fieldandstream.com/flinchfactor.

A horizontal move of 1/16 inch, shown actual size, will cause your shot to be way off.

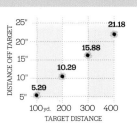

25"
20"
15"
10"
5"

DISTANCE OFF TARGET

21.18
15.88
10.29
5.29

100 yd. 200 300 400
TARGET DISTANCE

RELEASE MOTION Don't start and stop. Commit to a good follow-through, and the release will occur naturally.

THE MIND It's the most important aspect of shooting. You must deliberately focus on keeping your form perfect, shot after shot. If you think about aiming, accuracy will suffer.

RELEASE ARM Keep steady backward pressure with this arm until the arrow goes off. Think of it as pulling your bow apart.

176
NEVER MISS AGAIN

If you've hunted long enough, you know how humiliating it feels to send an arrow over a deer's back or put a bullet in the dirt. The good news: You may never feel that way again. Here's how to keep your shirttail intact.

BOW

Few skills rely so heavily on the connection between body and mind as does shooting a bow. From the soles of your feet to the position of your head, it all has to come together. —B.H.

BOW ARM A weak or tight bow arm causes most misses. You need to apply steady forward pressure here, right into the target.

STABILIZER Adding a stabilizer is the easiest way to steady your bow and improve your shooting. Don't skimp on weight.

STANCE Keep your feet lined up perpendicular to the target, which is the easiest way to maintain the same stance for each shot.

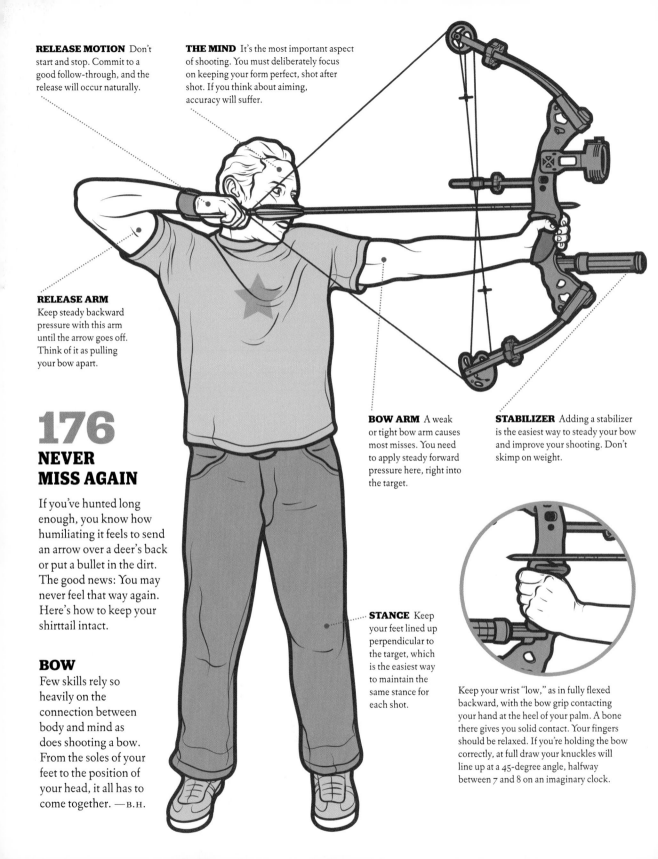

Keep your wrist "low," as in fully flexed backward, with the bow grip contacting your hand at the heel of your palm. A bone there gives you solid contact. Your fingers should be relaxed. If you're holding the bow correctly, at full draw your knuckles will line up at a 45-degree angle, halfway between 7 and 8 on an imaginary clock.

THE SWING You need to pick up the target, see it clearly, and decide where you're going to break it. When it's in the right spot, pull the trigger, and follow through.

EYES Don't ever take your eyes off the bird. Looking from bird to muzzle to bird will cause you to miss.

SWING HAND In order to maintain control of the muzzle, make sure your hand is forward enough on the fore-end to effect a smooth swing.

Start with the toe of the stock at waist level or a little above. The muzzle should be pointed where you expect to intercept the bird.

MOUNT Don't slap the butt into your shoulder; doing so will jolt the muzzle out of position and you'll need more time to pick up the target. Your shotgun mount must be fast and consistent. Good shots don't waste any motion.

The gun should describe a slight arc outward as you bring it up to keep it from catching on your clothing. Your head stays erect as the stock meets your cheek.

SHOTGUN

As athletic an endeavor as drilling a 50-yard field goal or sinking a 30-foot putt, shooting a shotgun requires focus and coordination. —D.E.P.

FOOTWORK Your feet should be pointed at an angle to the target so you don't have to fight to get the muzzle around.

When the butt is in your shoulder, your head should have to come down very slightly to be in shooting position. Your right elbow should be parallel to the ground, left elbow a bit lower.

SHOULDER Pull the buttstock securely into your shoulder.

THE ZONE To find your natural point of aim, put the crosshairs on the target, close your eyes, relax, breathe, and open your eyes again. If you're no longer on target, you have to adjust your position.

RETICLE Focus on the intersection of the crosshairs, not the target, when aiming.

ELBOWS Keep your elbows angled down at about 45 degrees.

HANDS Twist both hands downward slightly as if wringing a towel. This allows you to control the rifle as it recoils.

STANCE Stand nearly square to the target, angled slightly toward your strong side (here, the right side). Keep knees slightly flexed and lean into the rifle with the weight on the balls of your feet.

RIFLE

Nothing comes closer to the heart of American hunting than this: Hit the target. Precisely where you aim. Every time. —P.B.

KNEELING POSITION Take one step toward the target with the support-side leg (here, the left). Pivot on the ball of the strong-side foot and kneel as shown. The flat part of the supporting elbow rests on the supporting knee, with the rifle held directly above.

SQUATTING POSITION From your natural point of aim, squat straight down, with feet flat on the ground. Turn toes outward if necessary. Points of elbows are forward of the knees, with flat part of the supporting elbow resting on the knee directly below the rifle.

177 DISAPPEAR WITH A WINE CORK

Toss a wine cork and a lighter into your hunting pack, and you'll never be without a way to hide one of the biggest warning signs to game—your face. First, give the end of the cork a pre-burn treatment. Hold the lighter flame an inch below the tip until it smolders and flames. Rub out the black smudge on a piece of paper and then repeat. Once you get a good charcoal tip, it takes just a few seconds with a lighter to rejuvenate the cork before you apply it to your face. Cork camouflage washes off much more easily than commercial paints. To carry your cork, store it in a zippered plastic sandwich bag. And be sure you're using real cork, not synthetic. —T.E.N.

178 PLOT A SHOT WITH YOUR COMPUTER

Use Google Earth's mind-blowing database of searchable satellite imagery to figure out shot distances long before you pull the trigger. First, call up Google Earth and pull up your hunting location. Go to the top toolbar and click on "Show Ruler." Next, click on the down arrow beside the blue window that says "Miles," and change the unit of measurement to "Yards." Now your cursor will function as crosshairs. Click on the starting point for measurement and move the cursor to the ending point. Distance will show up in the window. —T.E.N.

FIELD & STREAM CRAZY-GOOD GRUB

179 GRILL STUFFED BACKSTRAPS

The best venison backstrap you'll ever eat is also one of the most impressive cuts to serve—and very easy to master. Here's what you need.

INGREDIENTS
One piece of venison backstrap
Italian dressing
Cream cheese
Fruit chutney
Bacon
Sun-dried tomatoes (optional)
Onions, caramelized (optional)

Marinate backstrap in Italian dressing for 12–24 hours. Butterfly by slicing horizontally through the meat to within one-half inch of the far side.

Open the butterfly cut lengthwise, like a sub sandwich roll. Add quarter-inch slices of cream cheese and then cover each with the fruit chutney. (Cranberry and mango work well. For a more subdued version, replace the chutney with sun-dried tomatoes or caramelized onions.)

Close up backstrap and wrap with bacon.

Truss the backstrap with kitchen string. Begin by looping the string around one end and then tie it around that end with a double overhand knot. Next, stretch 2 inches of string along the backstrap. Hold it in place with your thumb, wrap the string around the backstrap, pass the string behind your thumb, and repeat to wrap the entire backstrap. At the end, pass the string on the other side of the meat, threading it under the wraps. Tie off to the first wrap, and you're done.

Grill until medium rare. Snip off the string, slice, and serve. —T.E.N.

180 IDENTIFY DRAKE MALLARDS FLYING

Here are four simple steps that let you tell a greenhead from a girl duck before you pull the trigger.

SIZE MATTERS At first light, before you can see the green of a mallard's head, shoot the larger duck. Nine times out of ten, the bigger duck in a pair is a drake.

BE PATIENT Hold back and let the birds work the decoys so that you can get a good look.

KEEP YOUR EARS TO THE SKY Listen before you launch a load of No. 2s. Mallard hens quack. Mallard drakes call with a low, reedy yeep-yeep call that will identify them instantly.

KEEP YOUR EYES ON THE BELLY Look for the "halter top," the hard line between the drake's brown neck and white belly. —T.E.N.

181 REMOVE A BACKSTRAP WITH PRECISION

Many hunters ruin the best cut of venison. To avoid doing this, begin by hanging the deer from its hind legs and removing the shoulders.

STEP 1 Insert the knife beside the spine right in the middle of the deer. Keep the blade tight against the vertebrae and cut down to the neck. Turn the knife around and extend the cut to the hindquarters until the knife hits the pinbone of the hip. Repeat on the other side of the spine.

STEP 2 Insert your knife out in the curve of the ribs, 4 inches from where you think the edge of the backstrap lies. Carefully work the knife along the curve of the ribs and the bottom of the vertebrae to meet your long cuts.

Be sure to bring all the rib meat out with the backstrap.

STEP 3 Make the final cut across the backstrap at the pinbone, connecting the two long incisions.
—T.E.N.

182 RIG A PRUSIK-KNOT SAFETY ROPE

When it comes to danger, climbing into your tree stand could be said to rank right up there next to hunting rhinos with a pellet rifle. Learn to climb with a safety rope tied with a Prusik knot clipped to your harness, and you'll dramatically increase your chances of one day being a crotchety old fart. Tie off a rope to the bottom of the tree and then to the trunk above the level of your head when you're standing up in your stand. Tie a Prusik knot around this safety rope, and slide it up and down as you go.
—T.E.N.

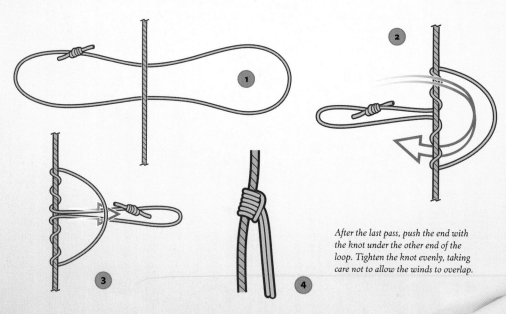

After the last pass, push the end with the knot under the other end of the loop. Tighten the knot evenly, taking care not to allow the winds to overlap.

183 ADJUST A SADDLE FOR AN ALL-DAY HUNT

After planning a horseback hunting trip for months, many desk jockeys finally arrive in big-game country barely able to walk, just due to the ride in. The secret to success is paying attention to the length of your saddle's stirrup leathers, which connect the stirrups to the saddletree. This is the primary factor that determines whether your trail will take you to lifetime memories or salty tears. Here's how to adjust your stirrups to fit your legs.

ON THE GROUND Get in the ballpark by running your hand under the seat to where the stirrup straps touch the saddletree. Adjust the length of the leathers so that the stirrup bottoms reach to your armpit.

IN THE SADDLE Fine-tune the fit by letting your legs hang down naturally from the saddle. Adjust the stirrup so the bottom of the tread is slightly below your anklebone. Now stand in the saddle. You should have a fist-size clearance between the saddle and your butt. If you're a greenhorn, it's wise to err on the shorter side.

IN YOUR MIND Adjust your expectations—riding over long distances hurts. There's an old saying: "If your knees are sore, your stirrups are too short. If your butt is sore, your stirrups are too long. If both your knees and your butt hurt like fire, then everything is just right."
—T.E.N.

184 HAUL YOUR DEER ANY DISTANCE

One tagged deer, no cart, no ATV, no dragging harness, and miles to go before you sleep. So what's the most efficient way to haul that animal out of the woods? Here are two methods to try. Both get your deer's head, neck, and shoulders off the ground, which results in less friction and easier dragging.

ONE-PERSON DOE DRAG Cut a sturdy stick of about ¾-inch diameter to an 18-inch length. Whittle a point on one end. Stab an inch-long slit through the animal's muzzle with your knife, just behind the black part of the nose and across the top of the nose bone. Work the knife blade under the cartilage and out the other side of the muzzle. Insert the stick into this slit. Grab the dragging stick with both hands behind your back.

TWO-PERSON BUCK PULL Pull the front legs forward and tie each tightly to the base of an antler. Then lash a stout 4-foot-long stick to the antlers at a crotch in the tines, leaving enough length protruding from either side for two people to stand beside the deer and pull, oxen-style. In addition to easing the burden, this method protects the cape from dirt and abrasion. —T.E.N.

185 FACE A DUCK BLIND IN THE RIGHT DIRECTION

Sometimes there's no choice, but on a cloudless day, an east-facing setup will force you to shoot into the glaring sun during the critical first half hour of legal light.

A front-lit blind also stands out from its surroundings more than a blind set in the dark shadows. Some hunters argue that drawing a bead on birds silhouetted against the light in the eastern sky is easier, but you'll disagree after five minutes of frying your retinas once the sun has topped the horizon. —T.E.N.

186

TEACH A BIRD DOG TO POINT

Getting a bird dog pup to start pointing feathers has as much to do with training as instinct.

GET THE PUP IN FEATHERS For the first year, it's all about getting the dog into birds. You want your pup to find so many birds that he figures out there's no way he can actually catch them.

GET TO THE DOG Once the dog points, get there fast. Your pooch needs to see the bird shot in front of him. That's the positive reinforcement.

GET THE POINT ACROSS Never shoot at a bird that he hasn't pointed. Teach your dog that the only way he's ever going to get a bird in his mouth is to point it so you can shoot it.

—T.E.N.

187 KILL A WILD PIG WITH A KNIFE

For centuries, Hawaiian natives dispatched wild pigs with little more than gumption and a 6-inch blade. As wild pig populations explode across the country, hunting them with dogs and a knife is growing in popularity. Here's the drill—if you dare.

STEP 1 Approach the pig from the rear, while it's focused on the dogs. Move slowly and avoid getting between your quarry and anything that would prevent you from backing away.

STEP 2 Grab the pig's hind legs just above the hooves. Lift the animal up like a wheelbarrow. The pig will fight for a few seconds and then stop. Flip him over on his side. Have a buddy secure the dogs away from the pig.

STEP 3 Let go with your knife hand and get a knee on the pig's shoulder. Unsheathe your knife. Sink it low and behind the shoulder, so it enters the heart, and then remove the blade immediately. Keep your weight on the pig until the deal is done. Pull this off correctly, and it takes mere seconds.

—T.E.N.

188 DISSECT THE WIND

Wind patterns are insanely complicated. One common mistake hunters make is misreading how currents react to landscape features. Missouri whitetail guide Kevin Small takes wind patterns apart with surgical precision.

It doesn't take a canyon wall to make the wind do flips. A hill, a ridge, a line of thick timber—all of these can have a dramatic effect on wind direction. Pick apart a buck's travel routes to find the one narrow window at which the wind is temporarily wrong for his nose but he has no other travel option. In this scenario, a west wind can work against you.

WIND WAVE When a breeze comes into contact with a large landscape obstruction, the wind will rise and then roll back over itself.

COULD BE TOO GOOD TO BE TRUE In theory, this is the perfect stand location (a) when dealing with a west wind. "But the wind will be rising at this point," Small says. "It will pick up your scent here and bring it right back to the bedding cover and the trails. You'll be busted 99 percent of the time."

SWEET SPOTS The only time to safely hunt these trails is in a north or south wind. In a north wind, hunt here (b). In a south wind, hang a stand here (c). —T.E.N.

189 WALK LIKE A DEER

Moving whitetails generally stop on odd-numbered steps—three, five, seven, and so on. It's an irregular cadence that you should try to duplicate when tracking over crunchy snow, tricking deer into thinking that the intruder has four legs instead of two. —K.M.

190 LET A YOUNG DUCK HUNTER CALL DUCKS

Duck species that routinely whistle include bluewing and greenwing teal, pintail, wood ducks, and wigeon. But mallard drakes will also make a sharp, single- or double-noted whistle, and, though the call is typically tied to breeding, it's a deadly finisher for shy greenheads during hunting season. For early-season teal hunting, a five-peep whistle is the go-to call. Since it's easy to learn, duck whistling is a great way to get a kid started. —T.E.N.

191 KEEP FOG OFF YOUR SCOPE

Be careful as you bring your rifle up to aim that you don't exhale a cloud of moisture-laden breath onto the cold scope lenses. This will fog your scope in an instant. It's very easy to avoid making this basic mistake once you know what to do. Simply hold your breath as you bring the rifle up, aim, and shoot. Then exhale.

—D.E.P.

FIELD & STREAM CRAZY-GOOD GRUB

192 TRY REAL BRUNSWICK STEW

You could argue forever over the birthplace of the famous Brunswick stew. Perhaps it's Brunswick County, North Carolina. Brunswick County, Virginia? Brunswick, Georgia? The state legislatures of Virginia and Georgia have even passed proclamations boasting bragging rights. But no one fights over its original primary ingredient. Squirrel it was, and squirrel it still is. Earmark a bitter-cold Saturday for stirring up a simmering pot of Brunswick stew. It's best cooked over an open fire. This recipe makes about 10 servings. Tell no one about the squirrel until after they beg for the recipe.

INGREDIENTS
4 large onions, diced
5 tbsp. bacon fat
6 to 8 squirrels, parboiled and deboned
6 cups water
One 28-oz can diced tomatoes
1 cup sherry
2 tsp. Worcestershire sauce
2 pounds fresh or two 10-oz. packages frozen lima beans
2 cups fresh or frozen corn kernels
Salt and pepper to taste
2 tsp. red pepper flakes
1 cup seasoned bread crumbs
4 tbsp. melted butter

In a Dutch oven, fry the onions in bacon fat and then remove them. Without draining the fat, add the squirrel meat and cook until it's browned. Add the water, tomatoes, sherry, and Worcestershire sauce. Simmer partially covered for 30 minutes. Add the lima beans and corn and simmer for 30 minutes. Add salt, pepper, and red pepper to taste. Sprinkle the bread crumbs, drizzle the butter over the top, and then stir. Cook uncovered for 15 to 20 minutes more. It's ready when a sturdy wooden stirring paddle will stand straight up in the pot.

—T.E.N

193 HOST A SUMMERTIME BACKYARD ARCHERY TOURNAMENT

Between the last bite of watermelon and the campfire, you've got a lot of afternoon to fill, so break out the bows for a few rounds of Archer's Horse. In this version, you'll spell A-P-P-L-E-P-I-E (or U-S-A for a quick game). First, set up a few 3-D targets at various distances and angles. On each, designate a small high-risk marker by sticking a high-visibility adhesive dot (or leftover hamburger bun) on, for example, the neck of the deer or the throat of a bear. Next, establish a line that shooters can't cross when it's their turn. When you've arranged the course and shooting order, here's how to play:

CALL IT Shoot from anywhere along the line and however you'd like—standing, kneeling, singing the national anthem. And you must call your shot: "Vitals, whitetail target."

SHOOT IT If you hit your target, the second shooter has to match the shot. If he makes the same shot, it falls to the third shooter to do the same, and so on until either someone misses or everyone makes the shot, at which point the first shooter takes a new shot.

MOVE IT If someone misses the shot, he is assigned a letter and moves to the last slot in the shooting order. The shooter who's next in line becomes the new leader and decides the next shot.

RISK IT To make things interesting, a shooter may call a high-risk shot during his turn. If he misses, he automatically gets a letter. But if he hits the target, it's worth two letters to the first player to miss the shot.

WIN IT When a shooter is assigned his final letter, he's not written off yet. He's gets one more attempt at the shot—but this time he must hit the high-risk marker. If he nails it, he loses a letter. If he misses, he has to fetch hot dogs for the remaining shooters. —T.E.N.

194 PICK THE RIGHT GUN

The type of mechanism used to load, fire, and eject rifle cartridges and shotgun shells is called the "action." Single-shot firearms must be reloaded after each shot. Repeating firearms fire each time the trigger is pulled, with additional cartridges or shells held in a magazine or tube under the gun barrel. Choosing which action you want in a firearm is critical, and the right decision balances speed, safety, accuracy, gun-handling characteristics, and aesthetics. —T.E.N.

SHOTGUNS

BREAK-ACTION SINGLE BARREL With a hinge at the receiver, break-action firearms open like a door to expose the breech for loading. Because single-barrel guns of this type can be made short and light, they are often a young shooter's first firearm.

SIDE-BY-SIDE This break-action shotgun features a pair of barrels mounted beside each other. Quick pointing and elegant, short and well balanced, this is the traditionalist's go-to gun, especially for hunters of upland birds such as quail. Many are made with double triggers—one to a barrel—for an instant choice of which choke to use.

OVER/UNDER A more modern variant of the break-action double-barreled shotgun, the over/under is a favorite of American shooters. It offers a quick follow-up shot, a choice of chokes for varying shooting conditions, and a single sighting plane down the top barrel.

PUMP A repeating shotgun, this action is worked by the shooter cycling the fore-end back to remove the spent shell and cock the firing pin and then forward to chamber the fresh shell and close the action. Fast, smooth, and dependable, pump shotguns are a favorite of waterfowl hunters due to the relative lack of moving parts and ability to work even when wet and muddy.

SEMIAUTOMATIC Also known as "autoloaders," these actions automatically cycle new shells into the chamber each time the shotgun fires. Gas-operated semiautomatic shotguns use some of the gas created when the shell is fired to work the action. Recoil-operated actions use the force of recoil to move the bolt and chamber a new shell. Autoloaders are quick to fire numerous shots and have less recoil than other actions but are generally heavier and bulkier than other actions.

RIFLES

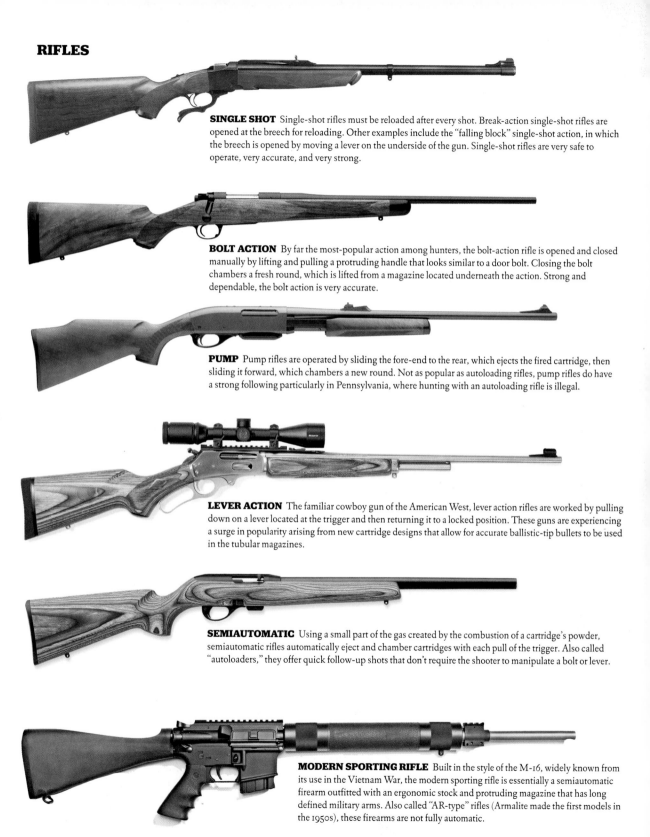

SINGLE SHOT Single-shot rifles must be reloaded after every shot. Break-action single-shot rifles are opened at the breech for reloading. Other examples include the "falling block" single-shot action, in which the breech is opened by moving a lever on the underside of the gun. Single-shot rifles are very safe to operate, very accurate, and very strong.

BOLT ACTION By far the most-popular action among hunters, the bolt-action rifle is opened and closed manually by lifting and pulling a protruding handle that looks similar to a door bolt. Closing the bolt chambers a fresh round, which is lifted from a magazine located underneath the action. Strong and dependable, the bolt action is very accurate.

PUMP Pump rifles are operated by sliding the fore-end to the rear, which ejects the fired cartridge, then sliding it forward, which chambers a new round. Not as popular as autoloading rifles, pump rifles do have a strong following particularly in Pennsylvania, where hunting with an autoloading rifle is illegal.

LEVER ACTION The familiar cowboy gun of the American West, lever action rifles are worked by pulling down on a lever located at the trigger and then returning it to a locked position. These guns are experiencing a surge in popularity arising from new cartridge designs that allow for accurate ballistic-tip bullets to be used in the tubular magazines.

SEMIAUTOMATIC Using a small part of the gas created by the combustion of a cartridge's powder, semiautomatic rifles automatically eject and chamber cartridges with each pull of the trigger. Also called "autoloaders," they offer quick follow-up shots that don't require the shooter to manipulate a bolt or lever.

MODERN SPORTING RIFLE Built in the style of the M-16, widely known from its use in the Vietnam War, the modern sporting rifle is essentially a semiautomatic firearm outfitted with an ergonomic stock and protruding magazine that has long defined military arms. Also called "AR-type" rifles (Armalite made the first models in the 1950s), these firearms are not fully automatic.

195

DROP THE MOST DIFFICULT DOVES

As a nation of dove hunters, we take five to seven shots for every bird bagged. With the price of shotshells what it is, few of us can afford to miss that much. If you shoot at everything that comes into range, a good average is one out of three shots. Although doves zipping randomly around a field present a wide variety of shots, most of the toughest shots fall into five main categories. —P.B.

 THE INCOMER YOU SEE FOREVER

A bird that comes all the way across the field to you is surprisingly easy to screw up. It's even worse if you announce (and we've all done this) to the person next to you: "I'm going to shoot this dove." Avoid the temptation to mount the gun early and track this bird all the way in. Inevitably you'll look back at the bead to check your lead and stop the gun, or the dove will dip down below the muzzle and you'll have to scramble to find it again. Instead, wait for it with the gun ready, butt tucked loosely under your arm. As the bird comes into range, look at the beak and make a smooth mount and shoot the bird in the nostrils.

 THE DOVE WITH ITS JETS ON

When you're in a crowded field, sometimes you have to root for a dove to get past other people so you can shoot it yourself. Problem is, when that bird reaches you, it's speeding and juking all over the sky. This one is a no-brain reaction shot—you have to trust your eye-hand coordination and get your conscious mind out of the way. Try an aggressive swing-through system for these birds, which can duck out from under a maintained lead–style swing. Sweep past the target from behind and shoot when the muzzle clears the beak. Keep a tight focus on the target, and your eyes will send your hands to exactly the right place.

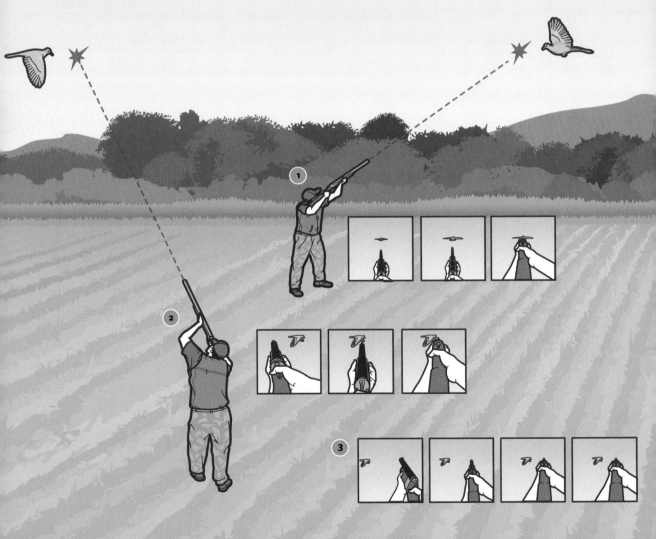

3 THE LONG CROSSER

The dove that loafs along unalarmed, crossing at 35 yards, requires a lot of forward allowance. The sustained lead system is the easiest way to connect on such shots. Keep your eye on the dove and mount the muzzle in front of the bird. Swing, matching the dove's speed. Trust your subconscious mind to tell you the instant the lead is right. If you try to measure the lead, analyze it, or double-check it, you will miss. Remember: lead doesn't have to be precise—you've got a wide pattern on your side. Focus on the bird, let the blur of the muzzle drift ahead of it, and shoot.

4 THE SURPRISE DOVE

The bird that takes you by surprise requires a little lead underneath. If you're a skeet shooter, you've made this shot hundreds of times at High House 1. If not, here's what to do: Resist the temptation to rush. Before you begin your mount, raise the muzzle, keeping it just to the right of the bird (if you're right-handed). That way, you won't lose sight of the bird behind the gun. Move the muzzle down through the bird while raising the stock to your face. Shoot when you see the dove above your barrel. Instead of shooting right at the bird, try to miss it underneath, as if you wanted to graze its belly with your pellets. It'll hit the ground.

5 THE HIGH OVERHEAD DOVE

Birds coming into a field over the treetops look impossibly high. In reality they aren't as far up as they appear to be (it's a very tall oak or pine that measures 90 feet). That 30- to 35-yard shot is well within the capability of even an improved cylinder choke. Plus, a dove straight overhead is presenting all of its vitals. Start with the muzzle behind the bird as you raise the stock to your face and swing through the target. Your back leg should be straight, and your weight should be on your back foot. When you can't see the dove behind the muzzle, keep the gun moving and shoot. The dove will fall, almost as if from the stratosphere.

196 TURN A UTILITY TABLE INTO A BUTCHER SHOP

Butchering a deer can be a chore that will make a mess of your basement and send you limping up the steps with a backache. This DIY butchering table will make your meat cutting a more pleasant experience. It's cheap, easy to store and clean, large enough for two people to work at together, and raised to a spine-pleasing height. Before butchering, clean the table with a 50-50 mix of bleach and water. Rinse it with distilled water. —T.E.N

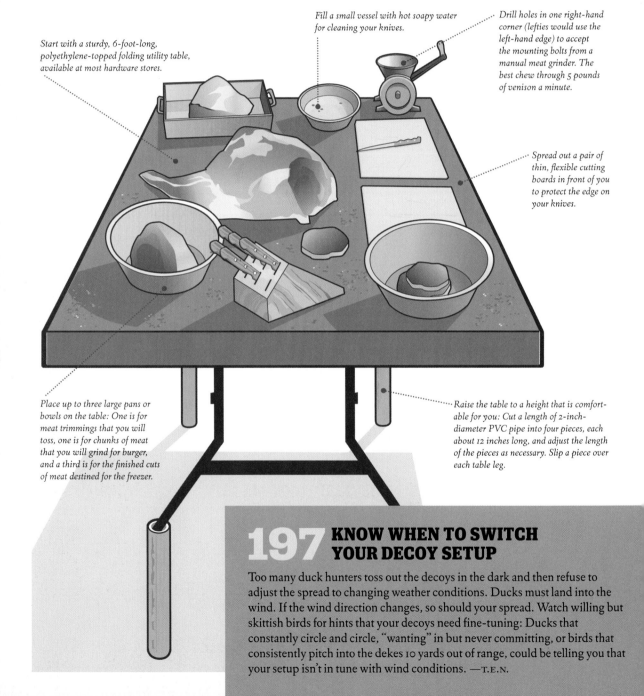

Fill a small vessel with hot soapy water for cleaning your knives.

Drill holes in one right-hand corner (lefties would use the left-hand edge) to accept the mounting bolts from a manual meat grinder. The best chew through 5 pounds of venison a minute.

Start with a sturdy, 6-foot-long, polyethylene-topped folding utility table, available at most hardware stores.

Spread out a pair of thin, flexible cutting boards in front of you to protect the edge on your knives.

Place up to three large pans or bowls on the table: One is for meat trimmings that you will toss, one is for chunks of meat that you will grind for burger, and a third is for the finished cuts of meat destined for the freezer.

Raise the table to a height that is comfortable for you: Cut a length of 2-inch-diameter PVC pipe into four pieces, each about 12 inches long, and adjust the length of the pieces as necessary. Slip a piece over each table leg.

197 KNOW WHEN TO SWITCH YOUR DECOY SETUP

Too many duck hunters toss out the decoys in the dark and then refuse to adjust the spread to changing weather conditions. Ducks must land into the wind. If the wind direction changes, so should your spread. Watch willing but skittish birds for hints that your decoys need fine-tuning: Ducks that constantly circle and circle, "wanting" in but never committing, or birds that consistently pitch into the dekes 10 yards out of range, could be telling you that your setup isn't in tune with wind conditions. —T.E.N.

198 BE A FAMOUS HUNT VIDEO DIRECTOR

Filming your buddy's deer hunt can be as exciting as pulling the trigger yourself. And who knows? You might just end up being the Next Big Thing on YouTube. To crank out a video that will get you noticed, here's a "shot list" of must-have scenes.

• Hunter or narrator discussing date, season, quarry, and location [include wide location shots]

• Hunter getting ready

• Hunter's feet walking to stand

• Hunter spotting game [include panning shots connecting hunter to animal]

• Close-ups: hunter looking through scope, the tip of broadhead or muzzle, a finger pushing the gun safety off, fingers clipping release to bowstring

• "Re-creates" after the shot: reenact hunter aiming in direction of game, looking intensely, shifting feet to take position

• Hunter finding arrow

• Hunter trailing prey

• Hunter posing with animal with no talking for closing shot —T.E.N.

199 THREAD AN ARROW THROUGH COVER

The tight cover that holds big whitetail bucks is tough on bowhunters. Say a good buck stops 40 yards from your stand, but there's a tree branch 20 yards in front of you—between your stand and the deer. Here's how to tell if you can make a clean and safe shot:

STEP 1 Put the 40-yard pin on the deer's vitals, as if you were taking the shot. Hold this point of aim.

STEP 2 Focus on the 20-yard pin. If the sight pin is above or below the branch, your arrow will clear. If the sight pin is on the branch, hold your fire. Your arrow's trajectory will carry it into the obstruction, leading to a spooked and educated deer or, worse, a wounded animal that will be difficult to track. —T.E.N.

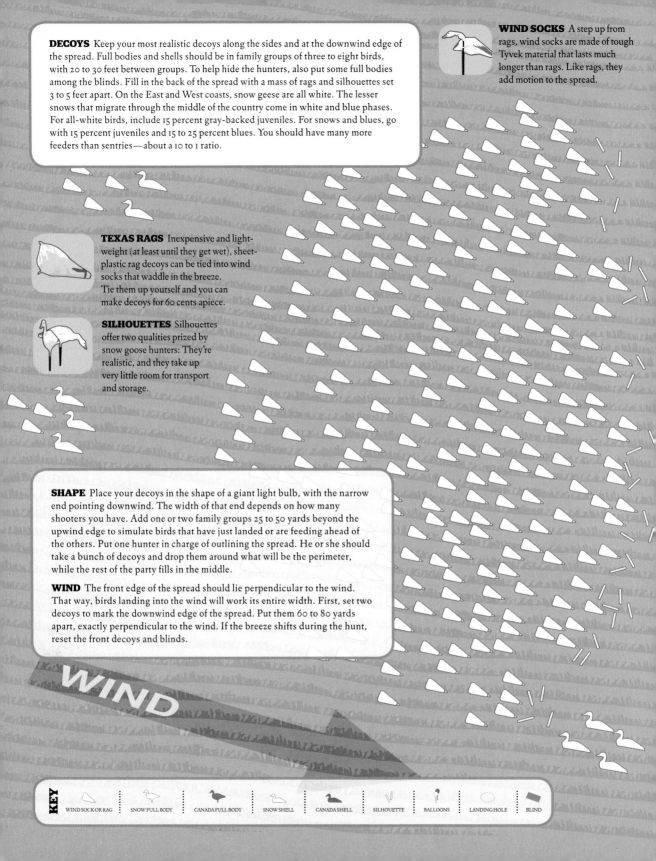

DECOYS Keep your most realistic decoys along the sides and at the downwind edge of the spread. Full bodies and shells should be in family groups of three to eight birds, with 20 to 30 feet between groups. To help hide the hunters, also put some full bodies among the blinds. Fill in the back of the spread with a mass of rags and silhouettes set 3 to 5 feet apart. On the East and West coasts, snow geese are all white. The lesser snows that migrate through the middle of the country come in white and blue phases. For all-white birds, include 15 percent gray-backed juveniles. For snows and blues, go with 15 percent juveniles and 15 to 25 percent blues. You should have many more feeders than sentries—about a 10 to 1 ratio.

WIND SOCKS A step up from rags, wind socks are made of tough Tyvek material that lasts much longer than rags. Like rags, they add motion to the spread.

TEXAS RAGS Inexpensive and lightweight (at least until they get wet), sheet-plastic rag decoys can be tied into wind socks that waddle in the breeze. Tie them up yourself and you can make decoys for 60 cents apiece.

SILHOUETTES Silhouettes offer two qualities prized by snow goose hunters: They're realistic, and they take up very little room for transport and storage.

SHAPE Place your decoys in the shape of a giant light bulb, with the narrow end pointing downwind. The width of that end depends on how many shooters you have. Add one or two family groups 25 to 50 yards beyond the upwind edge to simulate birds that have just landed or are feeding ahead of the others. Put one hunter in charge of outlining the spread. He or she should take a bunch of decoys and drop them around what will be the perimeter, while the rest of the party fills in the middle.

WIND The front edge of the spread should lie perpendicular to the wind. That way, birds landing into the wind will work its entire width. First, set two decoys to mark the downwind edge of the spread. Put them 60 to 80 yards apart, exactly perpendicular to the wind. If the breeze shifts during the hunt, reset the front decoys and blinds.

WIND

KEY   WIND SOCK OR RAG   SNOW FULL BODY   CANADA FULL BODY   SNOW SHELL   CANADA SHELL   SILHOUETTE   BALLOONS   LANDING HOLE   BLIND

MOTION Feeding snow geese are always moving, hopping over one another to get to uneaten grain first. Jig flags up and down from the blinds to simulate their movements. Fly black-and-white helium balloons, about half a dozen of each, 4 feet off the ground, weighted with decoy anchors or tied to stubble.

SHELLS Shells look like geese, they're stackable, and you set them out simply by throwing them on the ground.

FULL BODIES The ultimate in realism, full bodies take up lots of trailer space but help close the deal when the birds are hanging 70 yards outside the spread, deciding whether to stay or go.

200 FOOL FIVE THOUSAND GEESE

Why bother with the giant decoy spreads required to hunt snow geese? Because when you get it right, the reward is a tornado of geese 10 yards over your head—thousands of them yipping and barking so loud you can't hear yourself shout.

Start by finding the field where the birds want to be. Follow them from the roost ponds to feeding fields in the afternoon. If you can, wait until the geese have left the field for the evening and then mark the exact spot where they were feeding with an orange traffic cone. Come back well before dawn and come ready to work. You'll need a minimum of 400 to 500 decoys, but 800 to 1,000 are better. If you follow this blueprint, it's not that hard to build a killer spread. —P.B.

OTHER BIRDS Canadas and specklebellies often feed in the same field as snows. Set a few dozen Canada or speck shells and full bodies downwind of the spread. You can put out duck decoys too, but white spreads will suck in flocks of mallards and pintails whether they see other ducks or not.

BLINDS Set the blinds about three steps apart, in a line 15 yards from the downwind edge of the spread. If flocks consistently come close, inspect the decoys, and then slide off to one side or the other, move the blinds 50 yards downwind of the spread and shoot the geese as they're looking. Wearing white coveralls and becoming one with the decoys is the classic way to hide. You can also use a goose chair, which is a combination decoy and field chair. Laydown field blinds blend in best and are the most comfortable way to hunt.

LANDING ZONES Leave gaps of 10 to 15 yards in front of and behind the blinds where the birds can land. Snows and ducks will aim for the holes.

201 WET-AGE A DEER

Aging venison allows naturally occurring enzymes to break down the structure of collagen and muscle fibers. That helps tenderize the meat and gives it distinctive, complex flavors. But early-season deer hunters—and deer hunters all season long in the sunny South—have a tough time hanging deer when the outside temperatures are warm enough for short sleeves.

To age venison in balmy weather, try wet-aging. Cool the carcass with ice for at least 12 hours; butchering a deer before rigor mortis sets in can turn even tender cuts chewy.

While butchering, remove as much silverskin and connective tissue as possible; keep whole muscles as intact as you can. Drain off any blood, pat the cuts dry with a paper towel, and then package cuts of butchered meat in vacuum-sealed bags. Store in a refrigerator for five to eight days. After aging, freeze the cuts as they are or finish butchering them into portion sizes.

Wet-aging won't give your venison the complex, concentrated flavors that would accrue during a week in a frosty barn. But even in the fridge, enzymatic action will go to work on silverskin and tendons, turning a warm-weather September buck into a meal worth bragging about. —T.E.N.

202 SEE IN THE DARK

If you've ever wished that you could see in the dark, you're in luck! With these simple steps, you'll soon be able to maneuver in low-light conditions.

PROTECT In the critical minutes of dawn and dusk, shield your eyes from the sun. When moving your field of vision, allow your eyes to travel below the horizon line or shut your eyes as you move them. Before dawn, use the least amount of light required for the task; a low-level red or green light is best. Practice walking at night to increase your comfort level and clear favorite trails so you won't need a flashlight.

BOOST Use peripheral vision by focusing to the side of an object. Scan when you can; when your eyes linger on a particular object, they will adapt to whatever light is available. Try to get lower than the target to see its contours better. —T.E.N.

203 TAN A DEER HIDE

Tanning a deer hide with the hair on is work but it is manageable. Here's the drill.

Stretch the skin over a 2x6-foot board. With a dull knife held at 90 degrees to the surface, scrape off all remaining muscle, sinew, and membrane. Rub copious amounts of noniodized salt into the flesh side, roll it up, toss it into a plastic bag, and freeze. Two to three days later, let the skin thaw, flesh it again, and wash out the salt.

Prepare a tanning solution of 4 gallons of water, 1 pound of granulated alum, and 1 pound of salt. Soak the hide in the solution for a week, stirring once a day.

Remove it from the tanning bath and squeeze it dry. Lather the flesh side with neat's-foot oil; let this soak in for a few hours. Stretch the wet hide over a hard, straight edge such as a sawhorse or table, and work it back and forth over the edge, as hard as you can, to soften it.

Use a rounded dowel or butter-knife handle for the hard-to-reach corners. If you think you're finished in less than eight hours, you're not. —T.E.N.

204 HELP A KID GUT A FIRST DEER

Now it gets tricky: You have a deer on the ground and a kid at your side with a face white as biscuit batter. Think carefully about how you introduce a young hunter to the labor of turning what was once a living, breathing animal into bundles of neatly labeled meat.

Don't make a fuss. Approach the animal as next year's supply for spaghetti and stew, and you'll send a subtle message: What happens after the shot is just another part of the process. Gutting and skinning is nothing to dread. It's as much a part of hunting as lacing up your boots, so treat it that way.

Don't push it, either. On the other hand, recognize that the notion of removing the organs and severing joints from an animal with a saw is not exactly a stroll through Candy Land. Go easy. You're not out to prove a point or toughen up a soft kid. Also, if you think you might have crippled an animal, get your child out of the picture immediately. Dealing with a wounded animal is difficult under the best conditions, and watching while you dispatch your quarry at close range might just be enough to send a kid into early retirement from hunting.

Be methodical. Talk through every step, pointing out the animal's body structures. And give your child a job. Even if she (or he) is too young to handle a knife, she can hold a leg while you open up the body cavity or pull back the rib cage as you remove the lungs and heart.

See it through. The learning experience shouldn't end with field dressing. Involve your child in butchering, freezing, and other preparation tasks. If a pile of bloody meat gives your kid pause, then assign another task. Ask for help running the vacuum sealer, turning the grinder handle, or loading the freezer. Help your child understand that a large part of killing an animal is devoted to sustaining another life—their own. —T.E.N.

205 IDENTIFY TRACKS BY GAIT

Language teachers have discovered that the fastest method of learning a foreign tongue is to focus on phrases rather than attempt to translate each word. Tracking is similar. Studying the details of a single print in order to identify its source can be a daunting task. Instead, noting the pattern or "phrasing" of the tracks, which reveals the traveling gait of the animal, as well as the overall shape of the impressions helps you narrow the possibilities.

Note that animals use many different gaits; what is shown are their most common.

—K.M.

DIAGONAL WALKERS-TROTTERS (deer, elk, moose, wolf, coyote, fox, mountain lion, bobcat, lynx)

bobcat
deer
coyote

WALK

TROT

SHAPE Deer, heart shaped. Canids, egg shaped. Cats, circular.
GAIT Diagonal walkers move the opposite sides of the body simultaneously (front left with rear right and vice versa). This leaves a straight line of tracks with the hind feet falling into or near the impressions of the forefeet. Trotting is an elongated stride with less stagger between the left and right sides.

PACERS-AMBLERS (bear, raccoon, badger, skunk)

black bear

WALK

AMBLE

SHAPE Boxed-off toe with fuzzy leading edges and an elliptical rear (humanlike).
GAIT Pacers have wide bodies and move the feet from the same side of the body simultaneously. The impressions of the front and rear feet are roughly side by side. In a leisurely amble, a common pace, the back foot oversteps the front foot.

FULL BOUNDERS OR HOPPERS (tree squirrel, ground squirrel, chipmunk)

tree squirrel

FULL BOUND

SHAPE Star-shaped. **GAIT** Full bounders keep their rear feet side by side and their front feet side by side. The rear feet land ahead of the front feet.

HALF BOUNDERS (rabbits, hares)

cottontail

HALF BOUND

SHAPE Front round, rear oblong. **GAIT** Half bounders place their hind feet side by side, whereas their forefeet are staggered. The rear feet land ahead of the front feet.

GALLOPERS (most weasels, including marten, wolverine, ferret, mink, fisher)

fisher

4X4 GALLOP
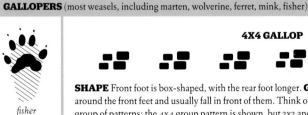

SHAPE Front foot is box-shaped, with the rear foot longer. **GAIT** In galloping, the rear feet swing around the front feet and usually fall in front of them. Think of it as skipping. Tracks are composed in a group of patterns; the 4x4 group pattern is shown, but 3x3 and 2x2 are also common.

206 HOIST ANY LOAD WITH A BACKCOUNTRY BLOCK AND TACKLE

Maybe you're all alone and need to lift an elk quarter off the ground, hoist a food bag beyond the reach of bears, or hang a deer. Maybe you should know how to rig a backcountry block and tackle using nothing more than rope or parachute cord and a couple of lightweight rock-climbing carabiners.

STEP 1 Find a tree with a strong, live branch that is at least 2 feet higher than you want to suspend the load. Throw a rope over the branch. Tie a loop in the rope about 5 feet from the standing end by making an overhand knot and pulling a short section of standing line through. Clip a carabiner to this loop.

STEP 2 Thread the running end of the rope through a second carabiner and then through the first.

STEP 3 Pull the end of the rope that goes over the branch until the first carabiner is near the branch. Tie this end of the rope to the tree trunk.

STEP 4 Clip the heavy object to the second carabiner. You may need to fasten a rope around the object.

STEP 5 Haul the load as high as required, using the tree as a block by passing the hauling end of the rope around the trunk. Pad it with a jacket or pack to lessen friction. Last, tie the hauling end of the rope around the tree.
—T.E.N.

207 SHOOT YOUR OWN BIRD

Doubling up on one bird is the mark of the rank amateur—and a mistake even seasoned waterfowlers make too often. You and your partners need to discuss a strategy to avoid pulling the trigger on the same duck or goose. The gunner on the left might agree to take birds on the left of the flock or to shoot the trailing bird in a pair. Based on wind conditions and your decoy spread, figure out where the birds are most likely to fly and then hand out the shooting assignments accordingly.
—T.E.N.

208 AGE DEER IN A BIG COOLER

Not all hunters have walk-in coolers, and a lot of us kill deer when it's still 70 degrees F outside. Here's a way to age whitetails for four to five days even when you're wearing shorts in the backyard. All you need is a whopping big cooler and a supply of 2-quart juice bottles or 1-gallon milk cartons washed out, filled with water, and frozen solid.

STEP 1 Decide whether to keep the hide on or off. Keeping the hide on prevents some moisture loss, but you'll have to contend with hair on the meat due to quartering the animal with the hide on.

STEP 2 Remove the tenderloins, which don't need aging. Saw off the front legs at the knees and then remove the legs at the shoulder joints. Remove both rear quarters in one piece by sawing through the backbone just ahead of the pelvis—you'll lose just a bit of backstrap. Remove the lower shanks. You're left with four pieces: the double hams, two front quarters, and the rib cage and backbone.

STEP 3 Place four to five 2-quart bottles or cartons of ice in the bottom of a large cooler; the absolute minimum size cooler you should use would be 160 quarts. You can use bags of crushed ice or small blocks of ice instead of cartons or bottles, but you'll need to monitor water levels carefully, and drain meltwater to keep it off the meat. Arrange the deer in the cooler—the double hams go in first and then the rib cage. Then, work the shoulders around them. Now tuck a few more cartons of ice in the space around the meat. Cover the cooler with a couple of blankets or sleeping bags for extra insulation. —T.E.N.

209 BE THE CAMP BIOLOGIST

Every deer camp should have a jaw puller to use to estimate the age of deer, if for no other reason than to have something else to talk about. Two tools are required: a pair of long-handled pruning shears and an inexpensive jaw extractor.

STEP 1 First, you'll need to lay the deer on its back; then, insert the jaw extractor between the incisors and premolars. Pry the mouth open.

STEP 2 Work the extractor along the lower jawbone, pushing down hard to separate cheek tissue from the jaw.

STEP 3 Use the pruning shears to cut the jaw as it curves upward behind the last molar. Place the cutting bar to the outside of the jaw and keep the handles parallel with the roof of the mouth.

STEP 4 Push the extractor through the cut. Put a foot on the deer's neck and then firmly pull the extractor out of its mouth. It will slide along the lower bone. At the front of the jaw, rotate the extractor 90 degrees to separate the jaws. Remove the freed jawbone. —T.E.N.

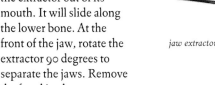

jaw extractor

210 TAKE THE TENDERLOINS

These are the long fillets that run parallel to the deer's backbone inside the rib cage, under the saddle. They are the most tender cuts and deserve the most tender care. All that is required is a sharp knife to remove them, a quick rinse, and a trip into a plastic baggie fast to prevent drying. Besides that, they simply call to be sliced into medallions, pan-seared in real butter seasoned with black pepper and rosemary, and eaten with the fingers. —T.E.N.

211 SHARE THE BIRDS

You know it, and your buddies know it: One side of the blind is the King Daddy seat—the coveted downwind edge where the shooting is easy as the ducks drift in with wings spread a mile wide. Don't hog it. Seat placement can make the difference between fast shooting and hard feelings, especially when three or more gunners are in the blind. If there's an obvious hot spot in the blind, rotate the seating. —T.E.N.

212 STOP A RUNNING BUCK

A low grunt or bleat will stop a close-in deer most of the time, but you'll need to minimize your movements. Make a call holder by sewing a loop of elastic cord on one side of the upper chest part of your jacket. Slip a grunt call under the loop, and you can easily reach it with your mouth. If you can't risk even that movement, try making a squirrel-like tch, tch-tch with your mouth. Have your gun or bow up and ready. Beyond 50 yards, a short, loud whistle sounds enough like a natural sound—a bird call, perhaps?—that it holds deer in place, intrigued but unalarmed, while they try to zero in on the source. If you can't produce an ear-splitting whistle with your lips, buy a referee's whistle and slip it on your grunt-call lanyard. Caught without a whistle? Holler "Stop!" and hope for the best. —T.E.N.

213 DISAPPEAR FROM DUCKS

With so much pressure on birds from north of the 49th parallel to the Gulf of Mexico, head-to-toe camouflage is critical for all but the earliest flights of the season. In a salt marsh or over open water, a shiny human face peeking over the blind is visible to ducks from a half mile or more away. In timber, ducks are doubly wary, and anything that looks out of place will send puddlers into the stratosphere. Why didn't they commit after a couple of passes? Take a good look at yourself. Hands, face, neck. Cover every inch, every time. —T.E.N.

214 FILLET A DEER QUARTER

Boning out a deer quarter is quick and easy, resulting in tender cuts of meat void of bonemeal and marrow formed when cutting through bone with a saw.

STEP 1 Place the skinned hind leg of a deer on a sturdy table, with the outside of the leg facing up. Slice through the silverskin along the natural seam between the top round and the sirloin tip, and pull the muscle away from the bone. Cut the top round off at the back of the leg.

STEP 2 Remove the remaining silverskin. Cut the rump roast away from the top of the hip bone.

STEP 3 Turn the leg over. Using your fingers, separate the bottom round from the sirloin tip at the natural seam. Cut the bottom round from the bone. Then cut the sirloin tip from the bone. Slice the shank meat away from the bone and trim off connective tissue. —T.E.N.

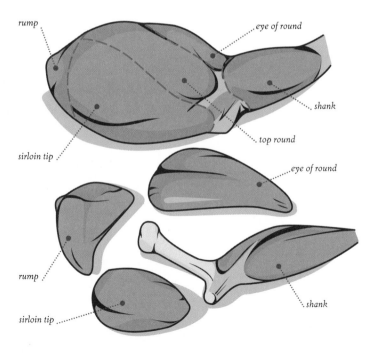

rump

eye of round

shank

top round

sirloin tip

eye of round

rump

shank

sirloin tip

215 WALK LIKE A SHADOW

Spring woods are noisy. A carpet of dead leaves and a winter's worth of ice-felled branches litter the forest floor. Learning how to walk silently will put you in a better position to call in the gobbler of a lifetime—and help you walk up to a hat-rack buck next deer season.

WALK LIKE A CAT Begin your step by lifting your foot straight up, toes pointing down to avoid snagging. Place the outside of your foot down first. Press the ball of your foot into the ground consciously, rolling from the outside in. Bring down your heel, then slowly shift weight to that foot. Be prepared to lift and shift whenever you feel any obstacle that might snap or crackle under your weight.

MAP YOUR STEPS To avoid having to watch your feet, make a mental map of the upcoming ground cover for the next 8 to 10 paces. Especially note where you might need to sidestep branches or high-step over fallen logs.

GO SLOW When looking for game, take three to four slow steps and stop. How slow? Three steps should take you at least 20 seconds.

HIDE YOUR NOISE Mask the noise of footfalls by moving whenever other sounds can muffle your own. Wind in the trees, moving water, and even airplane noise can all hide the sound of a human on the hunt. —T.E.N.

216 TUNE-UP YOUR TURKEY SKILLS

Often even the sweetest-sounding box calls come out of storage sounding a little flat. It's easy to ruin a call through overzealous tuning, so the secret is to go easy.

STEP 1 Cleaning comes first, but be very careful not to change the contours of the call's lips and paddle. Forgo the sandpaper. Instead try a light touch with a plastic-coated sponge of the kind usually used to scrub pots without scratching them. The plan is to remove hand grease, dirt, and old chalk, not wood.

STEP 2 Once the wood is cleaned, re-chalk the underside of the paddle. Many call-makers prefer to use railroad chalk, the type that is used to mark the sides of boxcars, but now there are many brands that are sold specifically for turkey calls. Stay away from blackboard chalk or any type of chalk made with oil.

STEP 3 Play the call, listening for the desired tone. Shiny spots on the lid's underside indicate that oil or dirt is still present. Repeat Step 1 until you get the sweet notes.

STEP 4 Adjust the tension screw on the paddle as a last resort. On most calls, it's right where it needs to be. Your goal is just to get the screw back into its original position if it has worked loose. Start by tightening it a quarter turn and then test the call. Repeat if necessary until you feel that you are tightening the screw past the point where it was set. If you reach this point, back off. —A.L.

F&S Field Report: SHOWDOWN

It is my 14th stalk on a pronghorn buck, the second of our third morning on the hunt. This time it's Dan Frye and I on the ground, and already we've clawed through a creekbottom that heads up in a field where a goat and his harem are feeding in the early light. Paul Ellis saw them first, an hour ago and with his naked eyes, but it took 10X binoculars for me to figure out the story. Glassing from the roadside a mile-and-a-half away, I saw the buck just as he raced down a gumbo bluff and tore across a wide valley between three cookie-cutter red-shale buttes. The subject of the goat's ire had fled the scene, but the puff clouds of gumbo dust were unmistakable: This antelope was as hot as they get. "Let's get the blow-up doll and the kneepads and see if we can make something happen," Ellis said.

Now we're at it again, Frye, the decoy, and I, all cozied up so tight I feel a little dirty. We're picking our way across a grassy flat at the toe of a long ridge when suddenly a buck and a doe rocket from behind us, 80 yards out and hellbent-for-leather, dashing towards the base of a butte that rises from the plains maybe a quarter-mile away. Frye and I exchange glances, shaking our heads. Where'd they come from? But the commotion draws the attention of the first buck, the one we'd seen from the road, the one we'd intended on stalking. His head appears through the fringe of grass on top of the ridge. He ain't happy. He knows something's up.

Pinned down on a piece of flat ground, huddled behind the decoy, we can't move a muscle. But we don't have to.

Something catches my right eye, and I look out over the flats, into the middle distance, somewhere between a quarter-mile away and the place where the plains fall off the edge of the earth. It's a tiny contrail of dust—a pronghorn buck is charging through the sagebrush and tufted grass. I grab my binos. Even at 400 yards, I know the look on his face: *Boy, I'm gonna bust you one...*

I grab Dan Frye's shoulder.

"Buck, man! To your right, and he's coming fast!"

Frye cuts his eyes and instantly jerks the decoy to cover me.

"This is it!" he barks. "Oh, man, look at him come! This is the one, brother!"

We crab around to the right, Frye covering me completely with the shield of the decoy, like a modern-day Achilles of the Montana plains. In an instant I settle on both knees, left shoulder pointed at the puff of prairie dust now 200 yards away and closing. I try to control my respiration, my pulse, the shaking in my bow-arm, deep-breathing and contorted like some broadhead-armed yoga swami.

Frye's not helping, bless his heart.

"Holy cow, man! He ain't gonna stop!"

"He's in the creek bottom now!"

"Where is he? Where'd he go?"

I lift my head to peer through the window in the decoy's rump, just as the antelope charges over the creek bank. For the briefest moment, one thought flashes through my mind: I sure am glad that's not a water buffalo.

"Now! Draw and hold!" Frye spits. "Hold . . . hold." He takes a last-minute range through his binoculars.

"Thirty-four yards." Out of the corner of my eye I can see his grin flash.

"All yours," he says.

He presses the front end of the decoy down and to the left, clearing me for a shot. The buck is posted up and prancing, glaring, quartering towards me. It's not a shot I like. I freeze at full draw, and lock eyes with the animal. I couldn't tell you if the standoff lasted a half-second or 10. I do remember blowing a long breath out through puffed cheeks. Then he takes a single step broadside.

For two and a half days, we had parsed over the horns of every pronghorn buck that we saw. And although any antelope taken with a bow is a memory to cherish, we didn't want to invest precious stalking time on smaller animals. That's one of the engaging aspects of hunting like this. Like the bucks themselves, we could choose our fights.

Or so we thought. But as that buck barreled across the sage flats, face a black mask of violent intent, I never even looked at the horns. Stone-still at full draw, it still never occurred to me to judge the headgear. At that moment, I knew exactly how big the horns were. And despite looking at them on my wall a million times since, they've never diminished a bit: They were as tall as the buttes that soared over the plains, as broad as the valley where I crouched.

On my knees, I settle the bow sight, and let the arrow fly.

—*T. Edward Nickens*
Field & Stream, *"Speed Trap,"* September 2010

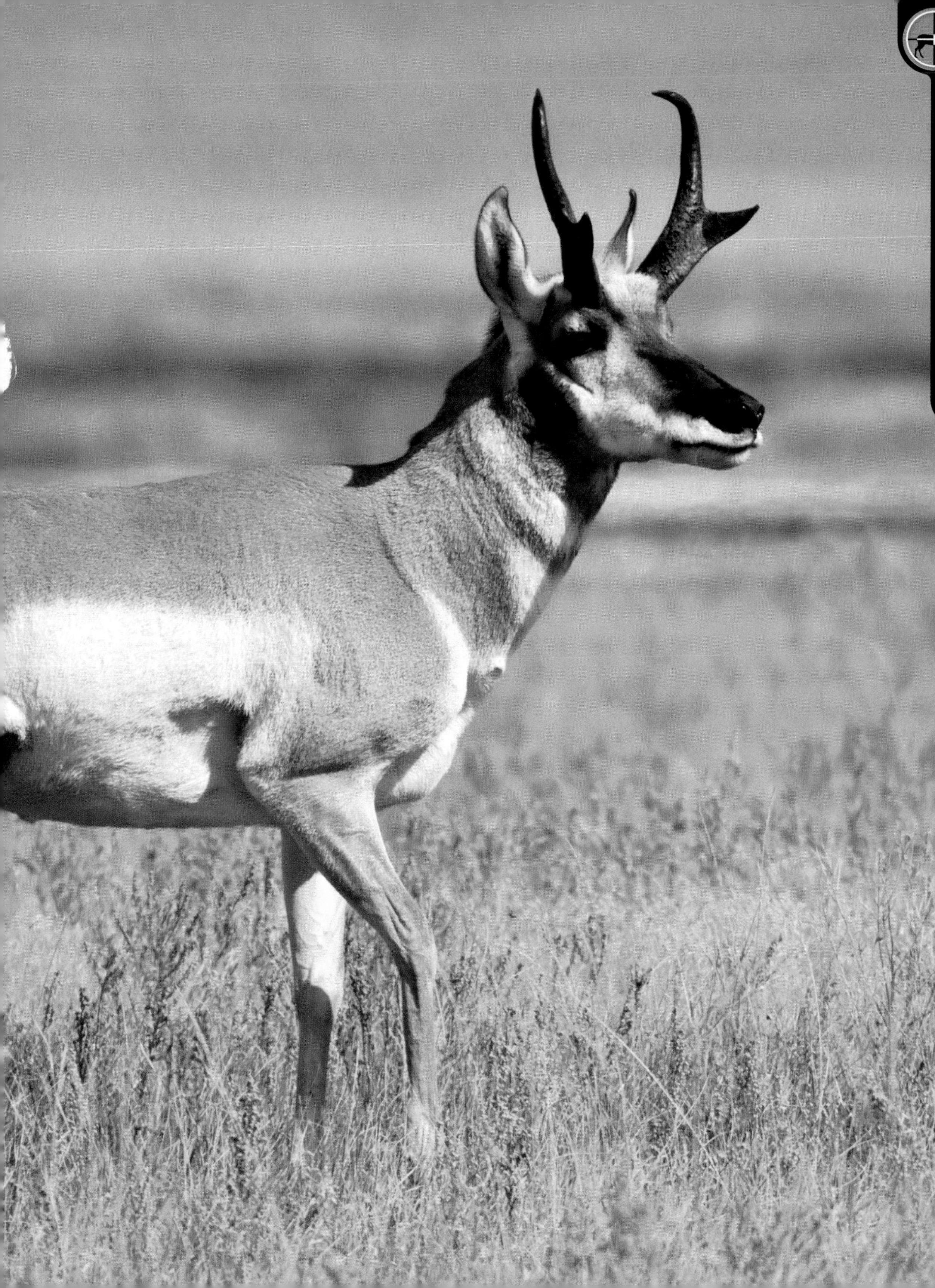

217 SKIN A DEER

The traditional skinning knife has an upswept blade and a high point, but a drop-point blade will do, if you take care not to puncture the skin with the tip. It's much easier to skin a deer when the skin is still warm. You can peel most of the hide away from the body by pulling on it, with your blade coming into play only to free the skin from the carcass at sticking points and for making initial cuts along the belly and chest, around the neck and hocks, and on the inside of the legs. Hold the blade so that the edge does not face your off hand, which grips the skin. Use shallow, careful slices to tease at the juncture of skin and carcass.

THE INITIAL CUTS
Make the cut along the inside leg with the blade facing up, so that it doesn't cut through hairs. If you do cut through the hairs, they can end up getting onto the meat, where they will be hard to remove.

FREEING UP STICKING POINTS
Most of your work will be done with just your hands. Use the knife sparingly to make small slices when the hide is sticking.

PEELING THE HIDE
Place a forefinger or thumb on top of your knife for precision while cutting. Peel the skin away from the meat with your noncutting hand.
—K.M.

218 SIT AND HIT

Practice getting into a sitting position quickly so you're not floundering around when there's game in front of you. First, point your left shoulder toward the animal and sit down. Bend your knees so your legs flare out like wings. You're now quartered away from the target. Next, place each elbow inside a knee joint and find that place where the elbows just lock down. Now your body is a tripod: your butt and two elbows form a stable platform for your rifle. The trick is to do this often enough that you don't even have to think.

In a tree stand, you're already sitting, but you still have prep work to do. Keep the rifle out of your lap; instead, rest the fore-end on the shooting rail and the butt on your thigh. Practice aiming with the fore-end held in your hand and your hand resting on the shooting rail. Make sure you have a clear sight picture. If you're hunting over a shooting lane, you might not have time to adjust. —T.E.N.

219 RELIVE YOUR CHILDHOOD WITH A FROG GIG

For many rural kids, frog gigging is a rite of passage. For some, it's a summertime fling they never grow out of. Bullfrogs freeze in the glare of a bright light like the proverbial deer in the headlights. Remember to check local laws before you hoist your trident. Some states, such as California, prohibit the use of frog gigs but do allow enterprising herp hunters to hand-grab frogs, as well as bag them with nooses, hooks, and tongs (which would be something to see).

GEAR UP Bullfrogs are tougher than you'd think, so sharpen each gig point with sandpaper or an emery board. You can find gigs at sporting-goods stores and in mail-order sporting goods catalogs.

EYES AND EARS Listen for the deep gaa-RUUMPH of mature bullfrogs and then sweep a bright light across the shoreline of ponds, lakes, and riverbanks. Check out thick mats of lily pads, fallen logs, and low mudbanks. Twin pinpricks of eyeshine and the telltale crescent white chin give the frogs away. Let the little ones grow.

STALK You'll need to get close, so be stealthy. In a boat, it's a two-person job. The paddler should move slowly to avoid creating frog-spooking wakes and to keep the light shining directly on the frog. Stay clear of anything that will scrape noisily against the boat. You need to get the gig within about 6 inches of the frog before you make your move.

FROG KABOB Jab the gig hard. You have to pin the frog to the pond bottom, through muck and mud, so give it all you've got. Now, slide your hand down the gig handle to the spear points and grasp the frog firmly around the belly. Bring the frog and gig up together before removing the frog from the gig. If you're grabbing bare-handed, do it with gusto. Using a fish-cleaning glove can help you hang on. —T.E.N.

220 SHOOT DOWNHILL AND UPHILL

Let's settle this old argument right here, and we won't need cosine angles. This is hunting, not geometry. Gravity only affects a bullet or arrow along its horizontal distance, not the linear distance taken by the projectile. To calculate your hold, simply figure out the distance between you and the target on a horizontal line. If you're 20 feet high in a tree and the deer is 3 yards from the base of the tree, then hold for 3 yards. If the ram is 200 feet above you, on a ledge 300 yards away on a horizontal line, hold for 300 yards and pull the trigger. —T.E.N.

WIGEON

ON THE WING Look for the distinctive white upper-wing shoulder patches of the males. When overhead, both sexes display an elliptical white belly surrounded by the brown-gray chest and flanks. Slightly smaller than mallards, wigeon sport longer, wedge-shaped tails than other puddle ducks.

IN THE HAND The male's white crown patch, which gives the bird the nickname "baldpate," is nearly impossible to miss, but it can be indistinct until November. Both sexes have a short, wide, gray bill tipped with black. The hen wigeon can sometimes be confused with the hen gadwall, but the latter's bill is orange-red and its wing lacks the green stripe separating the speculum from the shoulder patch.

VOICE The drake's frequent whistle is unmistakable: three notes, the middle one rising in pitch—we-WEE-hoo. The similar whistling call of the pintail is on the same pitch.

FLOCK/FLIGHT PROFILE Wigeon fly in swift, bunched, twisting flocks, like pigeons. They're known for flying high, then dropping fast into the decoys.

DECOY SET Wigeon frequently raft up in large groups far from shore. If you set a large J-hook pattern for a shore blind, group the wigeon decoys along the farthest point of the J.

SCAUP

ON THE WING Greater scaup are slightly larger than lesser scaup—natch—but they're fairly close in size. Greaters prefer salt and sound environments, whereas lessers congregate on freshwater, but flocks can be mixed with both kinds. To distinguish them from ringneck ducks, look for the telltale white wing patches on the scaup and the distinctive double white ring on the ringneck's bill.

IN THE HAND The broad, blue bill is characteristic, and it's the reason both greater and lesser scaup are nicknamed "bluebill." White wing bars extend past the elbow joint on greater scaup and continue halfway out the primaries; on lessers, the white patch stops at the elbow. Greater scaup drakes have a greenish sheen on the head. On the lesser, the sheen is purple, and you can see a small bump behind the crown on the males.

VOICE In flight, bluebills utter a raspy, purring br-r-r-a-a-t, br-r-r-a-a-t. Listen for whistling wings, too.

FLOCK/FLIGHT PROFILE Scaup fly relatively low to the water, swerving back and forth in erratic, bunched groups.

DECOY SET Diving ducks frequently raft up in large numbers. For bluebills, set gang lines of 12 decoys in long rows parallel to the shore. Fill in the gaps with singles.

WOOD DUCK

ON THE WING Wood ducks fly with their heads held higher than their bodies. Look for squared-off tails and broad wings that display a white stripe on the trailing edge. In flight, woodies can be confused with wigeon because of their white bellies, but the wigeon's thin, narrow wings and white shoulder patches help set it apart.

IN THE HAND With its gaudy green-and-white crest and multicolored (red, black, white, and yellow) bill, it's hard to mistake the wood duck drake for any other kind of bird. The drab hens can be confused with hen gadwall, but you can identify a woody hen by its tear-shaped white eye patch.

VOICE A loud, upwardly pitched, squealing w-e-e-e-e-e-k is commonly heard when the birds are on the water; it is heard as well when they're being flushed.

FLOCK/FLIGHT PROFILE As they careen through timber, woodies twist and turn like leaves in the wind. In open country, they fly fairly straight with swift wingbeats. Although they're usually seen in pairs or small groups, flocks can number in the hundreds.

DECOY SET Groups of woodies tend to have a destination firmly in mind, but singles and pairs can be lured away, especially after the morning feeding flights. The classic set of two small groups of decoys to either side of the blind works well.

MALLARD

ON THE WING The drake's green head and contrasting white collar are unmistakable. A white rump and breast signal a mallard drake flushing in low light, whereas the hens' white underwings give them away. (Look-alike gadwall hens have a lighter belly.) Look for a slow wingbeat that takes place mostly below the horizontal plane of the body.

IN THE HAND The drake mallard is the most readily recognized duck, but the hen can be easily confused with the black duck, gadwall, and mottled duck. Look for a bright white stripe bordering a purple speculum—blacks and gadwall don't have it, and the white stripe is barely visible on the mottled duck.

VOICE The classic quack is the call of the mallard hen. Drakes give a seldom heard, guttural, rasping kr-e-k.

FLOCK/FLIGHT PROFILE Greenhead flocks can be anywhere—so high they're barely visible or so low they skim the treetops. Look for relatively lofty groups of 6 to 40 birds flying in a direct, steady pattern, often in the classic V or U shape.

DECOY SET The classic C pattern is very effective, and it can be tailored to many field situations. The open part of the C forms the landing zone, so arrange the pattern with the gap on the downwind side.

NORTHERN PINTAIL

ON THE WING With its long tail extension, or pin, the drake is rarely mistaken for another bird, but "sprigtails" can be confused with wigeon. Their slender bodies and long necks are a giveaway, and the thin, gull-like wings beat in a longer arc than a mallard's or a wigeon's. Hens sport dark scalloping on the underwing flanks, and the drake's white neck stripe is unmistakable.

IN THE HAND Brown-gray hens are similar to other pale, female dabbling ducks, but only pintails and wigeon have dark gray bills. Unlike those of wigeon, the upper wings of pintail hens are nearly uniformly brown or bronze, with no pale stripes along the upper edge of the speculum.

VOICE The pintail drake's call is a trilling whistle. Hens quack coarsely on the flush.

FLOCK/FLIGHT PROFILE Swift fliers, often grouping in classic Vs or long lines, pintails will descend to decoys from great heights, bombing into open water after dropping in zigzagging lines.

DECOY SET Pintail decoys are most often used to add visibility and species variety to a grouping of puddle duck decoys. Use drakes for their long-range visibility and then mix in three to five pintails for every two dozen mallards. Or group them in large loafing flocks in the shallows.

GREEN-WINGED TEAL

ON THE WING Look for its tiny size, sharply pointed wings, a wingbeat nearly as swift as a diving duck's, and a short neck and tail. In good light, the emerald green wing patches are visible. The white breast and light underwings—especially on drakes—are a good clue when the birds are overhead or twisting and turning, and these help distinguish between green-winged teal and the blue-winged variety.

IN THE HAND Early-season drakes in eclipse plumage may lack the typical red head and iridescent green eye mask and can be confused with hens. Females sport dark spotted bills and brown wing coverts; the wing coverts of the drakes are gray.

VOICE Drake green-winged teal are very vocal, with a high-pitched, trilling preep-preep whistle.

FLOCK/FLIGHT PROFILE Teal often fly in closely knotted groups, low over marshes but a bit higher over open water. Their erratic flight patterns and habit of swooping into the decoys like tiny rockets make them one of the most challenging birds to shoot on the wing.

DECOY SET Teal dekes mixed in with mallard and other puddle duck spreads are a deadly draw. Rig three together on dropper lines that lead to a single 6-ounce weight and bunch them in tight groups.

—T.E.N.

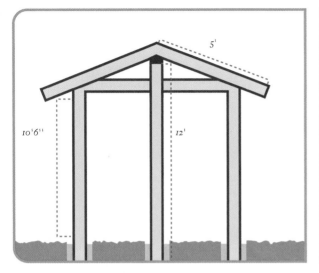

222 BUILD A ROOFED MEAT POLE

Most meat poles get the game off the ground but they don't protect it from rain or snow. This gable-roofed version does, and with style. The overall dimensions of the structure can vary, depending on the size of your club (and the construction skills of your hunters).

STEP 1 Mark the ground for four corner posts and two ridge posts constructed of 5x5 treated timbers. Sink the posts into 30-inch holes and anchor them with cement.

STEP 2 Attach a 5x5 ridge joist on top of the center posts. Allow for an 18-inch overhang on each end.

STEP 3 Nail in 2x4 or 2x6 rafters, allowing for an 18-inch overhang. Nail in roof sheathing of plywood or 1x6 boards. Cover with shingles or roofing tin.

STEP 4 Hang a 3-inch-diameter galvanized steel pole from the two ridge posts, about a foot below the ridge joist. Affix large eye screws or eyebolts to the ridge pole at 3-foot intervals. Attach a block and tackle to these when you're raising the deer up. —T.E.N.

223 BLAZE SECRET TRAILS TO YOUR STAND

Marking a trail to a favorite stand site or hidden blind is a dark art of the savvy hunter. Here's the secret formula.

CAMOUFLAGE THE TRAILHEAD Mark the entrance to the trail with a rock or other natural feature that is visible at night. Enter the trailhead from different angles to avoid wearing an obvious path in the ground.

BE TACK SHARP Flat thumbtacks reflect light at angles close to perpendicular, so they'll only show up if you're on the right trail. Cylindrical or cube-shaped tacks reflect light from all angles. Don't use them.

LEAVE CODED MESSAGES Use as few tacks as you can and devise a code only you and your hunting buddies can decipher. Three tacks in a triangle: Turn left. Single tack head high: Proceed straight. —T.E.N.

224

REMEMBER FOUR KNIFE "NEVERS"

1 Never store a knife in a leather sheath. It can cause rusting or discoloration.

2 Never use water to clean a horn handle. Horn absorbs moisture and can splinter.

3 Never use hot water to clean a wood handle. If the wood is cracked or dried, rub it with olive oil.

4 Never touch the blade or metal parts after oiling. This can leave behind salt and acids, which can cause oxidation.
—K.M.

225

ASSEMBLE A RIFLE REPAIR KIT

The most important 2 pounds you can carry on any (actually, every) hunt is a zippered nylon bag that measures 8x4x1 inches. It's a rifle repair kit, and it can save not only your bacon but the pork of other people who aren't so smart.

The cleaning rod is not for cleaning bores but for knocking stuck cases out of chambers. Any short and strong takedown rod will do. (A small-diameter rod works in all bore sizes.) Here are two other hints: Always carry a spare scope with a long tube that will fit a wide variety of mounts, and if you do work on a gun, do it over a bunk or a sleeping bag so when you drop small parts you can find them again. —D.E.P.

THE KIT SHOULD CONTAIN (a) a Lyman interchangeable-bit screwdriver, (b) a gunsmith bedding tool, (c) a Leupold multitool with Torx- and hex-head screwdrivers, (d) a set of small Allen wrenches (for working on triggers), (e) a collection of patches, and (f) a multisection .270-caliber steel cleaning rod.

226

JUDGE A TROPHY BUCK BY ITS EARS

The best way to tell the length of a whitetail's antler tines is by comparing them to the length of its ears, which typically measure about 8 inches. If the first or longest tine appears longer than the ear, and the second point is only a little shorter than the ear, you have all the information you need to make your decision. Shoot. —K.M.

227

HOLD A SHOTGUN TENDERLY

Some shooters clutch their guns almost tightly enough to leave dents in the wood. Relax your grip, and you might start breaking more clay birds—or downing more birds with feathers.

It's impossible to swing a shotgun smoothly if you strangle it. Try this: Put a death grip on an unloaded gun and mount it on an imaginary duck or dove. You'll feel the tension all the way up through your shoulders. Now hold the gun lightly in your hands and see how much more easily it flows to the target. How tightly should you hold a gun? Ever-quotable instructor Gil Ash says: "Just tight enough to squeeze a little toothpaste from a full tube." You may want to hold your gun even more lightly, tightening your grip only at the instant you make the shot so you can control the gun under recoil. —P.B.

228 SOUND LIKE A DUCK

A happy-sounding quack from a 10-pound hen is the foundation of duck calling, but there's more to it than blowing hot air. Blowing a duck call well requires forcing air from your lungs by pushing with your diaphragm, and using an open-throated calling style to get enough air volume to shred cattails. Here's the practice drill.

STEP 1 Learn to blow from your belly. Hold a small mirror a few inches from your mouth and fog it with your breath, blowing deep, sharp exhalations. Even the quietest clucks and quacks come from that hot, deep, fog-the-mirror air.

STEP 2 To open your throat, sit down, tilt your head back, and look up. Practice blowing a sharp quack straight up at the ceiling. Master one clean, happy-as-a-clam hen quack. This is the most essential duck call, and you have to get it right.

STEP 3 Once your craned-neck, staring-at-the-ceiling quack is solid, slowly bring your head forward a few inches at a time. Master the single quack in each progressive position until your chin is level.

STEP 4 When you can maintain an open throat in a normal posture, follow the single quack with a second clean one, then a third. Tone comes next: Use quacks to work your way from the bottom of the scale to the top, and back down. —T.E.N.

229 DECIPHER FLIGHT PATTERNS

Keep an eye on wingtips—when the ducks stop flapping and sail for a second or two, they're looking for the source of the calling, which means you're doing something right. Don't stop now. If a duck's tail is lower than his head, he's cruising and looking, and you've got a good shot at finishing him. But if he levels up, your chances are getting worse. Back off the call. Pull that jerk cord. And call hard "on the corners" as the birds are starting to circle and all you see are tail feathers. —T.E.N.

230 DECODE A DUCK QUACK

The best duck callers carry on a conversation. Here's what they're saying.

HAIL CALL Loud and nearly obnoxious, used when ducks are too far away to hear anything but the most raucous racket. Think Bourbon Street or spring break at Daytona.

GREETING CALL Warm and personal. "How ya doin'? What's going on tonight?"

COMEBACK CALL This is the party invitation. The gang's-all-here-and-you're-missing-it plea.

FEEDING CALL When ducks hear this, they should think about a bunch of guys scraping their plates with a fork.

HEN QUACK "Life is good, my friends. Grub a-plenty, and plenty to share." —T.E.N.

231 KNOW WHEN YOU'VE SCREWED A SCOPE HARD ENOUGH

One way that you can avoid endless trouble is by degreasing the base screws on your scope mounts and screwing them in hard.

How hard is hard? Hard is when you're turning the screwdriver for all you're worth and the next thing you know you're lying on the floor and the dog is pawing at you and whining. Hard is when you're twisting away and everything turns purple and silver. You get the idea. When tightening scope ring screws, however, you do not crank on the screwdriver until all the little blood vessels in your nose burst. You crank until, with a reasonable amount of effort, the screws will turn no longer. Then you stop. That's hard enough.

—D.E.P.

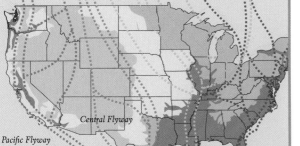

Pacific Flyway

Central Flyway

Mississippi Flyway

Atlantic Flyway

232 KNOW YOUR FLYWAY

Pouring down from the northern United States, Canada, Alaska, and the Arctic, migrating waterfowl broadly follow one of four migratory routes as they flee winter weather for their warmer southern wintering grounds. Knowing the flyway in which your favorite hunting spot is located will help you track the weather patterns that drive ducks south. Watch for big storm fronts bearing down in the northern reaches of your flyway. Ducks will be on the move. You should be packing decoys. —T.E.N.

FIELD & STREAM CRAZY-GOOD GRUB

233 MAKE A TEAL POT

A duck dish made with pancake syrup and a can of cola? This is no joke.

INGREDIENTS
6 plucked and cleaned teal, or
   3 to 4 mallards
One 12-oz. can cola
3 medium onions, quartered
Smoked sausage, 4 to 5 links cut into
   3-inch lengths
Pancake syrup
Cajun spice blend

Place ducks breast side down in a large Dutch oven–style pot.

Pour the cola over the birds.

Add onions. Place one piece of smoked sausage inside each duck. Scatter the remaining sausage pieces in the pot.

Squirt each duck with a dollop of pancake syrup.

Shake Cajun spice blend over the whole batch.

Cover and bake in 300-degree F oven for 3 hours.

Serve with rice and spiced rum.

—T.E.N.

234 SCORE ON BIRDS AFTER THE FIRST FLUSH

Often duck and goose hunters will spend the afternoons walking up pheasants or bobwhite quail with their duck dogs or pointing breeds. Everybody shoots the rise and then whoops afterward. That's when a handful of late flushers goes up, and you're standing with an empty gun and your mouth wide open. You need to think a few steps ahead to maximize your chances.

STEP 1 Check the location of other hunters. Folks lose their focus after the flush. Make sure the group knows you're going in.

STEP 2 After the initial volley, take a few steps out front in order to get a better angle on late flushers.

STEP 3 Turn your stock shoulder slightly away from the location of the flush. This will open up your stance and give you a better swing on birds that flush in the opposite direction. —T.E.N.

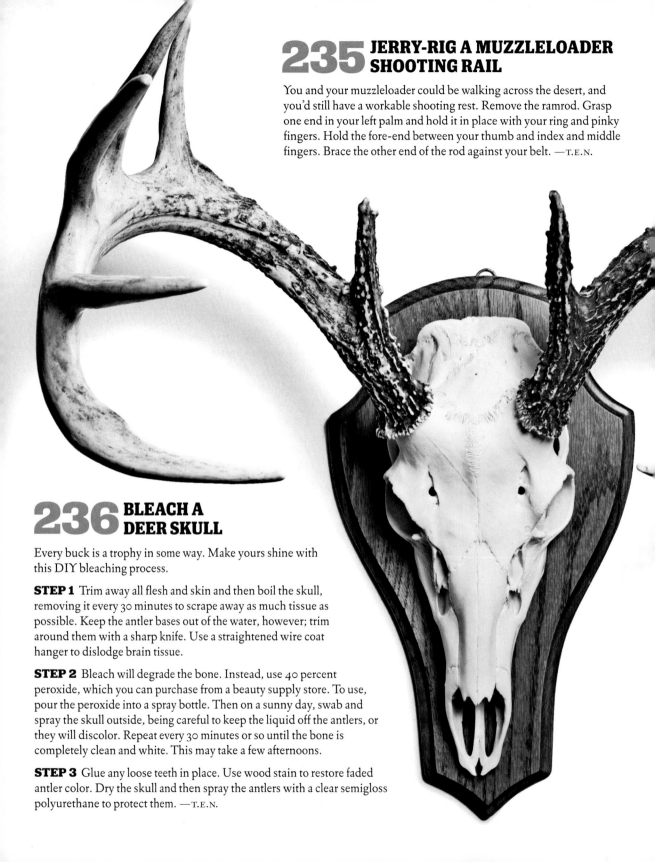

235 JERRY-RIG A MUZZLELOADER SHOOTING RAIL

You and your muzzleloader could be walking across the desert, and you'd still have a workable shooting rest. Remove the ramrod. Grasp one end in your left palm and hold it in place with your ring and pinky fingers. Hold the fore-end between your thumb and index and middle fingers. Brace the other end of the rod against your belt. —T.E.N.

236 BLEACH A DEER SKULL

Every buck is a trophy in some way. Make yours shine with this DIY bleaching process.

STEP 1 Trim away all flesh and skin and then boil the skull, removing it every 30 minutes to scrape away as much tissue as possible. Keep the antler bases out of the water, however; trim around them with a sharp knife. Use a straightened wire coat hanger to dislodge brain tissue.

STEP 2 Bleach will degrade the bone. Instead, use 40 percent peroxide, which you can purchase from a beauty supply store. To use, pour the peroxide into a spray bottle. Then on a sunny day, swab and spray the skull outside, being careful to keep the liquid off the antlers, or they will discolor. Repeat every 30 minutes or so until the bone is completely clean and white. This may take a few afternoons.

STEP 3 Glue any loose teeth in place. Use wood stain to restore faded antler color. Dry the skull and then spray the antlers with a clear semigloss polyurethane to protect them. —T.E.N.

237 CLEAN A SQUIRREL

Pound for pound (okay, ounce for ounce), squirrels are among the most difficult game animals to clean. Their skin is tougher than duct tape, and squirrel hair sticks to squirrel flesh with the tenacity of five-minute epoxy. Fortunately, you can create a simple device that makes stripping them a cinch. Here's how.

MAKE THE STRIPPER

STEP 1 First draw two lines across a 5x3 3/4-inch piece of 1/16-inch aluminum plate, sectioning it into thirds.

STEP 2 Cut three slots from the long edge of an outer third (see below for slot sizes). Smooth the edges with sandpaper.

STEP 3 Drill two holes through the middle of the other outer third. Then bend the two outer thirds up at a 90-degree angle, so that they form a U-shaped channel.

STEP 4 Using the holes that you drilled, nail the squirrel skinner firmly to a tree or post at shoulder height.

SKIN THE SQUIRREL

STEP 1 Hook the squirrel's rear legs in the two narrow slots, its back facing you.

STEP 2 Bend the tail over the back and make a cut between the anus and the base of the tail, through the skin and tailbone. Extend this cut about an inch down the squirrel's back, filleting a 1/2-inch-wide strip of skin away from the muscle, but leaving it attached at the bottom.

STEP 3 Make two cuts, each starting at the opposite sides of the base of this strip and extending laterally halfway around the squirrel, stopping just in front of the hind legs.

STEP 4 Now grasp the tail and loosened hide and pull firmly down. Except for the skin covering the back legs and part of the belly, the hide should shuck off inside out.

STEP 5 Flip the squirrel around, and slide its neck and two front paws into the slots. Grasp the edges of the remaining hide and strip the "pants" off the squirrel.
—T.E.N.

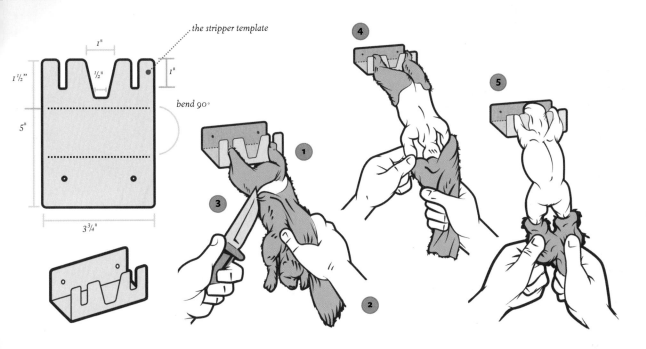

...the stripper template

1"

1 1/2"

1/2"

1"

bend 90°

5"

3 3/4"

238 SET MONSTER GANG LINES FOR BIG WATER DIVERS

Diving duck hunters often have to contend with extreme decoy-setting conditions. This heavily weighted gang line will hold decoys in place through Armageddon but still give hunters the option of moving them when the birds need tweaking.

Tie a 5- to 10-pound anchor to each end of 150 feet of decoy cord. (A tip for hunters with retrievers: Use lead-core line to keep this long mother line underwater and out of your pooch's paws.) Tie in 18-inch dropper lines for each decoy, spaced about 6 feet apart. Tie in a metal trout stringer clip to the end of each dropper. Set a number of gang lines parallel to one another and fill in the gaps with individual decoys. —T.E.N.

239 KNOW YOUR NUTS

Nothing draws game like mast crops, be they oak, beech, or hickory. The trick is knowing which crop is which, and what critters can't pass them by. —T.E.N.

WHITE OAK

In a good year, a mature white oak can produce upwards of 2,000 acorns. White oaks typically produce "bumper" crops every three to four years.

BEST FOR Deer, squirrels, turkeys, grouse, bears

CHESTNUT OAK

These sweet acorns are among the largest mast fruits in the woods and sprout soon after they fall. Deer can't eat enough of them.

BEST FOR Deer, squirrels, turkeys, bears

RED OAK

Red oaks are higher in tannin than white oaks, so deer target acorns of the latter first. But in years with a wet, cold spring or a late spring frost, white oak acorn production often plummets. A stand in red oaks pays off.

BEST FOR Deer, squirrels, turkeys, grouse

CALIFORNIA BLACK OAK

This western oak doesn't mind rocky slopes, thin soils, and dry climates. It's critical for muleys, and fawn survival rates are tied to its mast production. Look for pure groves loaded with acorns.

BEST FOR Mule deer, bears, quail

AMERICAN BEECH

Once the oily beechnuts are released from their prickly husks, smaller animals prize them. Wild turkeys will cover a lot of ground to find a good beech ridge; the extinct passenger pigeon once flocked to such spots.

BEST FOR Deer, squirrels, turkeys

SHAGBARK HICKORY

It's the sweetest hickory nut in the woods. Squirrels love them, and their gnawing sounds are a giveaway to knowing hunters. Wild turkeys swallow the nuts unshelled and let their gizzards do the hard work.

BEST FOR Squirrels, turkeys

240 SPATCHCOCK YOUR BIRD

You heard right. It's an Irish term that means to butterfly and nearly flatten a whole bird, so the meat cooks evenly. Use it to cook any gamebird over a fire.

Turn a dressed bird breast side down. With bird hunter's shears, cut cleanly up one side of the backbone and then the other, from neck to tail. Toss the backbone in the trash. Press the bird against a cutting board with the heel of your hand. Rub down with spices. Grill or spit it on a Y-shaped stick and roast it over the fire like a marshmallow. —T.E.N.

241 GLASS WITH A PLAN

Big, open country requires hunters to spend quality time behind good glass. Use spotting scopes and binoculars to visually pick the landscape apart to find that one memorable animal that offers a good chance for success. And you can't just lean over a spotting scope and rubber-neck distant ridges. Have a plan.

MAKE LIKE A PIRATE Spotting scopes can produce eyestrain-induced headaches. Consider wearing a patch over the eye you're not using.

BRACE YOURSELF You might be glassing for hours, so get comfortable and get rock solid. A backrest is key.

HAVE A FORMULA Be sure to avoid letting your eyes wander. Use binoculars first to pick apart the obvious cover. Then work a spotting scope over the rest of the landscape. Pick a viewing pattern and stick with it. Don't forget to look away from the glass every couple of minutes. Your trophy might have walked right up on you. —T.E.N.

242 REALLY, REALLY TICK OFF YOUR HUNTING PARTNER, PART I

A duck-hunting buddy finally caves in to your ceaseless whining and takes you to his new honey hole. It's on the back side of public land, so of course you cross your heart never to set a wader boot on the pond without him. And you don't—at least until you line up another hunt with someone else. There is nothing illegal about such two-timing promiscuity, but it is patently immoral. Such disloyalty may (or may not) be forgiven. But it is never forgotten. —T.E.N.

243 MAKE YOUR OWN DEER DRAG

Prevent rope burn and your own heart attack by using a homemade deer drag. You'll need two black plastic pallet sheets in good condition (try getting them from a warehouse), a grommet tool, 20 feet of parachute cord, and 10 feet of drag rope.

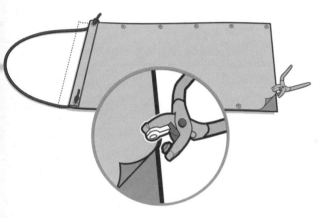

AT HOME Stack the two pallet sheets one on top of the other, slippery sides facing down. Attach them with grommets spaced about a foot apart all the way up both sides. Next, double over 2 inches of one of the short ends; secure with two grommets. Fasten the drag rope onto this reinforced edge with stopper knots.

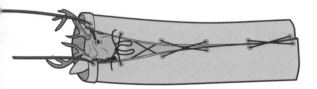

IN THE FIELD Place your deer on the plastic sheeting. Use parachute cord to lace the plastic around the deer, just like lacing up a shoe. Get dragging. —T.E.N.

244 SPOOK THE BULL YOU'RE HUNTING

One of the most common mistakes hunters make is trying to sound like a big bull. Throwing in half a dozen ringing grunts and a lot of chuckling at the end of the bugle might impress your hunting partner, but a herd bull's usual response is to round up his harem and nose them away from the intruder. —K.M.

245 GREEN-SCORE A WHITETAIL RACK

To gain entry into the Boone and Crockett (B&C) record book, your deer must be measured by an official B&C scorer after a 60-day drying period. But you can get your own score by using any measuring tape. It's called green scoring, and here's the formula for a typical whitetail. (All measurements are to the nearest $1/8$ inch.)

Measure the length of the longer main beam. Then measure the inside spread of the main beams; if this is less than or equal to your previous notation, it's your first number to keep. But if it is greater, discard it and use the original figure instead. Call whichever you retain A.

For each antler, add up the following: length of main beam; length of each normal point (the beam tip counts as a point, but do not include its length in your measurements here); the circumference at the smallest place between the burr and the first point; and the circumferences at the smallest places between the first and second, second and third, and third and fourth points (or halfway between the third point and beam tip). Add the two antler totals together to get B. Take A plus B to get your gross subtotal, C.

Now for the deductions: Take the differences between the corresponding measurements of each antler—that is, beam and point lengths, and the various circumferences. For example, if the right beam is 2 inches longer than the left one, write down that amount. Do the same for each individual measure; total them. To this figure, add the lengths of all abnormal points—those tines that don't project from the top of the main beam, or that don't have a matching tine on the other antler. This is D. Subtract D from C for the score. —T.E.N.

246 WORK A BEAVER POND OVER FOR DUCKS

Hunting a beaver pond starts with finding the right one. Young ponds and flooded swamps are a hunter's best bet, because rich, flooded soils produce a flush of edible plants, from duckweed to wild rice.

If your favorite pond seems to be drawing fewer ducks, look up and down the watershed for places where beavers have recently migrated.

Even older ponds, however, can produce a fine duck shoot. The surrounding trees produce more and more mast as they grow, a wood duck bonanza. As a beaver pond ages, it also tends to expand as the beavers add to the dam.

The deeper waters stay ice-free longer and can be a late-winter magnet when surrounding spots freeze up.

Always scout in the morning, not the evening. An older beaver pond or swamp that fills with ducks roosting at sunset might be empty of birds just a few minutes past legal shooting light as they depart for distant feeding grounds.

This two-person team (1) is set up near a creek channel. They have 8 to 10 decoys out in front of a blind, but they've moved back, temporarily, to the creek to shoot the first-light wood duck flights that follow the stream.

These hunters (2) are hunkered down for the long haul: well camouflaged in a fallen tree, comfortably seated at angles to each other to provide 360-degree views of the sky and using a jerk cord to create decoy movement.

This pair of hunters (3) is working birds that have lighted just out of sight of their decoy spread. One guy is in the blind, gun ready to mount.

His companion is stalking mallards on the far side of dense brush and blowdowns. They're doing a pinch maneuver: When the stalker flushes the birds, they'll fly over the guy still in the stand.

—T.E.N.

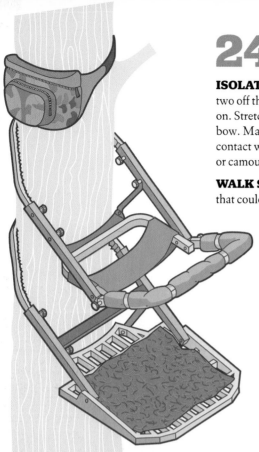

247 SILENCE YOUR TREE CLIMBER

ISOLATE THE PROBLEM At home, attach your stand to a tree a foot or two off the ground. Wear hunting clothes, grab your gun or bow, and climb on. Stretch your legs. Shoulder your gun and twist to each side. Draw your bow. Make a note of every place where metal or hard plastic comes into contact with the stand. Insulate the offending places with closed-cell foam or camouflage tape.

WALK SILENTLY Secure loose cables, buckles, and other noisemakers that could spook deer on your walk into the woods.

LUBRICATE MOVING PARTS Lube all squeaky hinges, welds, and joints with scent-free oil.

WAX SLIDING RAILS Run a scent-free candle across all rails that slide into larger-diameter tubes to dampen the sound of adjusting the stand.

LAY DOWN CARPET Glue a layer of marine carpet to the stand platform to silence scraping feet.

MINIMIZE ACCESSORIES The more gadgets you carry in your pockets, the likelier you'll sound like spare change clinking in the trees. Extra ammo, flashlights, and other small items should go into a daypack, to be fastened around the tree or hung from your stand. —T.E.N.

248 CHOOSE YOUR WEAPON FOR SQUIRRELS

Rimfire or scattergun? The decision is as much about philosophy as it is about ballistics. On the one hand, the squirrel is as sporting a .22 target as exists. On the other, they are tasty. Match the tool to the task.

USE A .22 RIFLE WHEN

• Hunting in a light rain. Stalking squirrels in the wet woods is a true joy.

• Hunting a dense population. Use .22 short ammo. It packs enough wallop out to 50 yards, but its softer report will keep squirrels active after a shot.

• Hunting fox squirrels. Slower and more prone to walk along the ground, these trophy-sized squirrels deserve a Boone and Crockett category of their own. Sniper them from 75 yards or better.

• There's a 48-hour *Rambo* marathon on television. Pack a semiauto and get it out of your system.

USE A SHOTGUN WHEN

• You hunt the early season. Leafy foliage makes rifle hunting exasperating.

• There's wind. Breeze-blown branches jack normally squirrelly squirrels into a level of physical schizophrenia unknown in the animal kingdom. Your only hope is a wide pattern.

• You want to walk. Follow creek banks and logging roads deep into the lair of the delicious tree rat. Shoot quickly and don't stop till something's falling.

• You're hungry. A hankering for squirrel is nature's way of telling you to forget sport and go big-bore. —T.E.N.

249 MAKE BUTTONS AND ZIPPER PULLS FROM A DEER RACK

Racks too small to show off are sized perfectly for handmade buttons and zipper pulls.

To make a button, use a hacksaw to cut off a tine at the diameter you need.

STEP 1 Using the tag end of the tine as a handle, sand the cut surface. Use 80-grit sandpaper first and then 120-grit. Next, saw off a disk about ³/₁₆ inch thick and buff the other side.

STEP 2 Drill thread holes with a ³/₃₂-inch bit, spacing the holes evenly.

To make a zipper pull, saw off a tine about an inch long.

STEP 1 Smooth the surface with sandpaper and drill a small hole into the center of the antler, about ¹/₂ inch deep. Fill this with a few drops of five-minute epoxy and thread a small screw eye into the hole.

STEP 2 Attach the pull to the zipper with a small loop of rawhide or ribbon. —T.E.N.

250 MAKE YOUR OWN SCENT WIPES

Make your own scent-killing wipes and use them to wipe down everything from body parts to binoculars.

INGREDIENTS
2 cups 3 percent hydrogen peroxide
2 cups distilled water
¹/₄ cup baking soda
1 oz. unscented shampoo (larger chain drugstores will carry this item.)

In a large bowl, mix together the hydrogen peroxide, distilled water, baking soda, and unscented shampoo. Stir, pour into a one-gallon milk jug, and loosely cap the jug. Let the mixture sit for three days.

While that's marinating, fill a small, lidded tub about two-thirds full with plain brown multifold paper towels—the kind that come in stacks, not on a roll. Cover the paper towels with your homemade scent killer and mush it all around so the paper towels absorb the liquid. Squeeze out the excess scent killer and replace the lid. You're good to go—undetected. —T.E.N.

251 HANG A MOOSE (OR ELK OR, HECK, EVEN A SMALL HERD OF DEER) FROM SKINNY TREES

THE SUPPLIES

Carry a hatchet, plenty of parachute cord for making lashings, and five 30-foot lengths of ³/₈-inch (or thicker) rope. That's one rope for the cape and head, and one rope for each quarter.

THE INGREDIENTS

Cut three poles 18 feet long; each pole should be 5 to 6 inches in diameter. Limb each pole. Lay the poles on the ground in the shape of a goalpost. The horizontal spar should be about 6 inches below the top of the two uprights, which should be the same distance apart as the two standing trees. Lash the poles at each juncture using diagonal lashings.

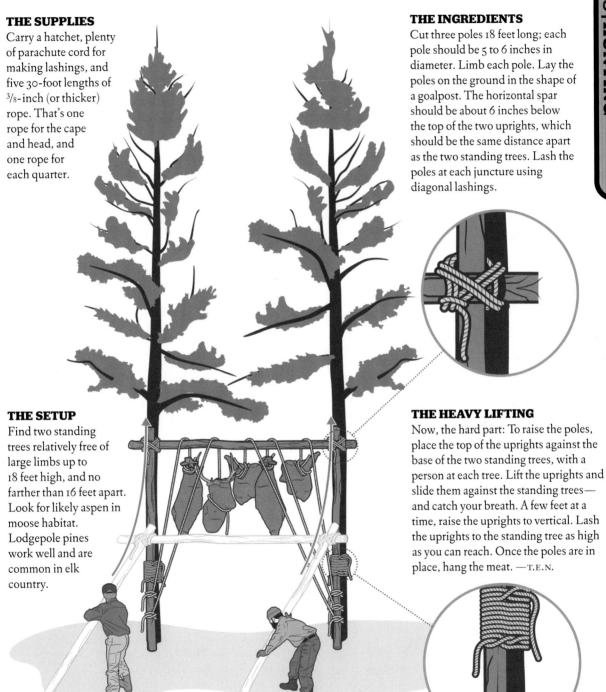

THE SETUP

Find two standing trees relatively free of large limbs up to 18 feet high, and no farther than 16 feet apart. Look for likely aspen in moose habitat. Lodgepole pines work well and are common in elk country.

THE HEAVY LIFTING

Now, the hard part: To raise the poles, place the top of the uprights against the base of the two standing trees, with a person at each tree. Lift the uprights and slide them against the standing trees—and catch your breath. A few feet at a time, raise the uprights to vertical. Lash the uprights to the standing tree as high as you can reach. Once the poles are in place, hang the meat. —T.E.N.

252 PRESERVE A TURKEY FAN

Wild turkey restoration has been wildly successful in recent years. Here's how to make a trophy out of a gobbler's breeding finery.

STEP 1 Remove the tail. Use a sharp knife to remove all flesh and fat from around the quill bases. Be careful not to cut the quills. The bases are ready when they're white and shiny.

STEP 2 Mold a wad of auto-body-repair filler. Lay the tail on a piece of plastic wrap, with the quill ends out, with enough plastic to fold over the quills. Apply the filler to the quills and cover them with the flap. Then work the filler between each quill.

STEP 3 Arrange the fan on a flat surface and spread the feathers, starting in the middle and moving to the outside edges of the fan. Tape the feathers down using masking tape. The filler should set in about 30 minutes. —T.E.N.

253 SHOOT STANDING WITH SHOOTING STICKS

STEP 1 Stand up straight. Adjust the height of the shooting sticks to adjust point of impact up or down. Never crouch or stand taller than whatever is comfortable.

STEP 2 Place the fore-end of the rifle in the V-notch of the sticks. Next, reach your fore-end hand across your body, under the gunstock, and into the opposite armpit. Gently clamp down on your hand to lock the arm in position. Now pull the stock into your shoulder, but not too tight. The goal is to be relaxed and put as little torque on the rifle as possible.

STEP 3 To fire, breathe deep and then let it out slowly. Squeeze the trigger just as you are running out of air. —T.E.N.

254 BARK A SQUIRREL

O.K., so the Kentucky rifle was developed in Pennsylvania. But John James Audubon saw Daniel Boone bark a squirrel in ol' Kaintuck, and soon the gun was synonymous with Kentucky. Here's how to make like Boone.

Hunt with a .32 blackpowder rifle—and be mindful of what, or who, is beyond your target. Aim at the branch under the squirrel's head. Place the bullet so it hits above the branch's centerline; it will splinter the branch and knock the squirrel silly. —T.E.N.

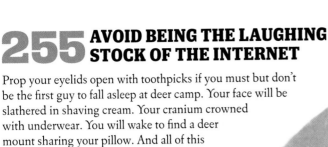

---

255 AVOID BEING THE LAUGHING STOCK OF THE INTERNET

Prop your eyelids open with toothpicks if you must but don't be the first guy to fall asleep at deer camp. Your face will be slathered in shaving cream. Your cranium crowned with underwear. You will wake to find a deer mount sharing your pillow. And all of this will be on Facebook. —T.E.N.

256 GRIND BURGER LIKE A PRO

The off taste in a bad venison burger often comes from fat, connective tissue, bone dust, and marrow. Want to get rid of it all? Be your own butcher.

TRIM LIKE A MADMAN Use cuts no lower than the shanks and trim as much of the fat, tendons, and connective tissue as possible. The thin, flexible blade of a pointed paring knife slides smoothly between connective tissue and flesh. Wash it frequently to keep it from sticking.

GRIND IT RIGHT Use the coarse blade for this. Electric grinders are easy to operate, but a high-quality hand cranker churns through 5 pounds of meat in a single minute and is a snap to clean.

HOLD THE FATS Despite all advice to the contrary, do not add extra fat at this stage. Instead, freeze packages of pure ground venison and mix it later, depending on the recipe, with binding agents such as ground chuck or pork, bread crumbs, or eggs.
—T.E.N.

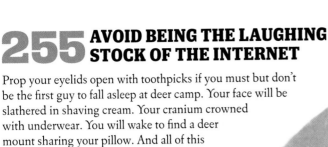

257 TURN A FARM POND INTO A WATERFOWL MAGNET

The best farm ponds for duck hunting tend to be located near rivers and other large bodies of water or in flyways where ducks are known to move. Here's how to build a sweet farm pond duck blind—and manage the pond for a big return in feathers.

THE LOCATION Assuming a northwest to west predominant wind, place the blind along the southwest shore of the pond. Most dams are along the southern edge, and the deeper water will stay open longer during freezing temperatures. You'll never be looking directly at the rising or setting sun, and you can rotate decoys based on wind direction.

THE FRAME Build your blind in the spring so native vegetation can regrow. Forego tall blinds—make yours 4½ feet tall in the front and 5 feet in back. Top it with a half-roof over the back so you can shoot behind it. Add two 2x4s at an angle from the edge of the roof to the top of the blind's front to create designated shooting holes.

THE DISGUISE Start with a base layer of burlap, tack on chicken wire, and then use zip-ties to attach bundles of native vegetation. Pin oak, white pine, and cedar hold leaves and needles long after they are cut. Transplant willows by clipping saplings at a 45-degree angle and sticking them in the mud. They'll reroot easily.

THE LANDSCAPE Mow the north or northwest shore close to the ground and arrange five full-body sleeping-geese decoys. Geese like to loaf and sun in the open.

THE PLUMBING Draw water down a foot or two in early summer. Weeds and grasses will root on the shoreline mudflats. Reflood a few weeks before the season. —T.E.N.

258 MAKE DUCK, DUCK, JERK

Slowly drying rich duck-breast fillets turns out pungent, densely flavored jerky. Just about any duck will work, except for mergansers. Start with a basic soy-teriyaki mixture, and personalize it with apple juice, Worcestershire sauce, jalapeño peppers, brown sugar, and ginger. —T.E.N.

INGREDIENTS

4 ducks
¾ cup teriyaki sauce
1 tsp. red pepper flakes
2 tbsp. freshly ground peppercorns
¾ cup soy sauce
1 tbsp. liquid smoke
½ tsp. onion powder
2 tsp. rosemary
1 cup red wine

Mix all marinade ingredients in a noncorrosive dish or plastic bag. Fillet the duck breast meat and then partially freeze or refreeze it; this makes the meat easy to slice. Carefully remove as much tendon and fat as possible. Slice ¼-inch strips along the grain. Marinate them overnight. To prepare the jerky, use one of the following three methods.

(Regardless of which jerky prep method you choose, check the jerky often. Cooking times will vary widely depending on the type of cooking equipment, thickness of jerky strips, and how close the meat is to the heat source.)

• Smoker: Use the lowest heat setting possible for 3 to 7 hours.

• Dehydrator: Dehydrate for 8 to 10 hours.

• Oven: Spray the oven rack with cooking spray and line the bottom of the oven with aluminum foil. Drape the meat strips on the oven racks. Prop the oven door open 2 inches with a toothpick or short pencil. Cook at 150 to 170 degrees F for 2 to 5 hours.

When done, each strip should bend but not break. Store jerky in your refrigerator or freezer.

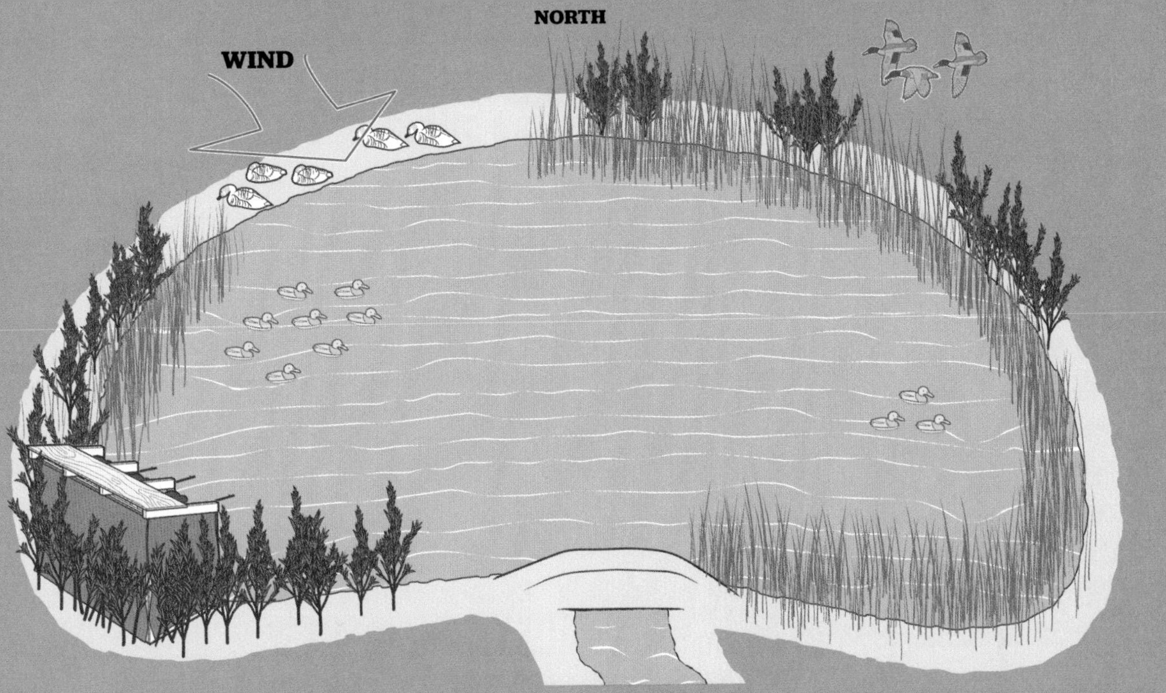
NORTH
WIND

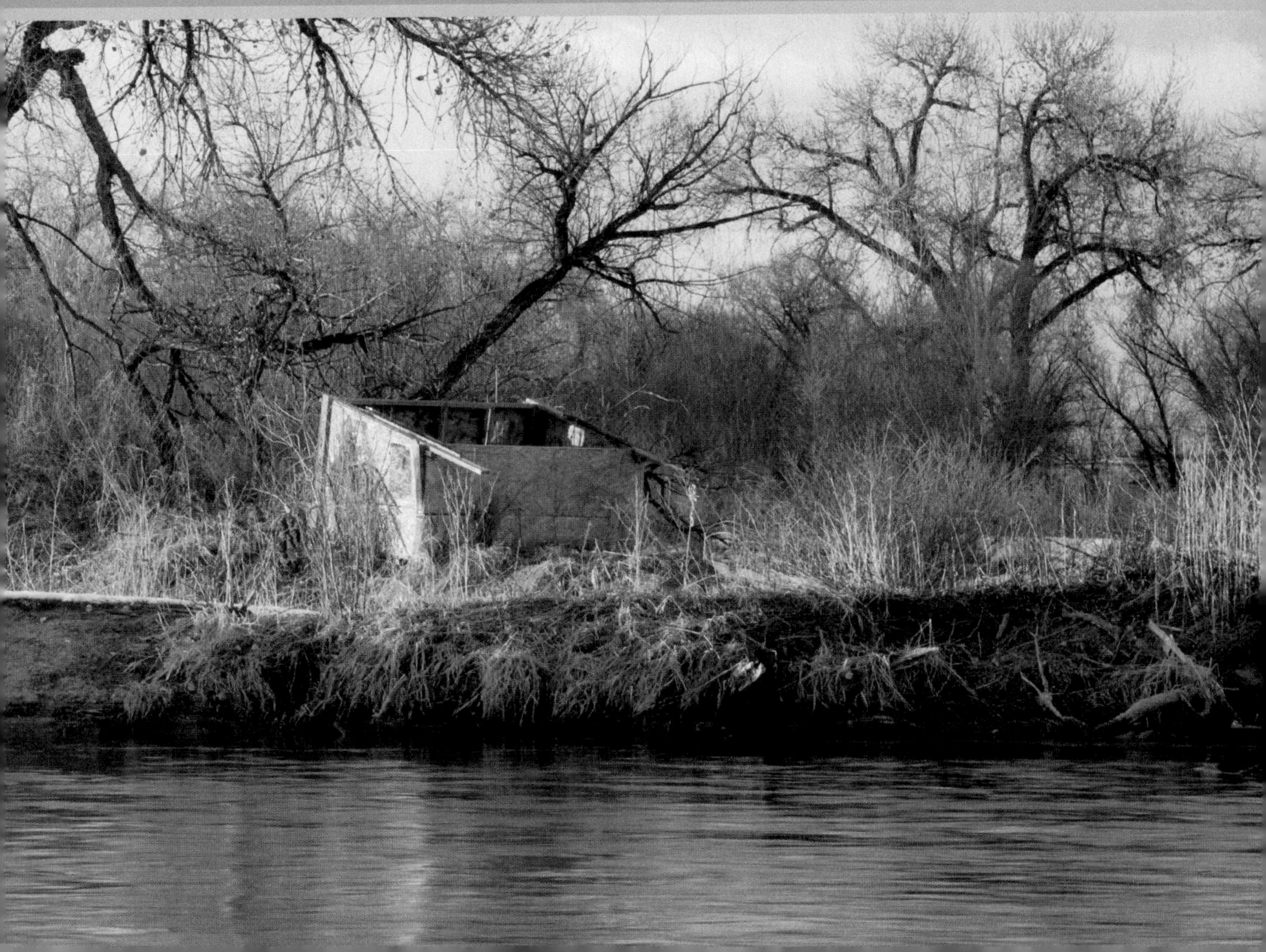

259 RAISE A LADDER STAND SAFELY

It is physically impossible to put up a ladder stand alone if you follow certain manufacturers' instructions. And what if you want to move an old ladder stand? But here's how a two- or three-person team can get it done.

READY IT Lay the ladder out with its base approximately 3 to 4 feet from the base of the tree for a one-person stand, or 4 to 5 feet for a two-person stand. The side of the stand that will touch the tree faces up. Tie a stout anchor rope to each back corner of the stand platform. The ropes should be 10 feet longer than the stand's height.

RAISE IT One person goes to the base of the stand and braces his feet against the ladder's bottom, holding an anchor rope in each hand. The others raise the platform end overhead and walk the stand up as the anchor person stays put and pulls in the slack on the ropes, keeping them tight so the ladder rises straight overhead.

RATCHET IT With the stand against the tree, crisscross the anchor ropes behind the trunk and tie them tightly to the bottom ladder rung. One person climbs the ladder, attaches a ratchet strap to the base of the platform, and secures it tight. —T.E.N.

260 MAKE THE BEST JERK CORD IN THE WORLD

Tired of lugging motorized decoys, remote-control units, and cumbersome mounting poles into the duck swamp? Then go retro with the best jerk cord you'll ever see in action. It gives up to five decoys a surprising amount of motion, with a minimum of movement on your part. The whole rig fits right in your pocket and goes up in no more than five minutes. And it's as deadly as it is simple.

You'll need 85 feet of decoy line, 15 feet of ⅛-inch black bungee cord, and six large black snap-swivels. Using overhand knots, tie five 6- to 8-inch-long loops into the last 20 feet of decoy line. These should be about 2 to 3 feet apart. Tie a snap-swivel to the end of each loop. Then tie one end of the bungee cord to the end of the decoy line near the last loop. Finally, tie the last snap-swivel to the other end of the bungee. To set up the rig, pass the bungee cord around a tree or sturdy stake (or a heavily anchored decoy) and hook it to itself using the snap-swivel. Run the decoy line to your blind and clip decoys to the loops. Pull the slack out, until the bungee cord just begins to stretch. A short, swift jerk will set the birds in motion, appearing as if they're splashing, content . . . and happy to have company. —T.E.N.

261 IDENTIFY A BUTTON BUCK AND HOLD YOUR FIRE

Many hunters want to protect buck fawns, those inglorious "button bucks." Identifying button bucks can be tough, but you can do it. Button bucks often travel alone; adult does rarely do. Buck fawns are squarish in body shape, whereas mature does are more rectangular. Glass the deer's head. Even if you can't make out the antler buds, a buck's head is flat between the ears compared with a doe's more rounded skull. —T.E.N.

262 DROP THE FOLLOW-UP DUCK

What's the toughest shot in waterfowling? "It's the follow-up shot in a big wind," says Missouri duck guide Tony Vandemore. After that first volley, birds have their wings out, and they're catching serious air. "It's an optical illusion. They're facing you, but actually moving backward." These directions are for a wind coming from the right; switch for a wind from the left.

If you're quick on the follow-up, put the bead to the left of the bird's butt and pull the trigger. You're trying to put shot in front of the bird's tail, not the head.

For the next shot, the birds are traveling faster and could be starting to turn. "They look like they're flying straight away, but they're banking to the left and gaining velocity." Increase the lead but keep shooting below the birds at the trajectory of their butts. —T.E.N.

263 HUNT A CROSSWIND

The standard advice is to still-hunt with the wind in your face. But this isn't always best. Bucks like to bed at the edge of cover, with the wind at their backs, so they can see what's coming in front of them and smell what's behind them. By hunting at right angles to the wind, you have a better chance of getting the drop on a bedded buck before it either sees or smells you. —K.M.

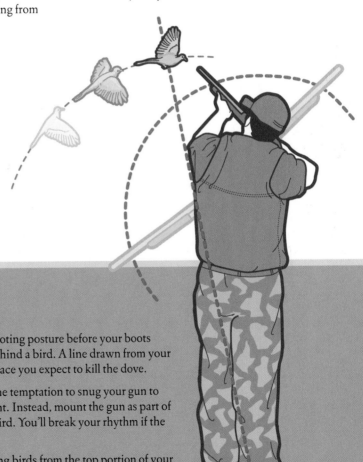

264 SET UP FOR A DOVE SHOT

WATCH YOUR FEET Think about good shooting posture before your boots tangle in cornstalks and you empty the barrel behind a bird. A line drawn from your rear heel to your front foot should point to the place you expect to kill the dove.

GET IN THE SWING OF THINGS Resist the temptation to snug your gun to your shoulder when the birds are 75 yards distant. Instead, mount the gun as part of the same fluid motion you use to swing on the bird. You'll break your rhythm if the buttplate hits your shoulder too soon.

KEEP YOUR HEAD DOWN Watch incoming birds from the top portion of your peripheral vision. That way your head will already be lowered when it's time to put your cheek to the gunstock. —T.E.N.

265 FLAG A GOOSE FROM START TO FINISH

Flagging geese from layout blinds is the pinnacle of big-bird gunning. Here's an energetic three-step plan to plot the perfect deception.

FAR When birds are 500 yards to a mile out, get the whole gang involved. Everyone waves a flag as high as possible and then brings it down to the ground. Run around the decoys. Make a fuss.

NEAR The geese have turned and are boring in at 200 to 400 yards. All of the hunters should get in the blind.

The mission now: Look like landing geese. When the flock veers, reach up with the flags as high as you can, flag them six to eight times, then lower slowly to the ground. Do it again, but start lower. And do it again, starting nearly at ground level.

CLOSE When birds are inside 200 yards, the most experienced flagger should close the deal: Hold the flag at a 60-degree angle and then drop it horizontal. Bring it up to 45 degrees and drop it horizontal. Then start almost horizontally, and drop it to the ground, feather pattern up. You're trying to mimic geese on the ground stretching their wings. —T.E.N.

266 PUT A WILD TURKEY TO BED

Daybreak in the turkey woods is especially bright when you've roosted a turkey the night before. If you know where the bird went to bed, there's no need to blunder through the woods hooting. You can sneak right in and start your hunt in his bedroom. Here's a complete plan, from late afternoon through bagging a bird at fly down.

LATE AFTERNOON

LOOKING Turkeys repeatedly roost in the same areas. The places you've heard birds before make good starting points for an evening expedition. On unfamiliar ground, look for feathers and droppings beneath trees with large, spreading branches. Find a place where you can see and/or hear a long way (1). Don't blow your locator calls while the sun is up. Toms won't answer until they're safely in a tree.

DUSK

LISTENING At dusk, turkeys start flying up. Listen for wingbeats and turkeys crashing through branches, as well as for yelping hens and gobbling toms. If you don't hear anything, use a locator call. When you get an answer, slip closer (2), pausing to call occasionally until you determine exactly where the turkey is roosted. Stay out of sight and try not to get closer than 100 yards from the birds.

DARK

GETTING OUT AND COMING BACK If you can see the bird, you're stuck. Wait until dark and tiptoe out. Mark the bird's location with surveyor's tape or punch it into your GPS. An hour before sunrise, set up 50 yards from the tree (3). Turkeys usually fly down to the uphill side, so cheat that way. Call softly and sparingly. If you got in undetected, the turkey will almost be in gun range as soon as his toes hit the ground. —P.B.

267 FLOAT FOR DUCKS

The best way to beat the duck hunting crowds is by float hunting. It's very effective during bitter cold snaps that freeze swamps and ponds. But there's more to it than just pointing a canoe downstream. You need some style, or all you'll see is the wrong end of flushed birds with few chances to pull the trigger.

QUIET DOWN Cutting the distance between you and duck Stroganoff begins with the proper craft. The quietest canoes are made of acrylonitrile butadiene styrene, or ABS, a common material for durable, general-purpose boats. (Royalex is a common ABS brand.) Fiberglass is next-best, as long as your stretch of stream is free of hull-shredding rapids. Far worse are aluminum canoes. They can hang up on rocks easily and sound as if you're paddling a tambourine. If you must float in a metal boat, dampen the decibels by lining it with outdoor carpeting or old carpet samples. No matter what you paddle, soundproof the rest of your gear: Zipper pulls, pockets full of shells, even the tiny metal tabs on glove cuffs will produce clinks and clanks loud enough to send a preening pintail scrambling.

Float hunting is a two-person game—a paddler in the stern and a shooter in the bow—and it requires close communication. Before you cast off, agree on simple signals for "ducks ahead," "ducks on left," "ducks on right," "move right," "move left," and "holy smokes, there's a whole flock of 'em!"

GET READY Knowing how ducks use rivers will help you see them in time to craft an approach. Often your best shots will come at sharp turns in the stream. The birds also tend to raft up behind fallen trees and trapped river debris, so keep your eyes open even after you pass a tangle of downed branches. Creek mouths are prime loafing spots, so approach them with the canoe held tightly to the bank and the bow gunner ready. It also pays to paddle up tributaries; off-channel beaver ponds and swamps often hold a load of ducks. Flush them from their hidey-hole and they might just pitch in downstream—which is where you're headed.

WORK THE BENDS The slow water on the inside of stream bends is a magnet for ducks, but these hard turns present a challenge for gunners faced with difficult shooting angles and a tipsy seat. Set up the shot by approaching with the canoe tucked close to the inside bank. Then, just before the bow clears the bend, the paddler uses sharp pry strokes to swing the stern of the boat towards the middle of the stream. The good news: The ducks will jump straight ahead. The bad news: The shooter has no excuses. —T.E.N.

268

PICK THE RIGHT RIFLE CALIBER

Most opinions about cartridges are formed by a combination of shuck, jive, ad copy, and friends' ill-informed advice. On these pages you will find the truth, always unglamorous, sometimes downright ugly. And one of the ugliest facts is this: Choice of cartridge ranks fairly low in determining whether you will succeed as a hunter. If you're a good shot, it doesn't matter much what you use. On the other hand, choosing the wrong round can screw you up royally. With that contradiction firmly in mind, here are top choices in each category.

—D.E.P.

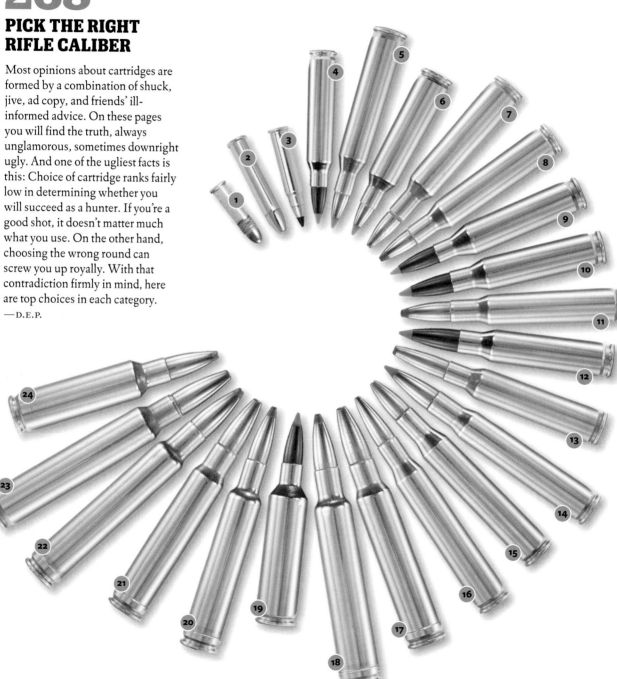

SMALL GAME Light in the hands, easy on the wallet, these rimfire rounds are the perfect choice for hunting squirrels and rabbits. These are also used on short-range varmints.

1 .22 Long Rifle

2 .22 Winchester Magnum Rimfire

3 .17 Hornady Magnum Rimfire

VARMINTS Long-range, flat-shooting, hyper-accurate calibers with light recoil.

4 .223 Remington

5 .220 Swift

6 .22/250 Remington

VARMINTS AND BIG GAME Heavier bullets than straight varmint rounds make these a choice for deer hunters as well.

7 6mm Remington

8 .257 Roberts

9 .243 Winchester

BIG GAME: THE LIGHT KICKERS These calibers are powerful enough to drop deer in their tracks but light enough to shoot enough to make you accurate enough to do it.

10 7X57 Mauser

11 7mm/08 Remington

12 .308 Winchester

13 6.5X55 Swede

BIG GAME: THE ALL-AROUND ROUNDS For everything in between antelope and moose, these calibers excel.

14 .30/06 Springfield

15 .270 Winchester

16 .280 Remington

17 .338 Winchester Magnum

BIG GAME AT LONG RANGE These calibers are ballistically capable of killing elk and bear some four football fields away. They demand similar capabilities from whoever pulls the trigger.

18 .300 Weatherby Magnum

19 .270 Winchester Short Magnum

20 7mm Weatherby Magnum

HEAVY OR DANGEROUS NORTH AMERICAN GAME These are large, tough calibers for large, tough game. Warning: They kick both ways.

21 .338 Winchester Magnum

22 .338 Remington Ultra Mag

23 .340 Weatherby

24 .325 Winchester Short Magnum

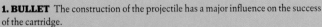

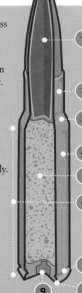

1. BULLET The construction of the projectile has a major influence on the success of the cartridge.

2. NECK Holds the bullet in place and aligns it with the rifling.

3. SHOULDER Modern cases have sharper shoulders—30 degrees or more—than older ones. It's thought that this gives a cleaner, more efficient burn to the powder.

4. CASE Always made of brass. There's nothing better.

5. POWDER It can be either spherical (ball) or extruded (log) and ranges in burning rate from fast to slow, depending on the bullet weight, case capacity, and case shape.

6. TAPER Modern cases have very little body taper; older ones have a lot. Low taper makes room for more powder, but cases with high body taper feed more reliably.

7. RIM Rimless cases have rims that barely extend beyond the extraction groove. Rimmed cases lack the groove and have wider rims.

8. BASE The base of the case carries the primer pocket and the headstamp, which designates caliber and make.

9. PRIMER Composed of a cup, anvil, and a small charge of explosive compound. Primers come in several sizes, and there are some with longer-sustaining flames, for magnum charges of slow powder.

269 ENTICE A SHY BULL

When bull elk give Wyoming guide Terry Search the silent treatment, he turns to a cow estrous call. Here's his plan:

STEP 1 When bugles are few and far between, listen for a distant bugle, a closer grunt, or a bull horning a tree. Get downwind, settle into a spot, and make an estrous-cow call just loud enough to be heard.

STEP 2 No response? Wait at least 15 minutes. It's all about

discipline now—do not call. Still no response? Make sure you can move without being seen by the elk and then relocate at least 30 yards away. You can move farther, but a 100-yard relocation, Search says, "would be pretty radical." Settle down and call again.

STEP 3 Play cat-and-mouse for two hours, calling and relocating every 15 to 30 minutes. If nothing happens in that time, back out carefully. The elk should remain close by as long as it has food, water, and shelter. Return later in the day or the next morning. —T.E.N.

270

PULL OFF A BUNNY HUNT ON YOUR BUCK LEASE

You have a deer lease but no bunny dogs? Now that whitetail season is over, you may be sitting on a world-class rabbit hunt in the making. Post a message on Craigslist (craigslist.org) or your favorite online message board saying that you'll trade access to your whitetail heaven in return for a rabbit hunt. The setup: You bring a couple of buddies and let the hound handler do the same. It's a win-win for everyone (except for the rabbits). Use your deer sense to fine-tune the rabbit hunt.

DRAINAGE DITCH Dominant bucks use these dense corridors to move across an open landscape. Rabbits will use the subtle trails as an escape hatch or a place to wait out the heat. Toss the dogs in or thrash through on your own.

BLOWDOWNS These were prime bedding spots, and you stalked close, moving as slow as molasses. Now, forget stealth: Jump on the trunks, bang on the limbs—even if the dogs have passed by.

LOGGING ROAD This was a scrape-line mecca during deer season. Use dirt roads and ATV trails to get standers into position without much noise.

SWAMP Just like deer, rabbits take refuge in the most tangled messes on the property. Use your hound pack to dislodge them from their safe places.

INNER WOOD'S EDGE Bucks love to rub saplings along the edge of pine thickets and open hardwoods. It's a great spot for standers as rabbits dash out of the thick pines to pour on the speed.

GROWN-OVER CLEAR-CUT This is core bedding cover for whitetails, and bunnies use it for that and more. Work it over thoroughly, and not just with the dogs. Get in there and worm your way around too. —T.E.N.

271 MAKE AN ELK-STOPPING BUGLE SCREAM

Wyoming guide Ron Dube walks softly but keeps a diaphragm call in his mouth all the time. His advice: When you bump an elk, call instantly. Call if he's seen you; call if he hasn't. Call even if you've shot at him. "Often I make this coarse bugle scream," Dube says, "nothing fancy, just rip a lot of air across the diaphragm so it screams, like the beginning of a bugle without all the chuckles. I'll scream until I'm out of breath and scream some more. I'll call loud and long until he's either dead or gone. I've had elk stop even after being shot at twice. It's extremely important to call after an elk has been hit by an arrow. Many times, that bugle scream will stop him and rather than go charging off, he'll just walk a little bit and bleed out." —T.E.N.

FIELD & STREAM-APPROVED KNOT #12

272 TIE A GETAWAY KNOT

Hunters on guided horsepack trips can help the wrangler out by knowing how to tie up their own mount. It doesn't sound like a very big deal until there's a game animal getting away and your guide has to deal with his horse, your horse, and whoever else's horse while you're all standing around. Learn a good hitch knot like the old getaway knot.

Start at chest level so the horse can't get a leg over the rope, and tie the horse with no more than 2 feet of rope slack between the halter and the tree.

STEP 1 Pass the rope around the tree on the right side (or over a rail).

STEP 2 As you bring the tag end of the rope around the tree, form a loop by passing the rope over itself. Lay the loop over the standing part of the rope.

STEP 3 Reach through the loop on the outside of the standing part and pull another loop of the working end through.

STEP 4 Snug the knot up to the tree.

STEP 5 To release the hitch, all you have to do is pull on the tag end and go. —T.E.N.

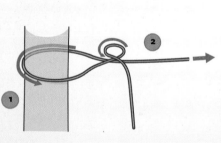

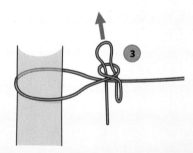

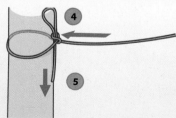

273 MASTER THE RUT

This is it. Thirty days to give it your all. When does are ready to breed, bucks are ready to do whatever it takes to line up a hot date. When they drop their guard, be ready to drop the hammer.

Pre-Rut Bucks are getting antsy as their testosterone levels rise and the amount of available daylight plummets. Mature deer move out of their swamp and thicket hideouts and nose around for does.

TACTIC–FIND A CORRIDOR Find a place where thick cover with food value, like greenbrier, edges into open woods near doe-feeding areas, such as crop fields or oak flats, and climb a tree. You might spot a buck doing a little pre-scouting on his own. Or put doe meat in the freezer before the rut kicks in.

Seek-and-Chase Does are coming into estrous right and left, and bucks are in pursuit. Deer will literally be running through the woods, all day long.

TACTIC–SIT TIGHT Does are like rabbits—they don't like to leave familiar habitat. If a buck chases a doe past you without giving you a shot, don't move. They could make another swing by, or, better yet, a bigger buck might storm the scene, ready to brawl. Scent bombs and other estrous scents can improve your chances.

Breeding Deer seem to have evaporated from the woods, because bucks and does are pair bonding. They might spend 24 to 48 hours together and move very little.

TACTIC–GO MOBILE Glass the edges of bedding cover thoroughly, looking for coupled bucks and does. If you find antlers, plan a stalk. You might also troll for bucks in between hot does by setting up in a funnel and using an estrous-bleat call.

Post-Rut Most bucks—but not all—are worn out and holed up in dense cover, seeking a safe haven where they can rest and refuel for the coming winter.

TACTIC–GO DEEP AND NASTY Put up a stand that overlooks swamp edges, the backsides of clear cuts, or steep brushy gullies where bucks feel cloistered. And check out old scrape lines. Does that didn't breed initially are coming into a second heat, and a few bucks will be on the prowl for their last dance of the year.
—T.E.N.

274 CLAIM THE SHOT ON A DOUBLE

STEP 1 Immediately upon pulling the trigger, feign in outright astonishment. Play up your acknowledged incompetence: "Holy crap! I can't believe I finally hit a going-away bird." Accompany your exclamation with a small fist pump.

STEP 2 Wheel around to face the dubious crowd. Shake your head and grin.

STEP 3 When you're met with the inevitable disdain, quickly give honor to others. "Did you shoot at that bird? I'm pretty sure I was right on that lower bird in the threesome. You, too?"

STEP 4 Cave in now and you lose. Offer an apology that puts the naysayers on the defense. "You can have that bird if it's really yours. I mean, if you're comfortable with that." —T.E.N.

275
MAKE YOUR OWN COVER SCENT

To collect urine while field-dressing your buck, puncture the bladder and fill a small glass bottle with the stuff. Store it in the freezer. Cut off the tarsal glands and trim everything away, leaving only the dark, malodorous centers. Chop these into small pieces—hide and hair together—and pack it into the bottom of a small glass bottle. Cover it with propylene glycol and keep the resulting solution in a warm place—the top of a water heater is perfect. A day or two before you hit the woods, strain out the solids and mix in a dollop of thawed urine. Urine plus tarsal scent is as natural as it gets. —T.E.N.

276 STEADY YOUR RIFLE

After hoisting your gun with a parachute-cord pull rope, tie one end off around the tree or stand, and toss the line over a limb above your stand. In the loose end that dangles down, tie a loop using a tautline hitch. You can now move the height of this makeshift shooting rail by moving the knot up or down the rope. When it's time to take a shot, thread your rifle through this loop. —T.E.N.

277 TRACK AN ELK

Tracking bull elk is primal and addictive. It requires all the woodsmanship, intelligence, and endurance you can muster. It's always possible that after you've hiked many miles, you'll be left staring at the tracks of a spooked elk that's already in the next county. But what makes it worth it is the feeling that comes with knowing that 1 mile down the trail stands an animal worthy of all your efforts. Here is a six-step game plan for tracking elk. Be warned: Once you start, you won't ever want to stop.

START IN THE PARKS Open parks and other sunny clearings in the timber are great places to find tracks. Elk feed and bed in these exposed areas only at night, pawing through light snow to search out sedges. The animals will be gone before dawn, but you will have a good chance of finding fresh tracks at first light. To make sense of the mess of prints you will find there, move a few yards back into the timber. Here you'll find where the trails funnel together, and you'll be able to isolate specific bands of animals.

TEST THE TRACK In powder snow, during a cold snap, or in deeply shaded areas, a three-day-old track may look fresh to the untrained eye. A hoofprint left in melting snow that quickly refreezes stays cookie-cutter sharp, though the animal that made it is long gone. Conversely, a recently made print drifting in with snow can appear old. Rely on your sense of touch instead. In powder, the edges and midline will set up and feel firm within an hour or two of the animal's passing. Fresh droppings are shiny, soft, and emit an organic, sweetish smell (a). Fresh lances of urine give to the slightest pressure. Crusty urine streaks, or pellets that crumble when squeezed, mean the trail is cold. Don't forget to use your nose. Elk beds retain a rank, barnyard odor that can fool even an experienced hunter, but a faint, clean scent of elk usually indicates a hot track.

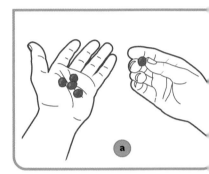

SIZE UP YOUR PREY It's difficult to predict the sex or size of an elk by looking at just hoofprints. More telling is the story that a trail writes in the snow: A large track accompanied by a small one invariably means a cow and a calf (b). A small band of elk, say five to six, will often include a spike but seldom a mature bull. A herd of 10 may indeed have a 6-point bull among it. Big bulls like to travel in pairs, so two sets of good-size tracks are always worth following. A lone track can be a bull or a cow, but if it's a bull of any size, you'll see where his antlers have made him skirt low-hanging branches. If a lone trail covers a lot of country but switches directions without apparent purpose, it likely has been made by a 2 ½-year-old bull. Young bulls will often stand from their beds and then hesitate before bolting away, affording the careful tracker a shot.

HEAD THEM OFF Elk rarely give hunters a second chance—and damned few first ones—so you need to follow them without alerting their acute senses. To better the odds, anticipate where they are heading. Often, elk heading to bed down for the day will walk along the side of a forested slope and then climb and circle back on a higher contour before lying down—choosing flat spots on side ridges where they hold the high ground on three fronts. They tend to divert from their course and feed before bedding, so look for circular depressions where they have punched their noses into the snow.

Don't be discouraged if you come to a freshly departed bed but the tracks don't indicate that the elk was spooked. A bull will often lie down awhile and then move off to find a better bed somewhere nearby. There's a good chance he's within range of your rifle.

SNEAK INTO THEIR BEDS When the track starts to waver and go uphill, slow way down because the elk is most likely preparing to bed. Stay 30 yards or so to the side of the track, cutting into it just often enough to stay on course (c). If you hunt with a partner, have one hunter take the track while the other takes a contour at a higher elevation, keeping the tracker just within sight. Try to circle and work down to the bedding elk from above. More often than not, you'll guess wrong, but a direct approach along the trail, no matter how carefully you place your feet, tilts the odds in the elk's favor.

TAKE THEM WHERE YOU FIND THEM If you finally catch up to elk, they're likely to be in heavy cover, revealing themselves only as pieces in a larger puzzle. Your eye may linger on a patch of color that resembles a peeled log, or a branch stub cocking at an odd angle might trigger a second glance. Then, like a trick picture, the animal comes into focus. If you've been scanning every inch of forest as it enters your view, the elk will be near the outer limit of your vision, its body striped by a picket of tree trunks. Don't try to stalk closer. Either you'll lose sight of the elk, or the elk will catch sight of you. This is why a powerful rifle with a good scope is a tracker's best choice. A lot of things can go wrong when tracking. The shot that ends the hunt shouldn't be one of them. —K.M.

278
MAP YOUR SPOT

Buy a U.S. Geological Survey (USGS) topographic map of your hunting camp. Or, better yet, print a topographic map or a satellite photograph from Internet sources.

STEP 1 Glue the map to a single sheet of foam-core board (a cardboard and Styrofoam laminate available at arts-and-crafts supply stores).

STEP 2 Mark the heads of pushpins with the initials of hunt club members.

STEP 3 Each hunter should mark his stand location with his pin upon arrival and remove it upon departure. —T.E.N.

FIELD & STREAM CRAZY-GOOD GRUB

279 ROAST A DEER HAUNCH

The 17th-century English poet and soldier of fortune Gervase Markham had this advice: "Stick it with cloves all over on the outside . . . larde it either with Mutton larde, or Porke larde, but Mutton is the best: then spit it and roast it by a good soking fire, then take Vinegar, bread crummes, and some of the gravy, which comes from the Venison, and boile them well in a dish: then season it with sugar, cinamon, ginger, and salt, and serve the Venison fourth upon the sauce when it is roasted enough."

Cut the shank off the hind leg of a dressed deer and bone out the haunch. Stuff the bone cavity with a 50-50 mixture of diced dried cherries and toasted pecans. Tie haunch with kitchen twine. Roll it in a spice rub made of the cumin, brown sugar, ginger, garlic powder, red pepper, and

Of course, Markham was writing in the England of 1615, when six servants were assigned to every respectable kitchen. Here's an easier way— if you're looking for an imaginative main course for your Christmas dinner, you can't do better than this. —T.E.N.

INGREDIENTS
1 haunch of deer
3 tsp. garlic powder
3 tbsp. brown sugar
Toasted pecans
2 tsp. Chinese five-spice powder
3 tbsp. ground cumin
Dried diced cherries
2 tsp. ground red pepper
3 tsp. ground ginger
(enough diced dried cherries and toasted pecans to fill the bone cavity; will vary) —T.E.N.

Chinese five-spice powder. Roast the meat at 350 degrees F until a meat thermometer reads 140 degrees F (rare) to 160 degrees F (medium).

Slice and bask in your own glory.

280 CLEAN YOUR KNIFE

Fixed-blade knives need only a quick wipe down with a damp cloth after each use and a light application of honing oil on the blade.

Folders and multitools collect blood and dirt at pivot points and locking mechanisms. If the tool has a plastic handle, immerse it in boiling water for one minute and then put it in a pot of warm water (so that quick cooling doesn't crack the handle). Scrub nooks and crannies with a toothbrush, working pivot points back and forth, and then air-dry the knife before oiling. Use compressed air to blast out gunk.

Wipe away surface rust with an oily cloth or oooo steel wool. Carbon blades naturally discolor with use. Bring them back to near-original luster by rubbing them with a cork dipped in cold wood ashes. —K.M.

281 TAKE A KILLER TROPHY SHOT

Tired of boring, dark, fuzzy photos of your best deer? Here's how to create a photograph every bit as memorable as the moment you fired.

STEP 1 Arrange the antlers in front of an uncluttered background. Situate the hunter to one side, holding the antlers with both hands. A big mistake is photographing a rack against the pattern of a camouflage shirt.

STEP 2 Stuff the deer's tongue inside the mouth or cut it off. Tuck the legs under the body. Cover wounds with your gun or bow. Wet the nose. Wipe away all blood. The final touch: Slip glass taxidermic eyes over the buck's eyeballs. They work like contacts and prevent those ugly glowing orbs. They're cheap and reusable.

STEP 3 Take some pictures with a flash, especially at midday. This will help light shadows, such as from a hat.

STEP 4 Try something different. Lie on the ground. Stage a photo of the hunter dragging the buck out. Experiment with unusual angles.
—T.E.N.

282 SHOOT A DOUBLE

You need presence of mind in the heat of excitement to get two birds with two consecutive shots. To execute the feat consistently, a hunter has to think like a pool player and set up the second shot with the first. You shoot one bird in such a way that the muzzle is in the right place to take the second. Here's how to do it in four hunting situations.
—P.B.

With incoming puddle ducks, you'll want to let the lead birds (a) come close, pick a drake, and shoot. The rest of the flock will react by climbing vertically to escape danger.

Look up, find a second bird (b) that's now heading upward and away from your decoys, and put your bead over its head. Always make sure the first bird is dead in the air before moving on to a second.

Diving ducks, on the other hand, will veer to either side when the guns go off. Adjust for this behavior by selecting a low bird (c) so that you don't lose track of the rest of the flock.

Verify you've hit the incomer and then look for your best second shot (d), which will likely be a low, 90-degree crosser. Swing through, give it plenty of lead, and finish your double.

When flushing birds fly in different directions, take note of their angles of flight. Shoot the most straightaway one first (e) and then swing back to shoot a bird that's angling to the side.

Shooting the birds in opposite order invites a miss. If you shoot the angling bird (f) first and then come back to shoot the straightaway, you stand a good chance of overswinging the target.

If the birds are flying away in the same direction, take the closer shot (g) first and then reach out for the far bird. Your gun will be in a perfect position to do so.

Go to the second bird (h) only after you drop the first. Make sure to keep the muzzle moving and to shoot in front of the bird—misses usually come from trying to get to it too quickly. —P.B.

283 SLIP INTO A STAND WITHOUT A SOUND

Bashing through the woods on your way to the stand is a great way to kill a spike buck. Here's the drill for getting in position without giving your position away—the first step toward hanging a rocking-chair rack on your wall.

CHOOSE YOUR PATH Before the season, clear trails to your stands by trimming away anything that might brush against your legs. Cut back old barbwire fences if they're no longer used, or mark fence crossings with a small piece of surveyor's tape.

WEAR GLOVES Some serious hunters pull on lightweight jersey gloves on top of rubber gloves. This keeps human scent off stand ladders and any vegetation you didn't clear away before the season.

PREP YOUR STAND Rings, buttons, and zippers can clink against metal ladder stands. Wear gloves here, too, and take your time climbing to avoid brushing against the rungs. Before you sit, scrape away loose bark from where your back will rest. Draw your bow or shoulder the gun, and swing at places a deer might appear. Snip away any branches that might snag and create movement.

—T.E.N.

284 SHOOT THE TRICKY OUT-OF-NOWHERE STEALTH BIRD

Ducks and doves have a nasty habit of acting like wild animals, such as appearing where you least expect them. That means overhead and coming straight from behind, presenting a very tough shot. Here's how to make it.

As you rise from your seat, point the muzzle at a spot halfway between the horizon and the bird (a) as it is flying away from you. Pull the gun swiftly up toward the bird. Keeping your head up and your eyes on the bird, bring the muzzle straight toward its beak. As the muzzle

approaches the bird on the upswing, circle the muzzle around and behind the bird (b). As the barrel reaches the top of this circle, bury your cheek into the stock as you prepare to swing down and past the bird.

Pull down and through the bird, accelerating the swing as you blot out the target (c). You'll lose sight of it momentarily but fire as soon as you see a slice of sky between the bead and bird. —T.E.N.

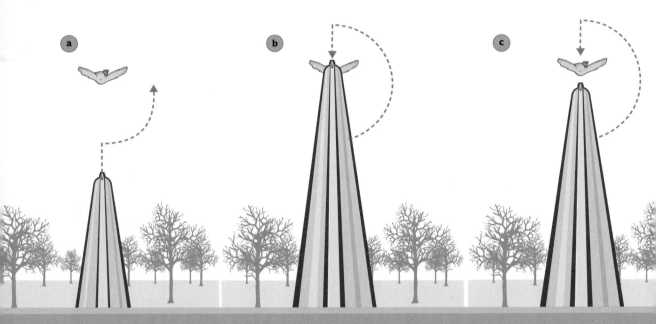

285 SIGHT IN A SCOPE ON A BOLT ACTION RIFLE

A bore collimator makes easy work of a complicated situation. But it isn't a requirement for whipping a bolt action into hunting condition. Here's a three-step process to sighting in a scope.

STEP 1 Set up a target 25 yards from your shooting position, at roughly the same height as your barrel. Remove the bolt and place the rifle firmly on sandbags or bags of kitty litter. Sight through the barrel and center the target in the bore. Then, adjust the crosshairs as needed to center the target, being careful not to move the rifle. Replace the bolt and fire one shot. Your point of impact should be less than 6 inches from the bull's-eye.

STEP 2 Readjust the rifle so that the crosshairs are centered on the target. Look through the scope and adjust the crosshairs to line up with the shot fired in Step 1; again, do it without moving the rifle. Now fire another shot. The point of impact should be within an inch or two of the target center.

STEP 3 Move the target out to 100 yards. Shoot a three-shot group, disregarding obvious fliers. Start with the elevation adjustment and move the point of impact to the desired location. (For most popular deer-size loads, a point of impact 2½ to 3 inches high at 100 yards allows for little to no holdover at hunting ranges. Check a ballistics chart for details.) Fire another three-shot group. If elevation is correct, adjust the scope for windage. Let the rifle barrel cool between groups. —T.E.N.

286 CUSTOMIZE BINOCULARS

Even the best (read "extravagantly expensive") binoculars on the market will give you a fuzzy view of the world until you correctly set the diopter ring. This adjustment, typically found on the right eyepiece or the center-focus knob, fine-tunes the binocular settings to compensate for any visual differences between your eyes. Set properly, a diopter will not only max out the performance of a high-end binoculars, but it will even boost the sharpness of budget glass. —T.E.N.

STEP 1 Set the diopter ring to the center of the adjustment scale. This is most likely marked with a zero; on some models it might be indicated with a hash mark or some other symbol. Cover the right lens barrel with a lens cap or duct tape.

STEP 2 Pick an object in the middle distance zone, about 50 yards away. Keeping both eyes open, move the focus ring (a) until the image is at its sharpest. Although you are focusing only with the left eye, keep both eyes open and relaxed. Do not squint.

STEP 3 Switch the lens cap or duct tape to the other lens barrel. Look at the same object and turn the diopter ring (see inset) to bring the object into sharp focus (b). Make sure the focus knob doesn't change. Keep both eyes open; do not squint.

STEP 4 Remove the lens cap or duct tape and look through both lens barrels. The image should remain sharp. Make a note of the diopter-ring setting, or place a small dot of fingernail polish on the correct adjustment. If your visual acuity changes during the year, you may need to reset the diopter.

Set focus for the left eye barrel.

Set diopter for the right eye.

287 PACK A WOODSTOVE FOR A SLOW, LONG BURN

You won't need to leave your cozy bunk to feed the stove if you load it right. Twenty minutes before sack time, rake all of the coals toward the stove's air inlets and stack large pieces of firewood tightly behind the coals. (Hardwood is best.) Open the ducts wide for 10 to 30 minutes—a large stove will require a longer burn time. Once the wood closest to the coals has burned to a thick layer of charcoal, cut back the airflow as much as 25 percent. Starved of oxygen, the burn will slow down and work its way through the stack overnight. —T.E.N.

288 HEAR WHAT YOUR RIFLE IS TELLING YOU

Were this the best of all possible worlds, we would fire three rifle shots at a target, peer downrange, and see three holes clustered within the area of a dime at precisely the right place. But this is not the best of all possible worlds, in that it has a place for chiggers, bad cholesterol, rabies, and abdominal fat. And in this vale of sorrow, we often look at our targets and see horror, chaos, and disorder.

In any event, we know that something is wrong, but what? Rather than burst into tears, you should regard this as a heart-to-heart talk with your rifle, which, if you can speak its language, will tell you what ails it.

DIAGNOSTIC TOOL Shooting from the benchrest will tell you just what your gun is thinking.

COMPLETE BREAKDOWN
Problem Your shots are all over the place, and you can't get a group to save your life. There could be several causes. First is a ruptured scope. The way to test this is to put a different scope on your gun and see if it groups better. Second is loose bedding screws on the rifle. Check to see if they're tight. Third is loose ring or base screws. Sometimes, one particular bullet weight will give results this bad. If this is the case, it's usually because the barrel's rifling twist is wrong for that bullet weight.

CONSISTENT FLIER
Problem Your ammo is almost, but not quite, right for your gun. Usually this shows up as two holes close together and the third one off to the side by an inch or two. At 100 yards, this is not a problem, but at farther distances, it will begin to cause some trouble. It's caused by bullets traveling just above or below the optimum speed for that barrel, causing it to vibrate inconsistently. Hand-loaders can cure it by raising or lowering the powder charge. Non-handloaders will have to try different ammunition.

INCONSISTENT FLIER
Problem Most of the time you get good groups, but sometimes you have one shot go astray, and then sometimes all three go where they're not supposed to. Most likely you're flinching, and if you don't think that it's possible to flinch from a benchrest, think again. You can buy or experiment with a sled-type shooting rest, which can virtually eliminate felt recoil, or try putting a soft gun case or sandbag between your shoulder and the butt. Or, if all else fails, get a less punishing rifle.

RISING GROUP
Problem Your groups are usually O.K., but they seem to keep moving up on the target, sometimes up and to the left or right, sometimes straight up. This is caused by an overheated barrel. When a tube gets too hot, it warps slightly, sending bullets errantly, and in addition, the heat waves rising from it give you a distorted view of the target, sort of like shooting through a swimming pool. The cure is easy: Let your barrel cool down. Start each group with a cold barrel and never let it get beyond lukewarm.

STRINGING
Problem In this situation, your groups string vertically or horizontally. First check the barrel bedding. Most barrels today are free-floating; there should be no contact from 1 1/2 inches forward of the receiver right out to the end. If there is, take the gun in for a rebedding job. The horizontal grouping can be caused by wind at the target that you don't feel at the bench. The vertical groups can be caused by the fore-end jumping on too hard a surface.
—D.E.P.

289 MAKE A BUCK SCRAPE

During the early phases of the rut, making a mock scrape is a great way to get the attention of the big bucks in your area.

WHERE Your ideal spot is a trail or edge near a doe feeding area, upwind of your stand site. Look for a place where a small branch or sapling extends over the trail at about head height.

HOW Don rubber boots and gloves. With a stick, hoe, or trowel, rake bare a 2-foot circle. Work a gel-based buck urine into the soil—the gel scents tend to last longer than the liquid scents—and drip a drop or two on an overhanging branch. —T.E.N.

290 CLEAN A PLUCKED DUCK IN 60 SECONDS

This method results in a fully dressed duck that retains its feathered head so it meets legal requirements for transport. Prepared this way, three mallards or six teal fit into a 1-gallon zip-seal bag.

STEP 1 Pluck.

STEP 2 With the blade of a hatchet, break the wing bones close to the body. Remove the wings with shears. Cut the feet off through the joint of the leg bones, taking care not to break the bones. This will leave a rounded bone at the end of the leg instead of a jagged tip. Remove the tail by snipping through the joint between the base of the pelvis and the tail.

STEP 3 Pick up the duck in one hand, with its head down and its back facing up. Run your shears along each side of the backbone and then snip the ribs down the back. If you do it this way, the backbone will stay attached to the body. Next, turn the shears perpendicular to the duck's spine and cut the backbone, windpipe, and esophagus at the neck.

STEP 4 Hold the duck over a bucket, feet down. Insert the shears under the backbone at the neck, open the blades an inch, and run the shears straight down the body. The backbone and all the organs will separate and fall into the bucket.

STEP 5 Fold the head back into the body cavity, and you're done.
—T.E.N

291 MAKE YOUR OWN WIND CHECKER

Several manufacturers produce effective, convenient, unscented wind-checking products. So does Mother Nature. The advantage of milkweed seed filaments is that you can see them for 50 yards—farther with binoculars—and get a real-world reading on what your scent is doing out there where the deer are.

STEP 1 Drill a ⅜-inch hole in the bottom of a film canister.

STEP 2 Remove the seeds from the plumes of half a dozen milkweed pods.

STEP 3 Stuff as many milkweed plumes as possible into the canister. Replace the cap.

STEP 4 Affix one strip of Velcro to the film canister, and the other strip to wherever you want to store it—gun strap, quiver, and so on.

STEP 5 Pluck a few plumes from the film canister and let them fly. —T.E.N.

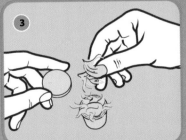

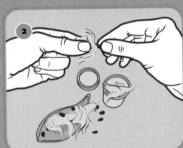

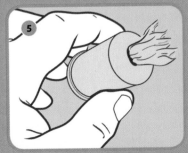

292 DROP A SINGLE BIRD OUT OF A FLOCK

STEP 1 Keep your gun off your shoulder and parallel to the ground. Point the muzzle toward the flock but don't mount the gun until you're ready to swing and fire.

STEP 2 Single out one bird from the flock and don't take your eyes off of it. Try to choose the highest bird or the trailing bird. Swinging on this target first will ensure good shooting form for the next bird as your gun naturally overtakes the flock.

STEP 3 Drill your eyes at your chosen bird and push the gun muzzle toward it. Fire on the swing and keep shooting until it drops. Only then should you go for the double, and your gun is already in position for the next swing through the flock. —T.E.N.

293 CLAIM THE BEST BUNK

Maybe you aren't the savviest hunter in the crowd, but putting your mitts on the comfiest bunk in the barn can score you points, as well. Here's how to always land the best bed available.

Half an hour before your ETA at deer camp, start whining about having to pee. Don't lay it on too thick quite yet. Unselfishly turn aside all offers for a quick rest stop: "Naw, guys, I can make it." (Wince slightly.) "Let's just get there. I know we're all in a rush."

When you're ten minutes out, start squirming. Say, "Man, I'm glad we're this close. I think something's about to rupture back here!"

As soon as the tires stop spinning, you're on the run. Don't forget to grab a small personal item on your way out of the truck. Don't hoist a large duffel bag—for cryin' out loud, your bladder's stretched beyond reason! Stake your claim to the prized mattress on your way to the privy. A slight limp on the way clinches the deal. —T.E.N.

294 SOUND LIKE A TURKEY

The biggest mistake novice turkey hunters make is calling too much. In the real world, the gobbler calls to a hen and expects her to come to him. You're trying to reverse the equation by getting the gobbler to come to you. You don't have to be perfect, and that's why the less you call the better. If the woods are quiet—no chattering squirrels or warbling songbirds—call once or twice and then hush up. Prolonged calling in this scenario is unnatural and will spook a big tom.

There are four basic calls you need to learn, but they're actually relatively easy to master. Of course, your gobbler will be the judge of that.

OWL HOOT The first call of the morning (or the last of the evening) helps to locate a roosting tom. It's simply hoot-hoot-hoot, done six to eight syllables at a time. If a roosting gobbler responds, you know how close or how far away your target is.

YELP The hen's basic call is a simple series of single notes—often five or six at a time—strung together. Use this call to let a gobbler know a hen is in his area. If you get a booming response, don't repeat. Let him come to you.

CLUCK If you think the gobbler is on the way and you feel a need to assure him that all is well, use this in place of the yelp. It's a short, sharp call put together in three-note clusters.

CUTT A call of last resort, this one is an attraction-getting series of loud clucks with an erratic tempo. This call carries a long way and might turn the head of a distant gobbler.
—S.L.W.

295 MAKE THE PERFECT YELP

To yelp on a slate call, grasp the base in your fingers and thumb. Hold the call off the palm to create a distortion-free sound chamber. Hold the striker like a pen, and be careful that no part of your hand touches the slate. Draw small circles and ovals on the slate surface, like writing in cursive, but in a single stamp-size spot. Work on creating a high tone and a low tone. Put them together, and you've got a yelp. —S.L.W.

296 CALL DUCKS WITH A PARTNER

You can double your chances at green-timber ducks by doubling up with another caller.

HAIL CALL Think "Row, Row, Row Your Boat" when team-calling to birds in the distance. As one caller hits his third or fourth quack in a descending hail call, his partner needs to follow with a similar descending hail call.

HEN TIME Once the birds are interested, dispense with the hail calls. Partners should blow a series of hen quacks that differ in pitch and cadence. If one caller starts off with a lazy hen, the other should cut in with a bouncing hen call.

THE CLOSER When birds are skimming the treetops in green timber, dial back the volume and try realistic feeding calls that simulate a single and very contented hen mallard. It doesn't have to be fancy. Just imagine a happy duck making soft little happy purring quack sounds. That usually does the trick.
—T.E.N.

297 AGE A DEER ON THE HOOF

Many deer hunters insist on shooting older bucks, not just judging a deer by the number of antler points. Aging a deer from a distance is never going to be an exact science, but it's definitely worth trying.

A 1½-year-old deer has smooth antler bases, few to no sticker points or tines, noticeably low antler mass, and a short, doelike face with a tapered muzzle. His rump appears higher than his shoulders, and his legs are thin. Bucks that are about 2½ years old have antler bases about 3 to 4 inches in circumference. Their back line is nearly parallel from front to hindquarters. During the rut, their neck begins to swell visibly. Three-year-olds have heavy, often rough, antler bases. They have a much larger neck and shoulders compared to the rest of the body. The back profile is still a straight line, but the belly begins to sag. When you see one of these older deer, you know it. —T.E.N.

298 HUNT PHEASANTS LIKE A COMMANDO

Most pheasant hunts are group affairs, but the solo gunner shouldn't be intimidated by the size of a piece of pheasant land. Going it alone means you get to do it your way. And this is the right way.

HUNT STRUCTURE FIRST The right way to start is to key in on smaller habitat elements that will hold birds, such as tree belts, ditches, and thickets. Once you drive the birds from cover, you'll be more apt to put them up in a field. One especially good pheasant magnet to look for: the grown-up banks of dams. The thick vegetation provides a windbreak, food, and cover—and the confined spaces a solo hunter needs in order to succeed.

MOVE QUICKLY Speed up your pace and sprinkle in stops and starts. Nervous birds will take to wing.

WORK ROAD DITCHES In the late afternoon, birds move to roads to pick up grit. They won't want to leave their safety zone—until they see your boots.

LEARN FROM YOUR MISTAKES It's inevitable that you'll flush birds out of range. Take note of which side of the food strip they flush from and what routes they use to escape to cover. Learn how the birds use a piece of land, and you can fine-tune your drive next time. —T.E.N.

299 KNEEL FOR THE BULL OF YOUR LIFE

When you finally get a shot at the bull elk you've been working, it'll happen quickly. It's vital that you practice shooting from realistic positions before the season. Here's how to make a shot from your knees, one of the most useful positions.

STEP 1 Start by dropping to both knees and lowering your butt to your heels. Some hunters prefer to drop to one knee only, but doing so can leave you susceptible to an unsteady side-to-side swaying movement, and this in turn can give you away or throw off your shot. The butt-to-heels drop creates a more compact and stable shooting position.

STEP 2 Keep the bow upright and rest the lower limb on one thigh (a). This leads to a lot less movement when you draw. If you were to lay the bow across the thighs, you'd have to move it upright to draw; at close range that's enough to spook a bull.

STEP 3 Depending on the length of your torso and the size of the bow, you may have to rise up off your heels as you draw (b). Doing this in one motion lessens the chance the bull will spot you—another reason to get used to this move in your backyard before your hunt.

STEP 4 To practice, staple 6-inch pie plates to your backstop. Move around, drop to your knees, and take the shot. Change angles. Go for accuracy first and then speed. —S.L.W.

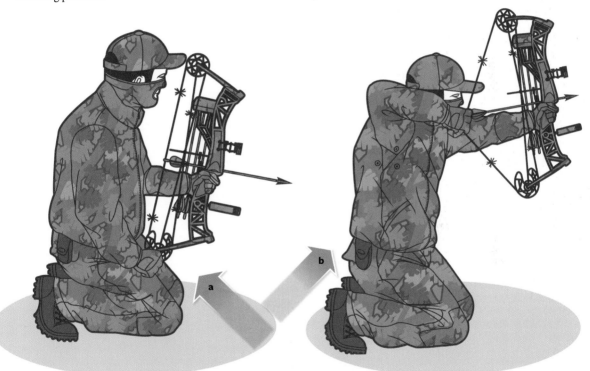

300 REALLY, REALLY TICK OFF YOUR HUNTING PARTNER, PART II

Timing is everything. Actually, the proper lead is everything, but that's another story; timing, however, is critical to knocking down birds. Nothing spoils the sight of a dozen quackers coming in on a string faster than the sight of some cowboy going solo—and too early—with his 12-gauge pump. Take turns, draw straws, whatever—but make it clear who's calling the shot.
—T.E.N.

301 HUNT SQUIRRELS LIKE A GROWN-UP

Everything you need to feel younger, eat better, and sleep through the night without having to use the bathroom is stuck in the far corner of your gun cabinet, gunked up with the last squirt of 3-in-One oil with which you bid farewell to your .22 rifle.

Well, almost everything. To turn squirrel hunting from child's play into a true rifleman's pursuit, you need to address two of the limitations of squirreling like a kid. First, get your rump off the ground so you don't end up squirming with back spasms a half-hour after you've hunkered down against a hickory. Lightweight, portable cushions and hunting seats might not make you feel like a kid again, but they'll keep you hunting longer and harder and prevent you from walking back to the truck bent over like Old Mother Hubbard. Next, pick up an adjustable shooting stick. It'll add serious range to your rimfire shooting, which makes sniping squirrels an even bigger—and more grown-up—blast.

Now, use all your big-boy deer-hunting smarts to hone in on the perfect ambush. The open woods are where children hunt. You want an edge where open woods butt up against younger growth full of tasty fox grapes and berries, thickets where a couple pounds of protein can move around without worrying about every red-tailed hawk in the county. From there squirrels will fan out into the oak and hickory woods, secure in the knowledge that all those fuzz-faced kids with their iron-sighted .22s are either down in the big woods or working on their Guitar Hero chops back home. If they're really paying attention, they might even hear the click of your trigger safety sliding into the red zone. —T.E.N.

302 STUMP SLUMP FOR GOBBLERS

Sitting against a tree seems a simple enough task. But if you do it wrong—and there are plenty of wrong ways—you might blow your shot at a gobbler. If you sit up, high and conspicuous, you may never get a chance to shoot. If you can't brace your arms on your knees, you'll have a difficult time holding the bead steady on the turkey or keeping the gun ready for long periods of time. If you have to move too much to prepare to shoot, the turkey will spook before you ever pull the trigger.

The hunter illustrated here isn't just slouched against a tree—he's hunkered down low to be inconspicuous to an approaching turkey. He's comfortable enough to stay in that position without moving. And he's braced to make a quick and accurate shot at a gobbler approaching from anywhere in front of him with minimum movement.

A great advantage of this "stump slump" is that you can balance the gun's fore-end on your knee and tuck the butt lightly under your shoulder, keeping the gun stable as you work a call or eat a granola bar. If a turkey comes in unexpectedly, all you have to do is reach slowly for the gun and lower your cheek onto the stock. Once you've assumed that position, your gun is solidly rested so you can wait for the perfect shot—and make it.

BACK Lean against the tree. The trunk protects your back, and it's your camouflage, too, because it hides your silhouette. Get comfortable; you may be there awhile. But don't slouch down so far and put so much weight on the trunk that you have to struggle and lurch upright in order to make a minor adjustment in aim.

LEFT HAND The back of your left hand lies flat on your knee. You can use it to make small adjustments in elevation and windage.

RIGHT ELBOW Brace your right elbow against the inside of your right leg. Having your shooting-side elbow supported helps steady your hold.

RIGHT LEG Splay your right knee out and down. It will provide a remarkably steady rest for your right elbow.

MUZZLE The muzzle faces just past your left foot. This is the natural point of aim, where no muscular effort is required to point the gun. Since it is much easier for a right-handed shooter to twist to the left than to the right, set up with your natural point of aim to the right of where you expect to see the turkey.

LEFT LEG Place your left foot flat so your lower leg is more or less perpendicular to the ground. That allows your gun to be supported by bone, not muscle.

FEET If the bird comes in too far to the right or left, wait until it goes behind a tree, then lean forward slightly to center your weight on your seat, not your back, and use short, choppy sideways "steps" to scoot yourself around to face in the right direction. —P.B.

303 SOUND LIKE A DEER

Calling deer adds an exciting element to whitetail hunting. Here are the most important deer sounds for hunters. Each can be duplicated by commercial calls, and each requires practice to make it field-ready.

BUCK GRUNTS The deer grunt establishes dominance and signals aggression, often in the presence of a doe, so the right buck grunt at the right time can provoke a buck to move toward your position. Use a soft grunt to get a buck to move out of cover or take a few steps from behind a tree. "Tending grunts" are deeper and more urgent, often used when a buck is trailing a hot doe.

BLEATS Doe and fawn bleats can be ordinary contact calls or alarm signals, and deer will often investigate out of pure curiosity. A "doe estrous bleat" is a louder, drawn-out bleat made when a doe nears peak breeding time. A can-type estrous bleat call can be a deadly buck tactic during the rut.

DISTRESSED FAWN BLEATS Used to target does for the meat cooler, these high-pitched, urgent calls can also pull in curious bucks who want to see which does respond to an anxious fawn.

BUCK SNORT-WHEEZE This contact call is heard when two bucks rub shoulders over a food source or a hot doe. Use it during the rut's peak to troll for a mature buck or to pull in a buck that comes to a grunt call but hangs up out of range.

BUCK GROWL-ROAR Calls to replicate the growl-roar are among the newest whitetail tactics. As a buck trails a hot doe, its state of arousal climbs. Some bucks turn a tending grunt into a rapid-fire vocalization with a bawling, growling sound. Other bucks will investigate the scene of such intense activity. —T.E.N.

304 MAKE RATTLING ANTLERS

Cut off brow tines and antler tips. Sand sharp edges or burrs. Drill a small hole at the base of each antler. Thread the ends of a 3-foot-long piece of black parachute cord through each hole and tie a stopper knot at each end. The week before opening day, toss the antlers into water to replenish lost moisture for the perfect tone, and paint a tine or two blaze orange. —T.E.N.

305 GET INTO A BUCK FIGHT WITH RATTLING ANTLERS

Rattling up a buck works best in areas with a healthy, almost even, buck-to-doe ratio. Here's the drill.

STEP 1 Factor in the breeze. Most bucks try to approach a fight from downwind. Set up with the wind at your back, overlooking open woods or a field.

STEP 2 Start slow. Rattle antlers lightly for 90 seconds. Wait five minutes and then repeat with louder rattling for up to two minutes. Sit tight for a half-hour.

STEP 3 Scrape the antlers against a tree and the ground and then rattle again. Give it another 30 minutes and then relocate. —S.L.W.

306 SHOOT WITH A "CHING SLING"

Shooting instructor Eric Ching's Ching Sling does away with the multiple loop adjustments and shoulder gyrations associated with the traditional military-style strap. It's essentially a standard rifle sling with the addition of a short strap on a sliding loop, and a number of shooting accessories companies make the slings. You'll need to add a third swivel just ahead of your trigger guard to use it, but that's it.

When you're ready to fire, insert your support arm (the left arm for a right-handed shooter) through the loop in front of the short strap, snug the short strap tight against your upper arm, and rotate your forearm back under the main strap to grip the forestock. Quick. Intuitive. Solid. —T.E.N.

307 SIT LIKE A KING ON A STYROFOAM THRONE

Nature's call can be a cruel song at 10 degrees below zero. One deer camp's savvy members have taken the edge off the frigid encounter between a bare bottom and the outhouse plank. First, they lined their john with three layers of cushy inch-thick Styrofoam and beveled the edges of the toilet seat for maximum comfort. Upon entering la toilette, you light a Coleman lantern, which provides light and heat. The lantern handle is raised upright for a makeshift towel rack. A baby wipe is draped over the handle. Voilà—a warm and soothing end to the business at hand. Or is that the end at hand? —T.E.N.

308 HANG NASTY WET BOOTS FROM THE RAFTERS

WHAT YOU'LL NEED

- PVC cement

- One 10-foot length of 1-inch PVC pipe, cut into the following sections: 8 @ 10 inches, 6 @ 2 inches, 1 @ 24 inches

- Three 1-inch four-way PVC pipe connectors

- Six 1-inch 45-degree PVC pipe elbow joints

- 1 No. 8 bolt, 1 inch long, with two nuts

- 1 eyebolt

- Clothesline or parachute cord, long enough to reach from your waist to the top of the tallest ceiling in your camp and back

- 1 large washer

DIRECTIONS

STEP 1 Cement the pipe pieces, connectors, and joints as shown in the photo.

STEP 2 Attach the bolt to the bottom end of the PVC frame.

STEP 3 Drill a hole through the top of the PVC frame. Attach the eyebolt to the ceiling and then run the clothesline through it and back down to the PVC frame, tying it off at the drilled hole. Tie the washer to the clothesline at a location that will stop the PVC frame at about waist height.

STEP 4 Raise the PVC frame like a flag and hook the washer over the bolt head at the bottom of the frame to hold it aloft. —T.E.N.

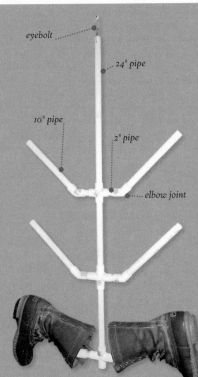

eyebolt

24" pipe

10" pipe

2" pipe

elbow joint

309 SNEAK A RIDGE READY TO SHOOT

When you're stalking over a ridge, think a few steps ahead. First, stop just below the crest. An inch is as good as a mile, so get as close to the top as you can. Get your breath under control there, not when you're looking through the glass at your prize. Next, look for a clump of grass, a rock, anything to break up your outline as you ease your head up. Take your hat off, chamber the rifle, and pull a small pack or some other rest along with you as you slowly take a look. If that muzzle is waving around, back down, get your head right, and get your breath under control, because you can't put that bullet back in the gun once you pull the trigger. —T.E.N.

310 SKIN A DEER WITH A GOLF BALL

No hair gets on the meat, and this method stretches the deer out and lays it right down on clean plastic. It's like taking its pajamas off. Don't laugh, because it works.

You only need to make a few cuts.

To tree

STEP 1 Lay the deer belly-up on a sheet of plastic or plywood. Make an incision through the skin all the way around the deer's neck about 6 inches below the ears. Make another incision from the neck cut down to a point between the front legs. Continue this incision out the inside of each front leg as far down as you want to skin the carcass.

STEP 2 Working from the top of the deer, free about 6 inches of skin between the top of the shoulder blades, and insert a golf ball or golf ball-size rock under the skin.

STEP 3 Tie the deer's head off to a sturdy pole or nearby tree. Make a slipknot in one end of another rope and cinch it over the golf ball, making sure it holds the deer's hide firmly. Attach the other end of this rope to your vehicle's tow hook.

STEP 4 Now just strip the hide from the deer by easing the vehicle slowly away from the carcass. —T.E.N.

311

FREEZE ANY GAME FOR CHEAP

You need two things to properly freeze game meat: a vapor barrier and a constant, supercooled environment. Here's the cheap, easy way to ensure a fine meal of venison or grouse come next summer.

Place small animals such as squirrels, doves, quail, and ducks into gallon-size resealable plastic freezer bags, and place the bags in a sink. (Many big game cuts, such as steaks and tenderloins, also fit.) Fill the bag two-thirds of the way with ice water—chilled water will hasten the freezing process—and swirl the meat gently to release any trapped air. Now press down slightly. While water spills from the bag, seal it tightly. You've created two barriers to freezer-burn-producing air: the plastic bag and a cocoon of protective ice.

So far, so cheap. Now you need to freeze those bags—quickly. The longer the freezing process, the larger the ice crystals that form, and large ice crystals will damage the cell walls of muscle tissue and degrade meat. A free-standing freezer is far superior to the traditional refrigerator freezer, which may or may not produce temperatures below the recommended 0 degrees F. Spread the packages out with at least two inches of air space between them. (Once frozen, they can be stacked.)

If your freezer sports wire grate shelving, line the shelves with newspaper to prevent the bag corners from drooping through the shelf grate and freezing into an icy hook. And don't freeze more than a quarter of the freezer's capacity at a time. Locked in ice, birds should keep six months or more; larger cuts last up to one year. By then you'll need to throw a wild game dinner party to clear out the freezer for a fresh delivery. —T.E.N

312   BECOME A GUN WRITER

Shoot constantly. Lose most of your hearing by your mid-30s. Pick out one cartridge that you admire and one that you despise and make this a leitmotif of your writing. It helps to be from the West or the South, but Easterners can be successful if they are eccentric enough. Escape death in Africa at least once.

—D.E.P

313 PLOT A YEARLONG AMBUSH

You can carve out a cookie-cutter food plot, sure. Even toss some seed on an existing field and hope for the best. Or you can think critically about how to design a food plot that provides yearlong nutrition and season-long shooting opportunities. Start with a footprint shaped like a Y—the branched design allows deer to approach across a wide variety of wind conditions. Even if you can't build a better food plot from the ground up, these strategies can help you fine-tune any piece of deer ground.

STEP 1 Plant dense browse such as blackberry or the strawberry bush known as hearts-a-bursting at the upper, outside edges of forks.

STEP 2 Inside the Y, one fork should be planted in early-maturing greens for bow season. Plant the other fork in forage greens for late gun season.

STEP 3 Position the open end of the Y to face the prevailing winds in your hunting area and put your deer stand at the bottom end of the Y. —T.E.N.

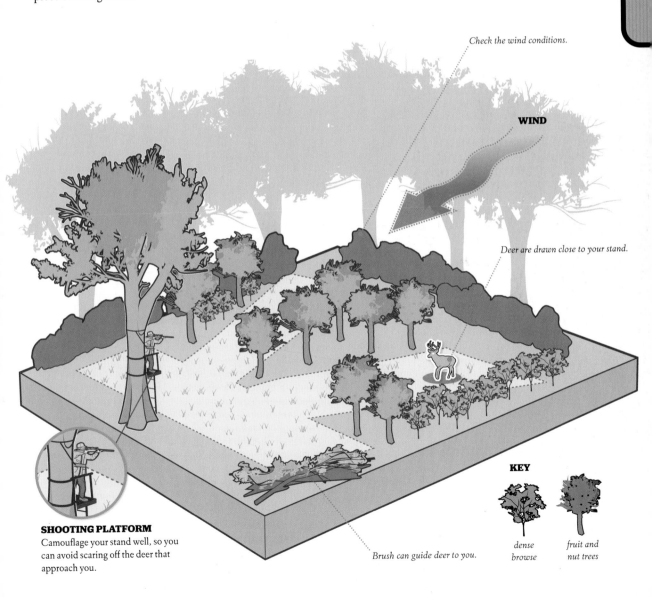

Check the wind conditions.

WIND

Deer are drawn close to your stand.

SHOOTING PLATFORM
Camouflage your stand well, so you can avoid scaring off the deer that approach you.

Brush can guide deer to you.

KEY

dense browse

fruit and nut trees

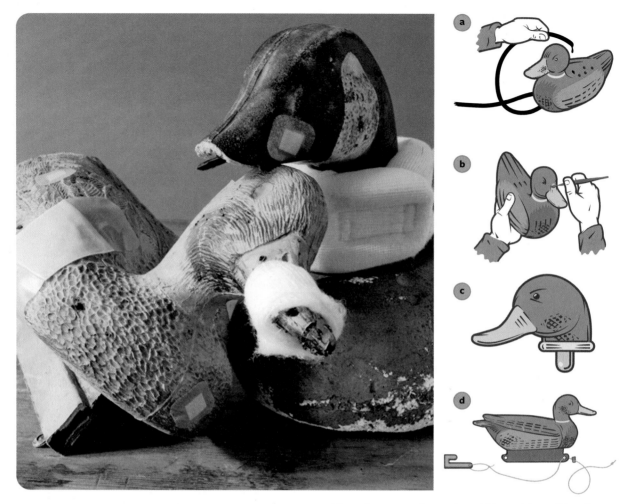

314 RESTORE GLORY TO YOUR DEKES

Faded, pellet-ridden decoys covered in sunbaked algae might attract a duck's attention on opening day, but Ol' Quack is a very quick study. In no time you'll wish that you had spent a morning or two in the garage sprucing up your spread. Here's a simple prescription for bringing your beat-up blocks back to life.

REPAIR Patch shot holes in plastic, hollow-body decoys by melting the end of a short length of black polypropylene cord and plugging the holes with a dab of the melted goop. (a) Or drill out each hole with a small drill bit and fill it with boater's silicone sealant.

REPAINT In most cases, a thorough touch-up will work wonders—after a bath. For faded plastic dekes, pressure-wash them or go to the nearest wand-brush car wash. Cork and foam decoys need a good scrubbing with a stiff brush. The trick to the makeover is to add realistic contrast, not close-up detail. To refurbish a mallard drake, use a flat-finish latex paint—black, white, and green should do the job. Concentrate on the head, upper rear tail feathers, double wing bars, and neck ring. (b)

REPLACE Battle-weary foam and cork decoys such as Herter's, L.L. Bean Coastal Corks, and many homemade blocks can be quickly revived with a new noggin. (c) Large sporting goods catalog stores and waterfowling specialty shops carry replacement heads.

RERIG Snarled and spliced decoy lines are a nightmare to deal with. Replace worn cords with specialty decoy line that resists tangles. (d) Thread the line through the keel hole and then add a cordlock between the keel and the stopper knot so that you can customize depth.
—T.E.N.

315 STAY HIDDEN IN THE WOODS

A whitetail deer has the advantage of a 310-degree view of the world, but experienced hunters know that deer see motion more readily than details and colors. The most successful stalkers learn how to camouflage their footsteps, silhouettes, and rifle and bow mounting. Here's how to move through the woods with as little movement as possible. —T.E.N.

SLIM DOWN Branches, twigs, and briers conspire to catch your clothing and telegraph your presence. Wear close-fitting clothes and snug down the cinch straps on daypacks and fanny packs for a slim profile. Cut off unnecessary webbing and loose laces that might dangle and snag a leafy branch. Avoid wearing wide-brimmed hats in the woods.

STAY IN THE SHADOWS Wolves, mountain lions, even predatory insects do it, and so should you. Look ahead and plot your route through the woods to take advantage of every gloomy copse of shrubs, every shady thicket, every tree shadow possible.

PUT YOUR BACK TO THE SUN When scent conditions allow, you'll want to move with the sun at your back. In other words, let your quarry do the squinting instead of you.

WATCH YOUR ROUTE It's not just ridges that threaten to expose your upright, bipedal silhouette to the forest world. Avoid routes that cut across meadows or that skirt in front of large rocks and expanses of forest edges and gaps. Instead of walking ridgelines, go along just below and take an occasional peek across the crest.

316 RELOAD IN THREE SECONDS FLAT

When you're jump-shooting ducks, the action can be over quickly. You need to be able to make superfast follow-up shots after the initial volley. A semiautomatic shotgun and this simple trick makes it easy. Before beginning the stalk, tuck a pair of shotgun shells into the Vs between the fingers of your fore-end hand. Once you've unloaded the first barrage, bring your trigger hand forward to snatch the shells from your fingers.

Keep your eyes focused on the birds. The shotgun action will be locked in the open position. Drop one shell into the open chamber, press the bolt return button, and either fire away or feed the second shell into the magazine tube. —T.E.N.

F&S Field Report: HEART TO HEART

As we turn our backs to the glow of the truck's headlights, the still deer lies half-darkened underneath our shadows. Blood flecks its muzzle like beads of rain. Mud coats the hindquarters—it was no easy drag up the hill. The air is steeped with the earth-and-sweat musk of a buck in rut.

My 7-year-old son, Jack, holds one hind leg as I open the belly with a knife turned blade up. The skin tears open with the sound of a zipper. Jack's eyes are like moons. He talked nonstop during the long sit in the stand and during the hour after the gunshot and the dragging to the old barn. But he has not said a word since I handed him the hoof to hold. He has seen deer before: in the wild, hanging under the deck, on the butcher table in the basement, on his dinner plate. He has not seen deer like this.

I point out the liver, the bladder, the windpipe, the rope of intestines.

"Where's the heart?" Jack asks.

With one hand I part the red lungs, clasped together like a mussel shell. The bullet tunneled through the upper lobes, pulverizing the tissues that stain my hands and wrists. I remove the heart and wipe it clean of blood. It is dark and hard, unlike the other organs, which seem to quiver of their own accord.

"That's a heart?" he asks. I nod. He looks at it for a moment.

"Cut it open."

This is a startling request, and I hesitate, for it seems almost sacrilegious. But when a little boy is struck with wonder, there's no time to trifle, and I want this moment to go wherever my son wishes to take it. I cleave the heart with the knife, top to bottom, so the two halves sag open in my palm. The hollows of the interior chambers are dark. I squeeze the heart to show Jack how it works—how it pumps blood from the lungs through the heart and then out the arteries that branch, again and again, into the dendritic vessels that feed each cell of the body.

He is quiet at first, and I fear I've lost him. "Just like ours?" he asks, low and husky like he speaks sometimes. I hear in his voice the man he will become.

"Just like ours."

—T. Edward Nickens
Field & Stream, "My Boy Jack,"
October 2006

"Difficulties are just things to overcome, after all."
—Ernest Shackleton

The Skin of Your Teeth

Now you've gone and done it. Gone too far or gone overboard. Lost your way, left your flashlight at camp, let darkness catch you in the woods without a single match. At the moment, it doesn't matter how you got here. What matters is that it's all up to you, bud. Live or die.

These days, it's all too easy to think that survival skills are a lost and useless art—techniques as practical as, say, knowing how to plow with an ox. The reality, however, is that modern life has figured out new ways to put the unprepared in precarious situations. For starters, it's easier than ever to gain access to remote, rugged country. Thanks to floatplanes, helicopters, even frequent-flyer miles, more and more of us are going farther and farther into the wilds. When we get there, we rely too heavily on things that go blank when the batteries die. And perversely, just when we really need to know how to signal with smoke or build a fire in the rain, the skills necessary to dig our way out of the hole have all but eroded away.

Only once have I come close to dying in the outdoors. Pinned underwater in a remote Alaska river, I clawed to the surface to face days filled with fear as my party portaged canoes through wilderness forest so thick we often couldn't see 10 feet into the woods. We swapped turns as point man, burrowing through the brush with a shotgun in one hand and bear spray in the other.

But I have to wonder: How often do truly skillful hunters and anglers skirt disaster—without even knowing it—because they know how to stay *out* of trouble? If you're smart enough to carry three ways to start a fire in your pack or pockets, you negate the necessity of a fire plough. Know how to find your way by deliberate offset, and you might not ever have to descend a cliff on a single rope.

The wolves have howled at my door only a time or two, but there have been plenty of instances when I was glad that I knew how to coax fire from damp wood, because it made life easier when I finally made it back to camp. I'm glad I know how to take a back bearing and navigate by map and compass because those skills mean I can plumb big woods with the confidence that I will be able to find my way back to the truck. The fact that I can run a whitewater rapid—or swim it safely if it turns out I'm not quite the paddler that I had imagined—

has opened up worlds of wilderness walleye and salmon and smallmouth bass.

Truth be told, having a few good survival skills is just as likely to come in handy when you need to whip up a quick, hot trail lunch as it is when you need to warm your frozen fingers enough to weave a brush raft that you will use to cross the swollen river before the raging wildfire burns you alive. Much of the value of knowing how to survive when you lose all your chips is that the knowledge helps you play a better hand when you're still holding a few decent cards.

And let's be honest: The ability to craft a back-country deathstar or use hot coals to hollow out a river cane blowgun—you're just plain cooler for having those aces up your sleeve.

So the next time some city slicker chuckles at the dryer lint you're saving for a DIY fire starter, just remind yourself: You may never need this stuff— until suddenly, critically, you do. Until you wander too far into the woods. Lose your way. Break down, fall down, or go down the wrong trail. Until you have to survive, for an hour or a long, cold night, or longer. Then you'll be happy you know how to survive. Lucky is the man who can spark flame and sleep soundly on a fire bed, a smile on his face, ready for the long hike home in the morning. —*T. Edward Nickens*

317 SURVIVE A FALL THROUGH THE ICE

Say "hard water" in northern regions, and folks know you're not complaining about rinsing soap out of your hair. In these cold climes, hard water is ice—as in ice fishing. And up here, you'd better know how to climb out when the water is not as hard as you thought. Here's a handy self-rescue device that has saved many a life.

HOW IT'S DONE Cut two 5-inch sections from a broomstick or 1-inch wooden dowel. On each of the pieces, drill a hole into one end that's slightly smaller than the diameter of whatever nails you have handy, and another hole crosswise at the other end. Drive a nail into each end hole. Cut off the nailhead, leaving 1 inch of protruding nail. Sharpen with a file to a semi-sharp point. Thread a 6-foot length (or a length that's equal to your arm span) of parachute cord through the crosswise holes and tie off with stopper knots.

Thread one dowel through both coat sleeves. When you slip the coat on, keep the dowels just below your cuffs. If you do go through the ice, grab the dowels and drive the nails into the ice to drag yourself out. —T.E.N.

318 MAKE EMERGENCY MUKLUKS

Keep toes and feet intact with makeshift mukluks. Find some insulating material—a piece of fleece, sleeping pad, or boat carpet—and do the following for each foot.

STEP 1 Cut it into a circle about 24 inches across.

STEP 2 Fold the circle of insulation into quarters.

STEP 3 Move one layer of the insulation aside and insert your foot into the folded material. There should be a single layer at the heel.

STEP 4 Alternate the remaining layers around your foot. Slip an outer shell—part of a tarp or even a pants leg cut from spare clothing—over the insulation.

STEP 5 Crisscross a piece of cord around the outer layer, or use duct tape to secure firmly. —T.E.N.

319 CALL FOR HELP IN ANY LANGUAGE

The international signal for distress is a sequence of short and long signals, designed for telegraph operators—three short, three long, three short. Adopted at the Berlin Radiotelegraphic Conference in 1906, the SOS sequence was based solely on its ease of transmitting. It does not mean "save our ship" or anything else you've heard. But you can transmit the code with just about any device imaginable: whistle blasts, car horns, gunshots, light flashes, even pots and pans. —T.E.N.

320 SURVIVE THE ROUGHEST NIGHT WITH A KNIFE

You can use a strong knife to turn a single conifer tree into an overnight bivvy. First, fell a 9-foot balsam or other evergreen and remove all the branches close to the trunk.

MAKE A BOUGH BED Cut the tips of the evergreen branches to 1 foot in length. Use wooden stakes to chock a 3-foot-long, 4-inch-diameter log (cut from the tree trunk) where you want the head of your bed to be. Shingle the boughs at a 45-degree angle pointing away from the foot of the bed. Compress tightly as you work your way down. Anchor with a second 3-foot-long log from the trunk chocked with wooden stakes.

GLEAN TINDER The low, dead branches and sucker twigs of conifers make excellent tinder. Carve a fuzz stick from the thickest branch. Gather wood shavings from the others by scraping with the knife held at a 90-degree angle to the twigs.

GIN POLE A FISH To cook a fish with no utensils, snip away all twigs from the longest branch. Sharpen the fat end and drive it into the ground at about a 45-degree angle. Chock it with a rock or Y-shaped stick. Run cord through a fish's mouth and gill like a stringer, tie it to the branch, and let it dangle and cook beside the fire. —T.E.N.

321 BUILD A FIRE IN THE RAIN

There are those who can and those who think they can. Here's how to be one of those who really can.

STEP 1 Allow three times as much time for fire building as you'd need in dry conditions. If you're hiking, gather dry tinder as you go along the trail.

STEP 2 Look down when looking for tinder. Dry tinder may be under rocks, ledges, and logs, and in tree hollows. The underside of leaning deadfalls can be dry in a downpour; chop out chunks of good wood. Conifer stumps hold flammable resins.

STEP 3 Look up. Search for dry kindling and fuel off the wet ground. Fallen branches that are suspended in smaller trees will likely be rot-free. Locate a dense conifer and harvest the low, dead twigs and branches that die off as the tree grows. Shred the bark with your fingers.

STEP 4 Make what you can't find. Use a knife or hatchet blade to scrape away wet wood surfaces.

As the fire sustains itself (a), construct a crosshatched "log cabin" of wet wood around it (b) with a double-layered roof (c). The top layer of wood will deflect rain while the lower level dries. —T.E.N.

322 AIM A MAKESHIFT SIGNAL MIRROR

The best commercial signal mirrors are made with aiming devices. But there are ways to aim a jerry-rigged signal mirror—aluminum foil wrapped neatly around a playing card, or the shiny interior surface of an aluminum can—that can also attract attention.

FOR A MOVING TARGET

STEP 1 Hold the mirror in one hand and extend the other in front, fingers spread to form a V between your fingers and thumb.

STEP 2 Move your hand until the target rests in the V.

STEP 3 Angle the mirror so the reflected sunlight flashes through the V and directly onto the target.

FOR A STATIONARY TARGET

STEP 1 Drive an aiming stake chest-high into the ground, or choose a similar object such as a broken sapling or rock.

STEP 2 Stand so the target, the top of the aiming stake, and the signal mirror are in a straight line.

STEP 3 Move the mirror so the reflected sunlight flashes from the top of the aiming stake to the target. —T.E.N.

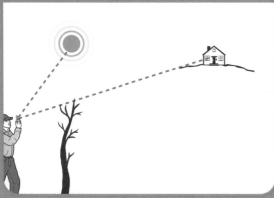

323
SPEAR FISH IN A FUNNEL TRAP

Make the walls of the funnel trap with piled-up stones or tightly spaced sticks driven solidly into the river or lakebed. Once fish are in the trap, close the entrance, roil the water, and either spear them or net them with a seine made by tying a shirt or other cloth between two stout poles. —K.M.

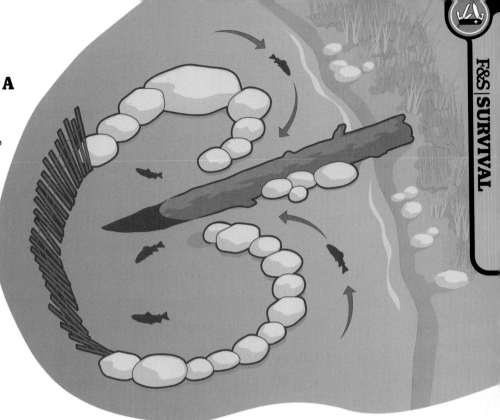

324
MAKE A TINDER BUNDLE

Fire making does not end with the birth of a red-hot coal, nor does a glowing char cloth ensure that you're going to get a flame. You must transfer the coal or char cloth to a bundle of fine tinder before blowing it into flame. Good sources include dried grasses; lichens (including old man's beard); shavings from the inner bark of aspen, poplar, and cottonwood trees (which burn even when wet); and windblown seed or fluff. The tinder bundle should be roughly the size of a softball and loosely formed to allow air circulation.

To blow the bundle into a flame, make a small pocket in the center. Tuck the glowing coal or char cloth into the pocket and then loosely fold the edges around it. Next, pick up the bundle and gently blow on it. Once it has burst into flame, place it under a tepee formation of small twigs and add larger pieces until you establish a strong fire. —K.M.

325 READ A BEAR'S MIND

A defensive bear (a) will appear stressed and unsure of how to act, pacing about and popping its jaws. Talk to it in a very calm voice. Don't throw anything. When it is not moving toward you, move away from it slowly and carefully. A stumble now could provoke a charge. If the bear continues to approach you, stop. Stand your ground and continue talking calmly. If the bear charges, use your spray or gun; wait until the last possible moment before hitting the dirt.

A predatory bear (b) isn't intent on rendering you harmless but rather on rendering you digestible. If a bear is aware of your presence and approaches in a nondefensive, unconcerned manner, get very serious. Speak to it in a loud, firm voice. Try to get out of the bear's direction of travel but do not run. If the animal follows, stop again and make a stand. Shout at the bear and stare at it. Make yourself appear larger—step up on a rock or move uphill. Prepare for a charge. —T.E.N.

326 BOIL WATER FOR SAFE DRINKING

Without chemicals or a filtering or purifying device, the only option for disinfecting water is to bring it to a boil. But how long to simmer plain ol' H_2O? Heat will kill bacteria, viruses, and parasites before the water reaches 212 degrees F, so once the liquid is roiling—and has cooled down a bit—it's safe to drink.

But there's more to the process than simply setting a pot on a fire or stove. First, bring a small amount of water to a rapid boil, swirl it around the pot to clean the sides, and pour it out. Refill the pot and bring the fresh batch to a roiling boil. Pour a quarter-cup on the ground to help sterilize the rim of the container and then fill water bottles as needed. And be sure you don't pour disinfected water back into the water bottle you used to dip the dirty stuff from the creek in the first place.

Boiling water removes much of its oxygen and gives it a flat taste, so add a drink flavoring agent or pour the water back and forth between two clean containers to aerate it as it cools. —T.E.N.

327 CARRY 50 FEET OF ROPE ON YOUR FEET

Real parachute cord is rated to 550 pounds. It's made of a tough outer sheath rated to 200 pounds, which protects seven interior strands, each rated to 50 pounds. Take apart a single 3-foot length of paracord, and you'll have almost 25 feet of cordage. Use it to rig shelters and snares, lash knife blades to spears, fix broken tent poles—you name it. If you replace both laces with paracord as soon as you buy a new pair of boots, you'll never be without a stash. Just make sure you buy the 550-pound-test cord. —T.E.N.

328 HURL A BACK-COUNTRY DEATHSTAR

Boomerang, schmoomerang. When you need to kill a rabbit, grouse, or squirrel with a stick, throw a backcountry deathstar. Cut two pieces of straight, wrist-thick hardwood about 2 to 3 feet long. Carve a notch in the middle of each stick and lash them tightly together with notches together. Sharpen each of the four points. Throw it sidearm for a whirling, slashing disk of death—or, in a survival situation, life. —T.E.N.

329 CREATE SMOKE IN THE MIDDLE OF THE OCEAN

Lose your motor miles from shore, and you'll need to attract attention in a big way. That means smoke on the water. Here's how to get noticed no matter where you are.

STEP 1 Grab a square throwable personal flotation device (PFD) or snap out a boat seat cushion. Tie a 10-foot line to one corner and tether the other end of the line to a downwind boat cleat.

STEP 2 Find something made of rubber that will hold a bit of fuel—a sneaker, dive fin, or foam drink insulator. Balance this item on the boat cushion or throwable PFD and siphon gas into it.

STEP 3 Light your signal fire and then use an oar or gaff to push it safely downwind from you. —T.E.N.

F&S Field Report: DEATH TRAP

Greenhill Rapids is a ¾-mile-long cauldron across the backbone of an esker, one of those weird rock formations created by the dragging fingers of a receding glacier. There's a dogleg turn in the middle and canoe-swamping pillow rocks all the way down. At low water it's too low, at high water it's crazy, and when the water is just right it is not to be taken lightly. We play it safe, portaging every bag, pack, and rod for a mile across hill and bog. Then Lee Bremer and Dusan Smetana slip into the river. Peter DeJong and I give them a half-hour to make it through the rapids, then we push off. When I lick my lips, my tongue is dry as toast.

We run the big upper drops cleanly, bashing through high rollers, then eddy out behind a midstream boulder. From here on out there are drops, rocks, and souse holes aplenty, but a straightforward line through the melee beckons. "A walk in the park," DeJong figures, nervously, as we guzzle a quart of water and congratulate ourselves on a textbook start.

That's when the wheels come off. I give the boat a strong forward stroke to reenter a hard current line but misjudge my downstream lean. The canoe responds by jerking violently to starboard. As I'm going over I get a glance at DeJong, high-bracing from the bow, but he knows the goose is cooked. In half a second we're both in the water, the boat between us, out of control.

For a couple of minutes it seems like no big deal. We roller-coaster for 300 yards, but then bigger boulders and nasty ledge drops appear. The canoe suddenly lurches to a stop, pinned against a truck-size rock. The current washes me past the canoe as I make a desperate grab for a gunwale. Upstream, DeJong slips over a ledge and bobs to the surface. My OK sign lets him know I'm unhurt, and he returns it with a grin.

Just then he slams into a subsurface boulder. He hits it hard, the kind of hard in which bones end up on the outside of skin and rescue operations commence. His grin morphs instantly into an O of pain. He slides over a hump of foaming water and comes to an instant stop, his body downstream, right leg pointing upcurrent. The look on DeJong's face is as alarming as his posture, one foot entrapped between rocks on the river bottom as the Missinaibi River pours over his shoulders.

Twenty yards downstream, I can do nothing but watch as he struggles to right himself and keep his head above water. If he loses purchase and his free leg slips, the current will sweep him downstream and break his leg, if it isn't broken already. DeJong strains against the river current, at times completely submerged as he tries to twist his leg out of the snare.

Suddenly he wrenches himself loose. Grimacing, he works across the river, and I gather a rescue rope in case he stumbles again. He makes it to the overturned canoe wild-eyed and panting, soaked and starting to chill. "I'm all right," he says. For a full minute neither of us speaks. "Strange way to catch a walleye, eh?" he says. We laugh the nervous laugh of a couple of guys who know they've dodged a bullet.

—T. Edward Nickens
Field & Stream, "Walleyes Gone Wild," May 2006

330 DRINK SNOW

Snacking on snow is fine until you're in a survival situation, when stuffing your face full of snow will consume critical energy reserves. To convert water from a frozen to a liquid state, choose ice over snow if possible, for it often contains fewer foreign objects that can carry pathogens, and ice will convert to more water than an equal volume of snow. Here are three ways to fill your water bottle from the hard stuff.

WATER MACHINE To melt snow or ice, snip a pea-size hole in the bottom corner of a T-shirt, pillowcase, or other makeshift fabric bag. Pack the bag with snow and hang it near a fire. Place a container under the hole to catch water melted by radiant heat. To keep the fabric from burning, refill the bag as the snow or ice melts.

FLAME ON Avoid scorching the pot—which will give the water a burned taste—by heating a small amount of "starter water" before adding snow or ice. Place the pot over a low flame or just a few coals and agitate frequently.

BODY HEAT You may have no other option than to use body heat to melt the snow. If so, put small quantities of snow or ice in a waterproof container and then place the container between layers of clothing next to your body— but not against your skin. A soft plastic bag works better than a hard-shell canteen. Shake the container often to speed up the process. —T.E.N.

331 START A FIRE WITH BINOCULARS

It's not easy, but it's not impossible. And if it has come down to this, you're probably running out of options, so there's no harm in giving it a shot.

STEP 1 Disassemble the binoculars and remove one convex objective lens. Gather tinder, a stick to hold the tinder, some kindling, and a Y-shaped twig to hold the lens in place.

STEP 2 Arrange the tinder on the end of the small stick and put this on the ground. Having the tinder slightly elevated will increase airflow and flammability, and having it on the stick will allow you to move it to the area where the sun's rays are most concentrated.

STEP 3 Drive the Y-shaped stick into the ground and settle the lens inside its fork—carving some grooves will help. Focus the smallest point of intensified sunlight onto the tinder. It is critical that this focused beam not wobble. Once the tinder smolders, blow gently, and have larger twigs ready to light. —T.E.N.

332 SURVIVE ON ACORNS

Stick with acorns from the white oak family (white oak, chestnut oak, bur oak), which have less tannin than red oak nuts. Cull any nuts with a tiny hole in the husk—this is made by an acorn weevil. Remove the cap and shell the rest with a knife or pliers from a multitool.

THE EASY WAY TO EAT ACORNS

To leach out the tannins, tie the nuts in a T-shirt. Submerge it in a running stream for several hours. Taste occasionally to test for bitterness. Or boil the nuts, changing the water frequently until it runs fairly clear. Then roast near a fire. Eat as is or grind into flour.

THE HARD WAY TO EAT ACORNS

Grind or pound shelled acorns, then mix with enough water to create a paste. Place a clean cloth in a wire sieve, scoop the acorn mush on top, and run fresh cold water over the mixture, squeezing water through the mush and out through the sieve. Taste occasionally, until the bitterness is removed. Use as a coarse meal like grits, or pound it into finer flour.

—T.E.N.

333 SURVIVE A FALL OVERBOARD

More than 200 sportsmen drown or succumb to hypothermia in boating accidents each year; most deaths occur when the boat capsizes or the sportsman falls overboard. Statistically, no other hunting or fishing activity has a higher fatality rate. Here's how to protect yourself.

THE CAPISTRANO FLIP

Because cold water conducts heat from the body much more rapidly than air, it's vitally important that you get out of the water. Canoes and narrow-beam boats can often be righted by a maneuver called the Capistrano flip. Turn your boat completely over (1) and then duck into the pocket of air trapped beneath it (2). Hold the gunwales at the center of the boat. If there are two of you, face each other a couple of feet apart. Lift one edge slightly out of the water. Then scissor-kick, push to break the boat free of the surface, and flip it upright over that lifted edge (3). —K.M.

334 BEAT BLISTERS WITH DUCT TAPE

STEP 1 Drain the blister with a sterilized needle or knife tip. Insert the tip into the base of the blister, then press out the fluid. Keep the flap of skin intact.

STEP 2 Cut a hole slightly larger than the blister in some pliable cloth. Put a second layer on top and seal this "doughnut bandage" to your foot with duct tape. No duct tape? Then there's little hope for you to begin with. —T.E.N.

FIELD & STREAM-APPROVED KNOT #13

335 TIE A HUNTER'S BEND

Unlike most knots, the hunter's bend is relatively new, invented only in the 20th century. It's perfect for joining two ropes, of either equal or dissimilar diameters, which makes it perfect for survival situations when odd scraps of cordage might be all you have at hand. And it's a great knot to use with slick synthetic ropes. —T.E.N.

1 Lay the two lines side by side, with tag ends in opposite directions.

2 Loop the lines, making sure neither rope twists on top of the other.

Keep lines from twisting.

3 Bring the front working end around behind the loops and up through the center.

Pull.

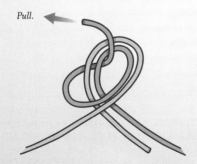

4 Push the rear working end through the middle of both loops.

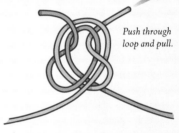

Push through loop and pull.

5 Seat the knot by holding the standing parts firmly and pulling both working ends. Pull the standing parts in opposite directions.

Pull both ends to set knot.

336 UPGRADE YOUR SURVIVAL KIT

Every personal survival kit should contain the fundamentals—waterproof matches, whistle, compass, knife, water-purifying tablets, a small flashlight. Think you have all your bases covered? See if you have room for a few of these low-volume lifesavers. —T.E.N.

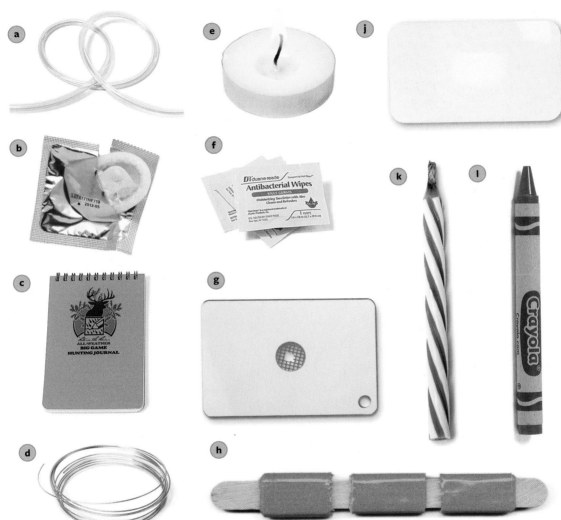

(A) SURGICAL TUBING Use it as a straw to suck water from shallow seeps, as a tourniquet, or as a means to blow a spark to flame.
(B) UNLUBRICATED CONDOM The best emergency canteen there is. **(C) WATERPROOF PAPER** Leave a note for rescuers—even in a howling blizzard. **(D) WIRE** If you can't think of 10 ways to use this, you're not an outdoorsman to begin with. **(E) TEA LIGHT CANDLE** The longer-burning flame will light wet wood. **(F) ANTIBACTERIAL WIPES** Stave off infection with a single-use packet. **(G) SIGNAL MIRROR** On a clear day, a strong flash can be seen from 10 miles away. **(h) BLAZE ORANGE DUCT TAPE WOUND AROUND A TONGUE DEPRESSOR** Tear off 1-inch strips of tape to use as fire starters or route markers. Shave wood with your knife to use as tinder. **(I) SMALL PHOTO OF LOVED ONES** Thinking of family and friends helps keep survival instincts strong. **(J) FRESNEL LENS** The size of a credit card, this clear lens will start a fire using sunlight. **(K) TRICK BIRTHDAY CANDLES** The wind can't blow them out. **(L) RED CRAYON** Mark trees as you move. You can also use the crayon as a fire starter.

337 MAKE A BLOWGUN

Drop your squirrel rifle in the river? It's time to channel your inner aboriginal and hunt squirrels with a blowgun and darts fletched with thistle.

STEP 1
Cut a piece of river cane 6 to 8 feet long. If necessary, straighten it by heating the bent parts over a fire and bending until straight. Leave it to dry in the sun for a week.

STEP 2 To remove the solid joints, heat the end of a straight steel rod until it's red-hot and burn out the joints inside your cane. Repeat until the cane is hollow. Smooth the bore by wrapping the steel rod with sandpaper and sanding the interior joints smooth. The smoother the bore, the faster the dart will fly.

STEP 3 To make a dart (opposite page), whittle a hardwood shaft to about 12 inches long and 3/16 inch in diameter. Then, whittle a sharp point on one end.

STEP 4 Tie a 2-foot string to the dart's blunt end. Hold a bundle of bull thistle or cotton against the blunt end, hold the end of the string taut in your mouth, and roll the dart shaft so that the thistle or cotton is held tight to the shaft but is still fluffy enough to form a fletching larger than the inside diameter of the blowgun. Tie off the string. —T.E.N.

338 USE SUPERGLUE TO CLOSE A WOUND

So-called "superglues" were used in the Vietnam War to close wounds and stem bleeding. Dermabond, a medical formulation, is a slightly different composition that minimizes skin irritation, but as many an outdoorsman will attest, plain ol' superglue will hold a cut together better than a strip bandage, and instances of irritation are rare. If you're stuck in the backcountry with no other way to close a wound, this will get you through until you can get to a doctor. Always use an unopened tube of glue. Clean the cut and pinch it shut. Dab a drop or two of superglue directly on the incision and then spread it along the length of the cut with something clean. The bandage is watertight and will seal out infecting agents. —T.E.N.

339 RESET A DISLOCATED SHOULDER

You wrench your arm out of its socket while taking a nasty fall, or your buddy screams in pain while hoisting a deer into the truck. If you're far from a hospital, try this method for resetting a dislocated shoulder in the backcountry.

STEP 1 Create a weight of approximately 7 to 10 pounds with a rock or stuff sack full of sand or pebbles.

STEP 2 Have the victim lie face down on a rock, large log, or upside-down boat and get as comfortable as possible. Drape the affected arm over the makeshift gurney's edge so it hangs free at a 90-degree angle. Tie the weight to the wrist of the affected shoulder, being careful not to cut off blood circulation. As the weight pulls on the arm, muscles will relax and the shoulder will relocate. This could take 30 minutes. —T.E.N.

340 MAKE A FIRE BED

It's cold enough to freeze whiskey, and you're stuck in the woods sans a sleeping bag? Make like a pot roast and construct a life-saving fire bed. Scrape out a gravelike trench in the dirt about 1 foot wide and 8 inches deep. Line it with very dry, egg-size to fist-size stones, if available. (Wet rocks from a stream or lake can explode when heated.)

Next, burn a hot fire into coals and spread a layer in the trench. Cover with at least 4 inches of dirt and tamp down with your boot. Wait one hour. If the ground warms in less than an hour, add more dirt. Now spread out a ground sheet of canvas, plastic, or spare clothing. Check the area twice for loose coals that could ignite your makeshift mattress. Ease onto your fire bed and snooze away. —T.E.N.

Tinder ignites as temperature rises.

341 MAKE A FIRE PLOUGH

This produces its own tinder by pushing out particles of wood ahead of the friction. Cut a groove in the softwood fireboard, then plough or rub the tip of a slightly harder shaft up and down the groove. The friction will push out dusty particles of the fireboard, which will ignite as the temperature increases. —K.M.

342 DRINK YOUR OWN URINE

Aron Ralston, the climber who amputated his arm with a pocketknife when he was pinned under a boulder, sipped his own urine during his ordeal. And while no one can say for sure whether it kept him alive, it didn't kill him. (Although it eroded his gums and palate.) If you find yourself in such a desperate fix, here's how to sip safely.

STEP 1 Morning urine may have more concentrated salts and other undesirable compounds. Avoid drinking this batch.

STEP 2 Treat urine with a water filter if available.

STEP 3 Take small sips.

—T.E.N.

343 TAKE A BACK BEARING

The reading from a back bearing gives you a compass direction to follow to return to your starting position. More important, it can correct lateral drift off of your intended direction of travel, which is what occurs each time an obstacle forces you to move off your intended line. Once you have your forward bearing, turn around 180 degrees and take a back bearing. (Say you're moving in a direction of travel of 45 degrees, or northeast. Your back bearing would be 225 degrees.) As you move toward your destination, occasionally turn around and point the direction of travel arrow on your compass back to your last location. The white end of the compass needle should point there. If not, regain the correct line by moving until the needle lines up. —T.E.N.

344 START A FIRE

BURNING SENSATIONS Always have a couple of these D.I.Y. options on hand.
—T.E.N.

DUCT TAPE A fist-size ball of loosely wadded duct tape is easy to light and will burn long enough to dry out tinder and kindling.

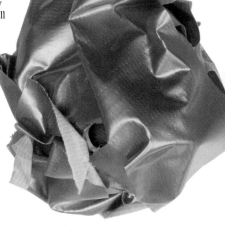

INNER TUBE Three-inch strips or squares of bicycle inner tube burn with a rank, smoky flame hot enough to dry small kindling. No bike? Try the rubber squares in a wader-patch kit (don't forget the flammable patch glue) or a slice from a boot insole.

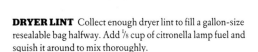

EGG CARTON AND SAWDUST Stuff each opening in a cardboard egg carton about half full of sawdust (collect this from your local school wood shop) and then add melted paraffin wax. Mix, let cool, and break apart.

EMERGENCY FLARE Cut a 2- to 4-inch section from an emergency road flare and seal the end with wax. It's easily lit even with wet gloves on.

DRYER LINT Collect enough dryer lint to fill a gallon-size resealable bag halfway. Add ⅛ cup of citronella lamp fuel and squish it around to mix thoroughly.

COTTON BALLS AND PETROLEUM JELLY It's a Boy Scout standby because it works. Stuff petroleum jelly–soaked cotton balls into a film canister or waterproof pill bottle and you have several minutes of open flame at the ready.

NATURAL WONDERS Learn to identify and gather natural tinder in your neck of the woods.

SPANISH MOSS Not a moist moss, at all, but an epiphytic, or "air plant," Spanish moss is a great tinder. But don't carry it around; it's notorious for harboring chiggers.

CEDAR BARK Common cedar bark should be worked over with a rock to smash the fibers. Pull the strands apart with your fingers, and roll the material back and forth between your hands.

BIRCH BARK The flammable oils in the papery bark of birches make this a time-tested fire catcher. Strip ribbons of bark from downed trees; it works just as well as bark from live ones.

SAGEBRUSH BARK Pound strips of bark with a rock and then shred them between your palms and fashion a tinder basket.

CATTAIL FLUFF The cottony interior of a cattail spike can be fluffed into a spark-catching blaze. Have more tinder nearby, because cattail fluff burns out quickly.

TINDER FUNGUS In northern areas, look for bulbous blotches of blackish wood on live birch trees. The inside of the fungus, which is reddish-brown, easily catches a spark. Crumble it for a quick start to a fire or use chunks of it to keep a coal alive.

PUNK WOOD Rotten, dry wood will flame up with just a few sparks. Use a knife blade held at 90 degrees to file off punk dust, and have larger pieces handy to transfer the sparks to larger punk wood that will burn with a coal. —T.E.N.

345 SKIN AND COOK A SNAKE

Mr. No Shoulders might give you the willies, but a hot meal of snake meat might also give you enough energy to make it back to civilization. This should be a last resort, as some of these creatures are protected.

STEP 1 Cut off the snake's head. Insert the knife tip into the anal vent and run the blade all the way up the belly.

STEP 2 Free a section of the skin. Grasp the snake in one hand, the freed skin section in the other, and pull apart.

STEP 3 Remove all of the entrails, which lie along the base of the spine.

STEP 4 Chop into bite-size pieces. Fry or boil. —T.E.N.

346 NAVIGATE BY DELIBERATE OFFSET

Say you climb a big hill to glass prime elk country. Now you have to bushwhack back, and even though it's no big deal to find the trail, moving in a straight line will be difficult. So, which way do you turn on the lakeshore or trail to find your original location?

Figure it out by using deliberate offset: Add or subtract about 10 degrees to your required compass bearing. Each degree of offset will move your arrival about 20 yards to the right or left for every 1,000 yards traveled. Hoof it back to the trail, and you'll know that you're off to one side. No guesswork. Make the turn. —T.E.N.

347 BUILD A FIRE ON SNOW

Go through the ice, over the bow, or into a blizzard and you'll need a fire—fast and before your fleece and fingers freeze. Let's assume you're not a complete moron: You have a workable lighter. Here's how to spark an inferno no matter how much snow is on the ground.

STEP 1 Start busting brush. You'll need a two-layer fire platform of green, wrist-thick (or larger) branches to raft your blaze above deep snow cover. Lay down a row of 3-foot-long branches and then another perpendicular row on top. Stay away from overhanging boughs; rising heat will melt snow trapped in foliage.

STEP 2 Lay out the fuel and don't scrimp on this step.

Collect and organize plenty of dry tinder and kindling and twice as many large branches as you think you'll need. Super-dry tinder is critical. Birch bark, pine needles, wood shavings, pitch splinters, cattail fluff, and the dead, dry twigs from the sheltered lower branches of conifers are standards. Place tinder between your hands and rub vigorously to shred the material. You'll need a nest as least as large as a Ping-Pong ball. Pouring rain and snow? Think creatively: dollar bills, pocket lint, fuzzy wool, and a snipped piece of shirt fabric will work.

STEP 3 Plan the fire so it dries out wet wood as it burns. Place a large branch or dry rock across the back of the fire and arrange wet wood across the fire a few inches above the flame. Don't crisscross; laying the wood parallel will aid the drying process. —T.E.N.

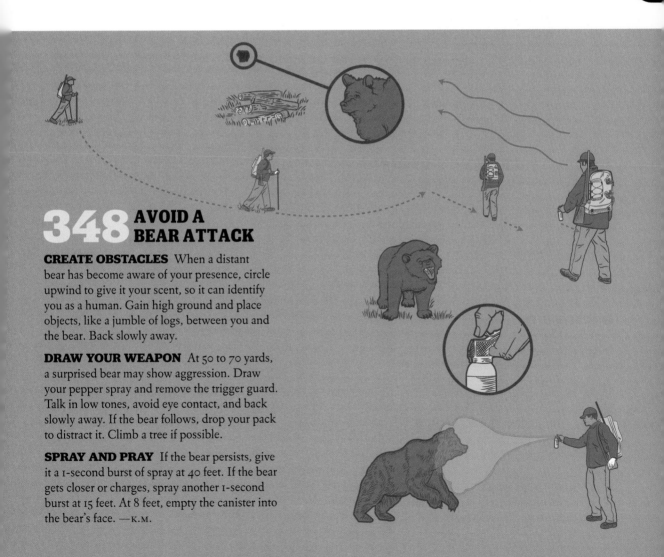

348 AVOID A BEAR ATTACK

CREATE OBSTACLES When a distant bear has become aware of your presence, circle upwind to give it your scent, so it can identify you as a human. Gain high ground and place objects, like a jumble of logs, between you and the bear. Back slowly away.

DRAW YOUR WEAPON At 50 to 70 yards, a surprised bear may show aggression. Draw your pepper spray and remove the trigger guard. Talk in low tones, avoid eye contact, and back slowly away. If the bear follows, drop your pack to distract it. Climb a tree if possible.

SPRAY AND PRAY If the bear persists, give it a 1-second burst of spray at 40 feet. If the bear gets closer or charges, spray another 1-second burst at 15 feet. At 8 feet, empty the canister into the bear's face. —K.M.

349 ATTRACT RESCUERS WITH SMOKE

A large plume of smoke can attract rescue attention better than any other method. Two basics: Unless you have plenty of energy and fuel, don't waste either maintaining a signal fire. Keep three fires ready to light when you spot a rescue plane. But don't waste matches trying to light a signal fire with a single match. Instead, ignite a longer-burning super-match. Look around: soda straws, plastic spoons, strips of rubber, and twists of duct tape all burn long and hot. Once lit, bring this super-match to bear on the signal fires.

Black smoke is usually better than white because it won't be mistaken for a campfire. Test green vegetation to make sure it produces plenty of smoke. To really pour out dark, billowing plumes, feed your blaze with anything petroleum-based: tires, oily rags, truck floor mats, and boat cushions.

White smoke is often more visible in country full of conifers. Feed wet foliage into the fire to produce white smoke. To make a large, billowing plume, build a big fire, and then nearly smother it with wet leaves or grass.

Try to build your fire in an opening where it can be seen easily from the air. —T.E.N.

350 SWIM WITH YOUR CLOTHES ON

The best strategy for drown-proofing is to stay with your boat. But what if your boat sinks at 4 AM and you go overboard with no hope of help? The best swimming stroke for survival is the breast stroke. It's the only stroke that provides forward vision, which keeps panic at bay, and relies on leg power, which will keep you moving much longer than crawl and side strokes. Here's how:

JUST SWIM! People drown trying to get their shoes off. A breast stroke remains efficient even when you're wearing bulky clothing. Keep your clothes on, roll over on your stomach, and get moving.

MAINTAIN FORWARD MOMENTUM The best way to do this is with an efficient glide. After each pull with your arms, regain an arrow shape with hands one on top of the other, straight out in front, and legs straight behind. As your glide slows, begin the next pull. Try to get a good 3-second count from each glide.

TAILOR YOUR STROKE TO THE CONDITIONS
In cold water especially, take it easy. As long as you retain forward momentum, you won't sink. —T.E.N.

351 BUILD A ONE-MATCH FIRE WHEN YOUR LIFE DEPENDS ON IT

If things are so bad that you're down to one match, then it's no time for you to be taking chances. The secret to last-chance fire building is attention to detail long before the match comes out of your pocket.

STEP 1 Begin with tinder. Collect three times as much as you think you'll need; don't stop looking until you have a double handful. Shred it well; what you're going for is a fiberlike consistency.

Conifer pitch, pine needles, cedar bark, birch bark, and dry bulrushes all make excellent natural tinder. Lots of other common items make good fire-starting material, too. Turn your pockets inside out to look for lint or candy bar wrappers. Duct tape burns like crazy; maybe there's a strip stuck to your gun case. Wader patch glue and plastic arrow fletching will work, too. The more variety you have, the longer the burn.

STEP 2 Gather twice as much kindling as you think you're going to need, and separate it into piles of like-size pieces. If you have to stop what you're doing and fumble for a pencil-size piece of pine at the wrong moment, your fire will go up in smoke. Your piles should consist pieces the diameter of a red wiggler, of a .22 cartridge, and of a 20-gauge shell. Use a knife to fuzz up the outer edges of a few sticks for a quicker catch.

STEP 3 Start small. Use two-thirds of your tinder to begin with and save the other third in case you need a second try with the dying embers of your first shot. Arrangement is important: You want to be able to get your match head near the bottom of the pile, and you also want to ensure that the slightest breeze pushes emerging flames toward your materials. Blow gently and feed only the fast-burning flames. —T.E.N.

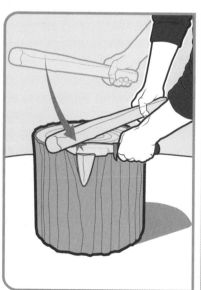

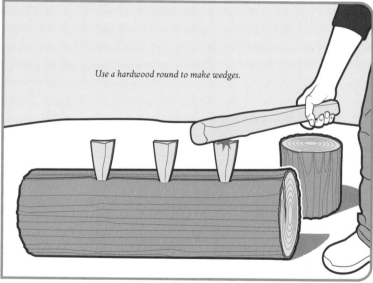

Use a hardwood round to make wedges.

352 SPLIT A LOG WITH A KNIFE

A knife is no replacement for an axe when it comes to rendering firewood. Still, you can use a hunting knife to expose the dry interior of a damp log by pounding the back of the blade with a wood baton.

Make several shingles this way, splitting thin, U-shaped wooden slices from the side of a round of firewood. Angle the edges of the shingles to make wedges and then insert the wedges into an existing lengthwise crack in a log. (If there isn't one, create one with your blade.) Hammer the wedges with a wood baton to split the log end-to-end and expose more surface for burning. —K.M.

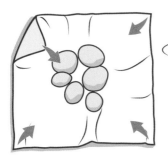

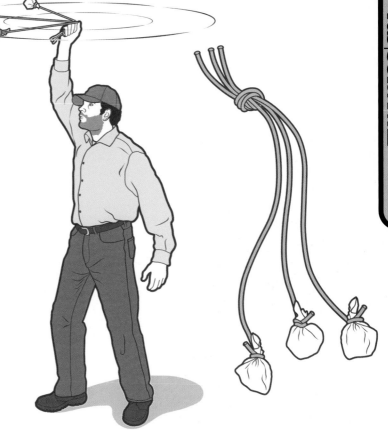

353 FLING A BOLA

Hey, if David took down Goliath with a single stone, you ought to be able to collect some meat with three handfuls of rocks and some parachute cord.

STEP 1 Tie the ends of three 40-inch lengths of parachute cord (or other 3/8-inch roping) together with an overhand knot. Secure a small pouch of rocks to each free end.

STEP 2 Take hold of the bola by the knot, twirl it over your head, and chuck this messenger of death into a flock of low-flying ducks, ptarmigan, or other, similar birds. —T.E.N.

354 EAT ROADKILL

If you make it to a road, rescue is likely just around the corner. If not, however, even the least-traveled highways can serve as a buffet for the feral forager. To separate plate-worthy roadkill from vulture food, follow these guidelines:

BODY CHECK Look for critters that have been clipped and tossed to the side of the road. If you have to use a flat shovel to retrieve your prize, well. . . .

SMELL TEST Any hunter knows what fresh dead meat smells like. Give the carcass a good sniff.

CLOUDY EYES Pass it up; it's been dead awhile.

FLEA CHECK If you find maggots, keep it out of your shopping cart. Fleas and ticks, however, are a good indicator of a fresh kill. —T.E.N.

355 TRACK BACK WITH A GPS UNIT

Most people treat a GPS like a digital toaster with a 100-page instruction manual—they use it only for the most basic tasks it's capable of. The track-log and track-back functions of most popular GPS units, however, are just the ticket for outdoorsmen who want to figure out how to return to a truck or cabin from a distant tree stand or duck blind. Here's how it works.

STEP 1 Turn on the GPS unit, leave it on, and leave it out where it can get a clear signal.

STEP 2 Activate the unit's track-log function. (Look for a menu choice called "Tracks" or "Trails.") Don't customize the settings, such as choosing how often the unit plots a waypoint. These will already be preset to monitor your rate of movement and lay down electronic crumbs at just the right time.

STEP 3 At your final destination, stop the track log and store and name the track before powering off. You can now easily follow that track back the way you came with your unit's return feature, or even download it to GPS mapping software. —T.E.N.

356 MAKE A BOW DRILL

Of all the friction fire-starting methods, the bow drill is the most efficient at maintaining the speed and pressure needed to produce a coal and the easiest to master. The combination of the right fireboard and spindle is the key to success, so experiment with different dry softwoods until you find a set that produces. Remember that the drill must be as hard as or slightly harder than the fireboard.

STEP 1 Cut a notch at the edge of a round impression bored into the fireboard, as you would for a hand drill. Loosely affix the string to a stick bow, which can be any stout wood.

STEP 2 Place the end of a wood drill about the diameter of your thumb into the round impression. Bear down on the drill with a socket (a wood block or stone with a hollow ground into it), catch the drill in a loop of the bowstring, and then vigorously saw back and forth until the friction of the spinning drill produces a coal.

STEP 3 Drop the glowing coal into a bird's nest of fine tinder, lift the nest in your cupped hands, and lightly blow until it catches fire. —K.M.

357 BE A BACKCOUNTRY DENTIST

Lose a filling in the backcountry and you might wish you were dead. Make a dental first-aid kit with dental floss, dental wax, cotton pellets, a temporary filling material such as Tempanol, oil of cloves, and a tiny pair of tweezers. To replace a filling, put a few drops of oil of cloves (be careful; it can burn) on a cotton pellet. Use tweezers to place the medicated cotton in the hole, then tamp down with a blade from a multitool. Cover it with the temporary filling material. —T.E.N.

358 SURVIVE A FRIGID DUNKING

An adult has a 50-50 chance of surviving for 50 minutes in 50-degree F water. In some parts of the United States and Canada, that's summertime water temperature. Go overboard in frigid water, and your first challenge is to live long enough to worry about hypothermia.

COLD SHOCK Hit cold water quickly and your body takes an involuntary few gasps of breath followed by up to three minutes of hyperventilation. You can literally drown while floating, before you have the chance to freeze to death. Keep your face out of the water. Turn away from waves and spray. If you're not wearing a personal flotation device (PFD), float on your back until you catch your breath. Don't panic. Cold shock passes after a minute or two. Only then can you plot your next steps.

HYPOTHERMIA The more of your body that you can manage to get out of the water, the better. Crawl up on anything that floats. Also, the more you flail around, the more your body will actually cool off. Unless you plan to swim to safety, stay still.

HELP Assume the heat-escape-lessening posture, also known as HELP. Hold your arms across your chest, with your upper arms pressed firmly against your sides; and your legs pulled up as far toward your chest as you can. This buffers the core areas of your chest, armpits, and groin. Remember that you can also lose a lot of body heat through your head, so try and find your hat if at all possible. The ultimate decision is whether to float or swim. Your ability to swim is severely hampered in cold water. Swimming increases the rate of heat loss up to 50 percent. It should be considered a last resort for rescue.
—T.E.N.

359 MAKE A TRAP OR DIE TRYING

Compared to the hours of energy expended while foraging or hunting in a survival situation, traps take little time to set, and, unlike firearms or fishing rods, they work for you while you sleep. But to trap animals with enough regularity to feed yourself, you need to heed these three principles as you set up.

1. LOCATION Rabbits, muskrats, groundhogs, and other animals make distinct trails that they use over and over. These trails are the best places to set traps, but they can be difficult to see in bright sunlight. Search for them early or late in the day when the shadows that define them are growing longer.

2. DIRECTION Where possible, narrow an existing trail—by brushing vegetation or driving a couple of small sticks into the ground—to direct the animal into the trap, or place a horizontal stick at the top of the snare so that the animal must duck slightly, ensuring that its head will go right into the noose.

3. SIZE Scale your trap correctly for what you're trying to catch. As a rule, the noose should be one and a half times the diameter of the head of the animal you wish to capture and made of material that will break should you inadvertently snare, say, a cougar's foot.

The most important tool you can carry if you're planning on catching your dinner is a spool of snare wire (26 gauge will be about right for all-purpose small-game snares; use 28 gauge for squirrels, 24 or heavier for beaver-size animals). Soft single-strand wire is superior to nylon monofilament because it holds its shape and game can't chew through it. You can also make snares from braided fishing superlines or 550 parachute cord, depending on the kind of trap you're making.

SQUIRREL SNARE

Make a small loop by wrapping the snare wire around a pencil-diameter stick twice and then turning the stick to twist the wire strands together. Pass the long wire end through the loop to form the snare (a). To build a squirrel snare, attach a series of small wire snares around a long stick propped against a tree (b). You can catch several squirrels at a time with this setup.

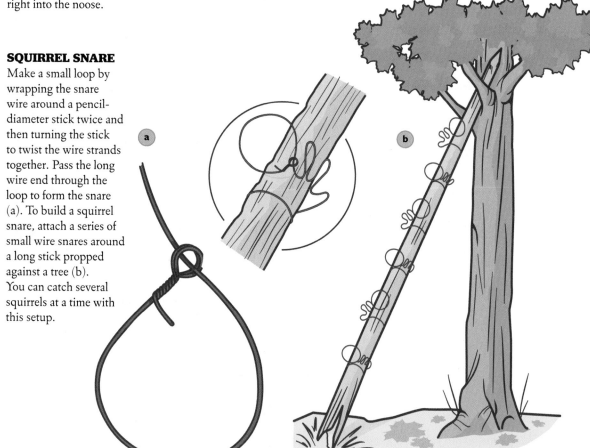

TWITCH-UP SNARE

Tie a small overhand loop knot in your parachute cord. Then fold the loop back on itself to form Mickey Mouse ears and weave the tag end through the ears (a). To build the twitch-up snare, use more cord to tie a spring pole or the branch of a small tree in tension (b). Set up a trigger mechanism like the one shown (c). When the animal's head goes through the loop, the trigger is released, and it snatches the animal into the air, out of reach of other predators. —K.M.

FIELD & STREAM CRAZY-GOOD GRUB

360 CHOKE DOWN BUGS

A fistful of bugs for dinner might seem a little crazy. And good? Not so much. But when the chips are down, this is the original MRE (meal, ready to eat), packed with enough nutritional punch to help get you through the night. The average grasshopper sports 20.6 grams of protein and 5 milligrams of iron—that's twice the iron and just 3 grams of protein less than a similar spoonful of lean ground beef. The FDA allows one rodent feces per sampling of popcorn. Wouldn't you rather eat a hopper?

START WITH THE LEGS Remove the grasshopper's legs to help control the bug and keep it from hanging up in your gullet. Some grasshopper gourmets remove the head by grasping the thorax and slowly pulling off the head. This pulls out much of the entrails, and the rest can be scraped away with a stick.

COOK BEFORE EATING Cooking is critical to kill internal parasites. Skewer insects on a thin stick and hold the stick over a fire, or roast the grasshoppers on a rock set close to the flame. A grasshopper is just like any other small piece of meat. In fact, once you get over the bug phobia, that's exactly what it is. —T.E.N.

361 STAY ON TOP OF THIN ICE

Crossing a frozen lake or pond, whether you're ice fishing or you're lost and trying to navigate back to camp, is one of the most dangerous outdoor activities. It's especially perilous in spring, when the ice pack is deteriorating and thickness alone is not an accurate gauge of safety. Here's how to travel safely.
—K.M.

Slushiness is a sign of a weakening pack; so is finding snow cover or water on top of ice. Depressions in the snow indicate a spring.

Stay away from inlet and outlet streams. Under-the-ice current can reduce ice strength by 20 percent or more.

Use your walking stick or ice chisel to test ice conditions.

Tow your equipment sled on a long rope. You can push it toward a victim who has fallen through.

Carry cutoff broom handles tipped with sharp nails and attached with 2 feet of cord. Dig them alternately into the ice to haul yourself out.

Cattails and other vegetation, as well as rocks and logs, conduct heat, weakening the ice.

Beware of black, gray, or milky ice. It lacks the strength of clear blue or green ice.

If you break through, face the ice you've already crossed. It will be stronger than ice in the direction of your fall. Crawl until you reach safe ice.

A 50-foot cord wrapped around an empty plastic jug makes a handy flotation device. Stand on sturdy ice and toss the jug to the victim.

Thin cracks may let you see whether the ice is thick or not.

Eroded shore ice is a sign of a thinning ice pack. Beware.

Ice sloping from a bank may trap air underneath, reducing its strength.

Pressure ridges are caused by fluctuating temperatures. Avoid them.

Open water is a red flag, pointing to a marginal ice pack nearer the shore.

362 NAVIGATE BY THE NIGHT SKY

The lost have turned their eyes upward for direction since long before man slew his first mammoth. Here is how the moon and stars can help you find your way home.

NORTH BY NORTH STAR

Polaris is the only star in the northern hemisphere that doesn't travel. It always points within 2 degrees of true north, making orientation simple. Locate the pointer stars on the bucket of the Big Dipper in Ursa Major. Observe the spacing between the two stars and then follow their direction five equal spaces to Polaris. You can also fix the position of Polaris, which is not a particularly bright star, using Cassiopeia.

DIRECTIONS BY MOONLIGHT

By noting when the moon rises, it's simple to tell east from west. When the moon rises before midnight, the illuminated side faces west. If it rises after midnight, the illuminated side faces east.

LET THE HUNTER BE YOUR GUIDE

During hunting season in the northern hemisphere, Orion can be found patrolling the southern horizon. This one is easy to spot because Orion rises due east and sets due west and the three horizontal stars that form his belt line up on an east-west line.

SIGHT ON A STAR

You can roughly calculate direction by noting the path of a star's travel (with the exception of Polaris, all stars rise in the east and set in the west). Face a star and drive a stick into the ground. Next back up 10 feet and drive in a second stick so that the two sticks line up pointing toward the star. If the star seems to fall after a few minutes, you are facing west; if it rises, you are facing east; if it curves to the right, you are facing south; if it curves to the left, you are facing north. Can't find a stick? Use the open sights on your rifle or the crosshairs of the scope to sight on the star and then track its movement by its deviation from the sights. —K.M.

363 DESCEND A CLIFF WITH A SINGLE ROPE

If you have to rappel down a cliff with a single rope, you won't get a second chance to do it right. Take notes.

CHOOSE AN ANCHOR POINT This can be a sturdy tree or rock outcrop near the edge of the precipice. Make sure the anchor point won't pinch the rope as you pull it down from below. Pass the rope around the anchor so that the two ends are even and meet the landing point with a few feet of extra rope.

WRAP YOUR BODY With your back to the cliff, straddle the double strand of rope. Pass it around your right hip and then across your chest and over your left shoulder. Grasp the ropes at your lower back with your right hand, and bring them around to your right hip. With your left hand, grasp the ropes in front at chest height.

DESCEND Keeping close to perpendicular to the cliff, walk down the precipice. Relax your grips periodically to slide down the rope. To arrest a swift descent, grip tightly with your right hand while pulling the rope to the front of your waist. At the bottom, retrieve the rope by pulling one end.

—T.E.N.

364 BREAK BIGGER BRANCHES

No axe, no saw, and here comes the bitter cold. In such a situation, knowing what to do can mean the difference between a cozy bivvy and a frigid one. The trick is to break unwieldy limbs of dead and downed trees into usable 18-inch sections When you need heartier fuel than what you can render by breaking a few branches across your knee, turn to these useful methods.

FIRE GIRDLE You can use your campfire to help you by digging a small trench radiating outward from the fire, then scraping hot coals into the trench to fill it. Place larger branches across the coals and rotate them. Once they are partially burned through, they will be easy to break.

TREE-CROTCH LEVER Find a sturdy tree crotch about waist high. Insert a dead tree branch into the crotch and push or pull the ends until the wood breaks. This is the quickest way to render dead branches up to 20 feet long into campfire-size chunks.

KNIFE NOTCH Cut a V-notch into one side of a branch, lean it against a tree trunk or place one end on top of a rock, and kick the branch at the notch.

TWO-MAN PUSH-PULL Two men can break a long branch into pieces by centering the branch on a sturdy tree and pushing or pulling against opposite ends. —T.E.N.

365 SPARK FIRE WITH A KNIFE

Use a high-carbon steel blade or scrounge up an axe head or steel file; stainless steel blades won't work. Find a hunk of hard stone. Besides flint, quartz, quartzite, and chert work well. The trick is to stay away from round rocks; you need one with a ridge sharp enough to peel minuscule slivers of metal from the steel. When they catch fire from friction, that's what causes the spark. Add highly flammable tinder. Start sparking.

STEP 1 Hold the stone with the sharp ridge on a horizontal plane extending from your hand. Depending on where the sparks land, hold a piece of char cloth, tinder fungus, dry grass bundle, or Vaseline-soaked cotton ball under your thumb and on top of the rock, or set the fire-starting material on the ground.

STEP 2 If you're using a fixed-blade knife or axe head, wrap the sharp edge with a piece of leather or cloth. With the back of the blade, strike the stone with a glancing, vertical blow. If the tinder is on the ground, aim the sparks down toward it.

STEP 3 Gently blow any embers or coals into a flame.
—T.E.N.

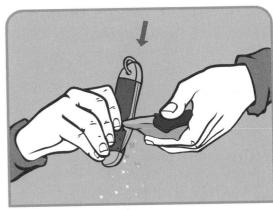

flint and knife blade

flint and file

flint and axe head

366 GET WATER FROM A TRANSPIRATION BAG

One of the quickest, easiest, and most effective ways of gathering emergency water in a vegetated environment is to mine the leaves of surrounding trees and bushes. It's a snap, and it can save your life.

Look for a leafy tree in bright sunshine. Place a small rock in a plastic bag, then shimmy the bag over a leafy limb. Be careful not to puncture the bag. Blow the bag up to create smooth surfaces for water condensation. Tie off the bag opening as tightly as possible. Work the rock down into the end of the bag so that one corner of the bag is lower than the ends of the limbs. As sunlight heats the bag and vegetation, evaporated water will condense on the bag's inner surface and drip into the lowest corner. Simply pour it out or insert a length of tubing or a hollow grass reed into the mouth of the bag so you can drain the collected water without removing the bag from the limb. Don't forget to purify water collected in the wild. —T.E.N.

367 TIE A WATER KNOT

You can repair blown webbing or make an emergency harness out of loose webbing with this never-say-die knot, the water knot.

STEP 1 Make an overhand knot in one end of the webbing.

STEP 2 With the second end of your webbing, follow the overhand knot backward through the knot. Make sure this second webbing does not cross over the first. Keep at least 3 inches of tail ends free.

STEP 3 Set the knot with your full weight against the webbing or in the harness. —T.E.N.

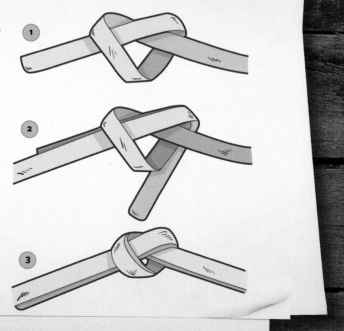

STEP 1 Drive sticks into the ground to outline an inner and outer circle. The diameter should be about half the poncho's width. Weave limbs, saplings, and other wood into a doughnut shape, using the stakes as a guide.

STEP 2 Secure the woven materials with whatever cordage is available—vines, peeled bark, bootlaces, strips from your shirt.

STEP 3 Place the brush raft on top of the poncho and put the hood on the inner side of the doughnut. Tie the neck with the drawstring so it won't let in water.

STEP 4 Draw the sides of the poncho up over the raft. Fasten to the brush via grommets or by tying cordage around small stones wrapped in the material.

368 BUILD A BRUSH RAFT TO CROSS A RAGING RIVER

You're thinking: "Build a survival raft? When will I ever need to do that?" So consider this: Not long ago, a hiker in New Mexico's Gila National Forest was trapped on the far side of the Gila River after it rose too high for her to wade back. She managed to survive five weeks before being rescued. In fact, crossing raging rivers is a survival situation outdoorsmen often face.

Here is an easy way to build a brush raft. It's designed to keep your gear dry while you swim and push it ahead of you. Though it's buoyant enough to keep you from drowning, it can't support your full weight. You'll need a poncho (or a tarp), which determines its size. Tie a rope to the raft to hold on to while crossing. —K.M.

F&S Field Report: TWO ALASKAS

The idea that there are two Alaskas came to me in a cold wave as my canoe was swept into the toppled trees and I was thrown overboard. I caught a glimpse of my pal, Scott Wood, sprinting toward me across an upstream gravel bar, knowing that this was what we had feared the most. Wood disappeared into the brush, running for my life, and then the river sucked me under, and I did not see anything else for what seemed like a very long time.

Every angler dreams of Alaska. My dream was of untouched waters, uncountable salmon and trout, and an unguided route through mountains and tundra. But day after day of portages and hairy paddling had suggested that mine was a trip to the other Alaska, a place that suffers no prettied-up pretense. The other Alaska is not in brochures. It is rarely in dreams. The other Alaska will kill you.

We'd had plenty of postcard moments, for sure: king salmon jetting rooster tails over gravel bars. Tundra hills pocked with snow. Monster rainbows and sockeye salmon heaving for oxygen as we held their sagging bellies. But day after day the four of us had paddled through the other Alaska, scared to death, except when the fishing was good enough to make us forget the fear.

Now the world turned black and cold as the Kipchuk River covered me, my head under water, my arm clamped around a submerged tree, my body pulled horizontal in the hurtling current. Lose my grip and the river would sweep me into a morass of more downed trees and roiling current, so I held on ever tighter as water filled my waders. The river felt like a living thing, attempting to swallow me, inch by inch, and all I could do was hold my breath and hang on.

I can't say how long I hung there, underwater. Twenty seconds, perhaps? Forty?

For long moments I knew I wouldn't make it. I pulled myself along the sunken trunk as the current whipped me back and forth. But the trunk grew larger and larger. It slipped from the grip of my right armpit, and then I held fast to a single branch, groping for the next with my other hand. I don't remember holding my breath. I don't remember the frigid water. I just remember that the thing that was swallowing me had its grip on my shins, then my knees, and then my thighs. For an odd few moments I heard a metallic ringing in my ears. A scene played across my brain: It was the telephone in my kitchen at home, and it was ringing, and Julie was walking through the house looking for the phone, and I suddenly knew that if she answered the call—was the phone on the coffee table? did the kids have it in the playroom?—that the voice on the other end of the line would be apologetic and sorrowful. Then the toe of my right wading boot dragged on something hard, and I stood up in the river, and I could breathe.

Wood crashed through the brush, wild-eyed, as I crawled up the river bank, heaving water. I waved him downstream, then clambered to my feet and started running. Somewhere below was my canoeing partner.

—T. Edward Nickens
Field & Stream, "The Descent," June 2007

369 FIND WATER IN THE DESERT

The old standby, a solar still, has fallen out of favor. Instead, search for water in the immediate area during the cooler hours of the day. First look in cracks and pockets in rocks and then dig into seep springs in side gullies. Then search for animal trails that converge—they will often lead to water sources. Find a high vantage point and glass for reflections in the desert that could indicate ranch pipelines or small stock ponds in the area. Truly desperate measures include wiping dew off a poncho or car hood. Such efforts may sound crazy, but every half-pint of water can buy you a few hours of lucid thought. —T.E.N.

370 SURVIVE IN FAST WATER

Maybe you fell out of your fishing boat, or maybe you slipped while wading the river. Either way, you're suddenly sucked downstream into a long, violent rapid. What do you do?

STEP 1 The safest way to ride a rapid is on your back, with your head pointed upstream, your feet pointing downstream, legs flexed, and toes just above the water's surface. Lift your head to watch ahead. Use your feet to bounce off rocks and logs.

STEP 2 Choking on water will unleash a panic reaction in even the most experienced swimmer. The surest way to avoid a sudden, massive gulp of water is to inhale in the troughs (low points) and exhale or hold your breath at the crests (tops) of the waves.

STEP 3 You will naturally look downstream to avoid obstacles, such as logjams, but don't forget to also scan the shoreline for calmer water, such as an eddy on the downstream side of a rock or river bend.

STEP 4 As the current carries you toward quieter water, paddle with your arms and kick with your legs to steer yourself toward shore. When you get close, roll onto your stomach and swim upstream at a 45-degree angle, which will ferry you to the bank. —K.M.

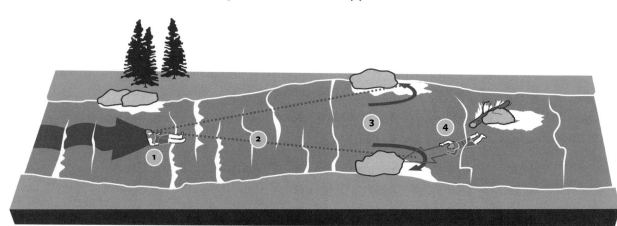

proper position

swim to eddy

371 SURVIVE A LIGHTNING STRIKE

There are lots of snappy sayings to help you remember lightning safety: When the thunder roars, get indoors! If you can see it, flee it! But what do you do when you're caught outdoors with almost nowhere to hide? Try this.

NEAR YOUR VEHICLE OR AN ENCLOSED STRUCTURE Get inside something—your car, a house, a barn. Open structures such as picnic shelters provide little to no protection.

OUT CAMPING Avoid open fields and ridgetops if camping during seasons when thunderstorms are prevalent. Stay away from tall, isolated trees, fence lines, and metal. Move into a lower stand of trees if possible; a tent provides no protection.

IN OPEN COUNTRY Avoid the high ground and points of contact with dissimilar objects, such as water and land, boulders and land, or single trees and land. Head for ditches, gullies, or low ground, and clumps of trees and shrubs of uniform height. Spread out: Group members should be at least 15 feet apart.

ON THE WATER Head inside a boat cabin, which offers a safer environment. Stay off the radio unless it is an emergency. Drop anchor and get as low in the boat as possible. If you're in a canoe on open water, get as low in the canoe as possible and as far as possible from any metal object. If shore only offers rocky crags and tall isolated trees, stay in the boat.

AT THE LAST MOMENT When your hair is standing on end, it's almost too late. Many experts believe that the "Lightning Crunch" provides little to no protection for direct or close strikes, but at this point, some action is better than nothing. Put your feet together and balance on the balls of your feet. Squat low, tuck your head, close your eyes, and cover your ears. —T.E.N.

372 CUT SAPLINGS FOR SHELTER

If you find yourself in need of a shelter, you can gather the wood to construct one by felling a tree. If you can bend a green sapling, you can cut it, but it helps if you bend the trunk back and forth several times to weaken the wood fibers before bringing your knife to bear on it. To cut a sapling, hold it bent with one hand and then press down on the outside of the curve with your knife blade angled slightly (a). Rock the blade as you cut, while maintaining steady downward pressure (b). Support the trunk as you work to keep it from splintering, which would make it difficult for you to finish the cut. —K.M.

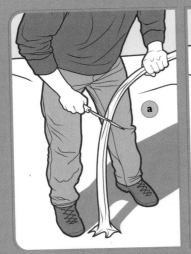

Bend the sapling to make the cut easier.   *Use straight downward force.*

373 PITCH A SURVIVAL CAMP

As a lost hunter or fisherman, your job is to make the search and rescue (SAR) team's job easier by staying put. But as you wait to be found, there are other things you should do to stay comfortable—and alive.

MIXED SIGNALS

1 Build a fire in an open area, such as a ridgetop. Stack green boughs beside it so you'll be ready to make a smoke signal to alert search aircraft.

2 Pack extra orange mesh hunting vests. Hang them from small trees or spread them on the snow, where they can be seen from a great distance.

3 Drag logs to construct an SOS sign with the sides of each letter at least 10 feet long.

4 Practice aiming your signal mirror so you can direct the flash when SAR aircraft appear. If you don't have a mirror, you can use a pot, a space blanket, or even a credit card.

When the SAR aircraft approaches, raise both hands to indicate that you need help. If you need medical care, lie down on your back with your arms stretched above your head.

THE ULTIMATE SHELTER

5 Pack a headlamp instead of a flashlight. It leaves your hands free to start the fire.

6 Gather a big pile of firewood to burn all night. Your supply should include wrist-diameter sticks, plus some 5-foot-long logs.

7 Night air flows downhill. Pitch your camp in a lee with the opening of your shelter parallel to the wind direction. That way, the shelter doesn't fill with smoke.

8 Pack a square cut from a closed-cell sleeping pad. It insulates you from cold ground. If you don't have a pad, sit on your pack.

9 Blow three whistle blasts at regular intervals to alert any nearby search teams.

10 Stay hydrated. A small titanium pot weighs less than an ounce and can be used to boil snow for safe drinking water.

WIND

11 If you don't have a tarp, one of the quickest shelters to build is a lean-to that uses a tree branch for the ridgepole. Break or saw branches for the framework and then lace smaller branches through the frame to make the shelter rigid.

12 Thatch the shelter with branches or pine boughs. Arrange them with tips pointing down to direct runoff. Tilt branches against the thatching to keep it in place.

13 Bank the lower sides of the lean-to with snow for insulation.

14 Once you build a fire, it's unnecessary to wrap up in your space blanket. Instead, tuck its edges into the shelter so the silver film forms a reflecting wall. It will provide warmth and cheery light.

15 Insulate your body from the ground and snow. Snap branch ends to make a bough bed at least 8 inches thick.

16 Place a retaining log across the shelter opening. It makes a comfortable seat and blocks the heat of the fire from melting the snow under the bough bed.

17 Use logs to build a wall in back of the fire, directing the fire's warmth toward your shelter.

18 Wet clothes quicken hypothermia. Hang your clothes by the fire to dry. —K.M.

BUILDING YOUR FIRE

If your hands are too cold to shave fuzz sticks or scrape bark for tinder, try getting your fire started with the following: tiny twigs (a), pine tips with rusted needles (b), and cut strips of a gamebag or your underwear (c), since cotton burns fiercely.

374

FIND A LOST PERSON

Lose a party member in the backcountry, and you shouldn't sit around until search and rescue arrives. Here's the drill for putting on your own manhunt while waiting for the pros.

PLOT THE POSITION

Mark a map with the letters PLS (for "point last seen") at the lost individual's last known position. Draw 3- and 6-mile radius circles around the PLS. Half of all lost persons will be found within the 3-mile circle, and 9 out of 10 within the 6-mile range. If the PLS is within a 10-minute walk, immediately hike there, yelling and whistling every 30 seconds.

CONTAIN THE DAMAGE

Make a list of likely high-traffic areas that the lost person might stumble across and send someone to mark the area with notes, day-packs, and directions back to camp.

USE YOUR HEAD

Get into the lost person's brain. Think of where he could have lost his way.

ESTABLISH SEARCH TEAMS

Make sure searchers have a way to navigate and communicate and then agree on specific times and locations for meeting up again. Send one team to the PLS and send the others to places identified as likely areas.

STOP AT NIGHT

If it's not a true emergency, suspend the search after dark.
—T.E.N.

RESOURCES

(a) Benchmade Activator +. www.benchmade.com
(b) Spyderco Gayle Bradley Carbon Fiber Folder. www.spyderco.com
(c) CRKT Big Eddy II. www.crkt.com
(d) Buck Special. www.buckknives.com
(e) Lone Wolf Trailmate. www.lonewolfknives.com
(f) DiamondBlade Pinnacle 1. www.diamondbladeknives.com
(g) Case Ridgeback. www.wrcase.com
(h) SOG Toothlock Black TiNi. www.sogknives.com

(a) Pinnacle Performa XT. www.pinnaclefishing.com
(b) Bass Pro Shops Pro Qualifier. www.basspro.com
(c) Redington Delta. www.redington.com

(a) Thompson/Center Encore Pro Hunter Turkey; www.tcarms.com
(b) Perazzi M Series. www.perazzi.com
(c) Beretta Silver Hawk. www.berettausa.com
(d) Browning BPS. www.browning.com
(e) Winchester Super X3. www.winchesterguns.com
(f) Ruger No. 1. www.ruger.com
(g) Kimber 84M. www.kimberamerica.com
(h) Mossberg 500. www.mossberg.com
(i) Marlin 308XLR. www.marlinfirearms.com
(j) Remington 597LS HB. www.remington.com
(k) Stag 7 Hunter. www.stagarms.com

(a) Heddon Spook. www.heddonlures.com
(b) Luhr Jensen Hot Lips. www.luhrjensen.com
(c) PowerBait HeavyWeight Thump Worm. www.berkley-fishing.com
(d) Rapala Original Floater. www.rapala.com
(e) Booyah Vibra-Flx. www.booyahbaits.com
(f) Mister Twister Curly Tail Grub. www.mistertwister.com
(g) Daredevle Spoon. www.eppinger.net
(h) Kalin's Triple Threat Grub. www.unclejosh.com
(i) Southern Pro Lit'l Hustler. www.southernpro.com
(j) Blue Fox Vibrax Spinner. www.bluefox.com
(k) Smithwick Rattlin' Rogue. www.smithwicklures.com

FIELD & STREAM

In every issue of *Field & Stream* you'll find a lot of stuff: beautiful photography and artwork, adventure stories, wild game recipes, humor, commentary, reviews, and more. That mix is what makes the magazine so great, what's helped it remain relevant since 1895. But at the heart of every issue are the skills. The tips that explain how to land a big trout, the tactics that help you shoot the deer of your life, the lessons that teach you how to survive a cold night outside—those are the stories that readers have come to expect from *Field & Stream*.

You'll find a ton of those skills in *The Total Outdoorsman Manual*, but there's not a book big enough to hold them all in one volume. Besides, whether you're new to hunting and fishing or an old pro, there's always more to learn. You can continue to expect *Field & Stream* to teach you those essential skills in every issue. Plus, there's all that other stuff in the magazine, too, which is pretty great. To order a subscription, visit www.fieldandstream.com/subscription.

FIELDANDSTREAM.COM

When *Field & Stream* readers aren't hunting or fishing, they kill hours (and hours) on www.fieldandstream.com. And once you visit the site, you'll understand why. First, if you enjoy the skills in this book, there's plenty more online—both within our extensive archives of stories from the writers featured here, as well as our network of 50,000-plus experts who can answer all of your questions about the outdoors.

At Fieldandstream.com, you'll get to explore the world's largest online destination for hunters and anglers. Our blogs, written by the leading experts in the outdoors, cover every facet of hunting and fishing and provide constant content that instructs, enlightens, and always entertains. Our collection of adventure videos contains footage that's almost as thrilling to watch as it is to experience for real. And our photo galleries include the best wildlife and outdoor photography you'll find anywhere. Perhaps best of all is the community you'll find at Fieldandstream.com. This is very much a place for the outdoorsman. It's where you can argue with other readers about the best whitetail cartridge or the perfect venison chili recipe. It's where you can share photos of the fish you catch and the game you shoot. It's where you can enter contests to win guns, gear, and other great prizes. And if you're not careful, it's a place where you can spend a lot of time. Which is OK. Just make sure to reserve some hours for the outdoors, too.

THE TOTAL OUTDOORSMAN CHALLENGE

So, you've finished the book. You've mastered all 374 skills. You're ready to take on the world—or at least the wild. Go for it. But you might also consider displaying your newly acquired skills in another arena: the Total Outdoorsman Challenge.

Since 2004, *Field & Stream* has ventured on an annual countrywide search for the nation's best all-around outdoorsman—the person who's equally competent with a rifle, shotgun, bow, rod, and paddle, the person who can do it all. And whoever proves he can do it all walks away with the Total Outdoorsman title, as well as tens of thousands of dollars in cash and prizes.

The Total Outdoorsman Challenge is about more than hunting and fishing, though. The event celebrates our belief that the more outdoor skills you have, the more fun you can have in the woods and on the water. It celebrates the friendships that can only happen between sportsmen—the type of bonds that inspire traditions and build hunting camps. Every year thousands of sportsmen compete in the Total Outdoorsman Challenge, and every year many of those competitors meet new hunting and fishing buddies.

So, now that you're ready, you should consider testing your skills in the Total Outdoorsman Challenge. (Visit www.totaloutdoorsmanchallenge.com to learn more about the event.) And if you're not sure you're quite ready, you can always read the book again.

INDEX

CONTRIBUTORS

T. Edward Nickens (T.E.N.) is Editor-at-Large of *Field & Stream* magazine. Known for do-it-yourself wilderness adventures and profiles about people and places where hunting and fishing are the heart and soul of a community, he has chased ptarmigan and char north of the Arctic Circle, antelope in Wyoming, and striped marlin from a kayak in Baja, California. He will not turn down any assignment that involves a paddle or a squirrel. Author of the magazine's "Total Outdoorsman" skills features, he also is host, writer, and co-producer for a number of *Field & Stream*'s television and Web shows, among them *The Total Outdoorsman Challenge* and *Heroes of Conservation*. Nickens has been a National Magazine Award finalist, and has won more than 30 writing awards, including three "Best of the Best" top honors awards from the Outdoor Writers Association of America. He lives in Raleigh, North Carolina, within striking distance of mountain trout, saltwater flyfishing, and a beloved 450-acre hunting lease that has been the cause of many a tardy slip for his two school-age children.

Anthony Licata (A.L.) is the Editor of *Field & Stream*, the world's leading outdoor magazine, fieldandstream.com, and all of *Field & Stream*'s television programming. Licata joined *Field & Stream* in 1998 as an Associate Editor, quickly moved through the ranks to Senior Editor in 2000, and was promoted to Editor in 2007. Licata, who is the 15th Editor in the 115-year history of the magazine, received recognition from the American Society of Magazine Editors in 2009 when *Field & Stream* won a National Magazine Award for General Excellence, the most prestigious award in all of magazine publishing. Licata has also served as the on-air host for the *Field & Stream Total Outdoorsman Challenge* television show and has appeared as a hunting and fishing authority on many national television and radio shows. A native of Dimock, Pennsylvania, Licata developed an early passion for hunting and fishing that he pursued with his father and brothers. He has hunted and fished across North America and in Europe and Africa, but his favorite activities are still bowhunting for whitetails at the family deer camp and fly fishing for trout in Pennsylvania spring creeks.

Phil Bourjaily (P.B.) sold his first outdoor story—on snipe hunting—to *Field & Stream* in 1985. Today, he is the magazine's Shotguns columnist and co-writer, with David Petzal, of "The Gun Nut" blog on Fieldandstream.com. He is the author of the *Field & Stream Turkey Hunting Handbook* and, as a turkey hunter, has renounced early mornings in favor of sleeping in and killing spring gobblers between the hours of 9 AM and 2 PM. A 1981 graduate of the University of Virginia, he makes his home today, with his wife and two sons, in his birthplace of Iowa City, Iowa. He has traveled widely in pursuit of upland birds, waterfowl, and turkeys, but his favorite hunts are for pheasants close to home with his German shorthaired pointer, Jed.

Kirk Deeter (K.D.) is an editor-at-large for *Field & Stream* and co-writer of the "Fly Talk" blog at Fieldandstream.com. Deeter is also the publisher and editor of *Angling Trade*, the trade magazine covering the flyfishing industry in North America. He is known for his "gonzo" story angles, from free-swimming Class IV rapids to flyfishing for mako sharks out of kayaks to fishing in the remote Bolivian jungle with natives in dugout canoes. Deeter has earned various awards, including "Excellence in Craft" top honors for his fishing and conservation stories from the Outdoor Writers Association of America. His most recent book, *The Little Red Book of Fly Fishing*, (co-written with Charlie Meyers), was released by Skyhorse Publishing in 2010. He lives with his wife, Sarah, and son, Paul, in Colorado.

Keith McCafferty (K.M.) writes the Survival and Outdoor Skills columns for *Field & Stream*, and contributes adventure narratives and how-to stories to both the magazine and Fieldandstream.com. McCafferty has been nominated for numerous National Magazine Awards over the years, most recently for his February 2007 cover story, "Survivor." McCafferty's assignments for *Field & Stream* have taken him as far as the jungles of India and as close to home as his back yard. McCafferty lives in Bozeman, Montana, with his wife, Gail. McCafferty loves to flyfish for steelhead in British Columbia and climb the Rockies in pursuit of bull elk.

John Merwin (J.M.) has been the primary author of *Field & Stream*'s fishing features and columns for the past 15 years. In 2008, he extended his angling expertise to Fieldandstream.com as the co-author of the fishing blog "The Honest Angler." Among other accolades, Merwin was nominated for a National Magazine Award for his story "*Field & Stream*'s Best of Summer Fishing," in the June 2008 issue. He is the former editor and publisher of both *Fly Rod & Reel* and *Fly-Tackle Dealer* magazines, as well as a former editor of *Fly Fisherman*. He served for several years as the executive director of the American Museum of Fly Fishing and has authored and edited a total of 15 books on angling, including the best-selling *Trailside Guide to Fly Fishing*. Merwin lives in Vermont with his wife, Martha.

David E. Petzal, (D.E.P.) the Rifles Field Editor of *Field & Stream*, has been with the publication since 1972. A graduate of Colgate University, he served in the US Army from 1963 to 1969, and he began writing about rifles and rifle shooting in 1964, during his service. He is a Benefactor Member of the National Rifle Association and a Life Member of the Amateur Trapshooting Association. He has hunted all over the United States and Canada, as well as in Europe, Africa, and New Zealand. Petzal wrote *The .22 Rifle* and edited *The Encyclopedia of Sporting Firearms*. In 2002, he was awarded the Leupold Jack Slack Writer of the Year Award, and in 2005 he received the Zeiss Outdoor Writer of the Year Award, making him the first person to win both.

Additional contributors: Joe Cermele, Bill Heavey, Peter B. Mathiesen, Tom Tiberio, and Slaton L. White

ACKNOWLEDGMENTS

From the Author, T. Edward Nickens
I would like to thank all of the talented people who made this book possible, including the *Field & Stream* staff editors who guided this project with great care and insight. *Field & Stream* field editors Phil Bourjaily, Keith McCafferty, John Merwin, and David E. Petzal, and editor-at-large Kirk Deeter, provided unmatched expertise. Just good enough is never good enough for them. I wish I could name all the guides, outfitters, and hunting, fishing, and camping companions I've enjoyed over the years. Every trip has been a graduate course in outdoor skills, and much of the knowledge within the covers of this book I've learned at the feet of others. And last, thanks to my longtime field partner, Scott Wood, who has pulled me out of many a bad spot, and whose skillful, detailed approach to hunting and fishing is an inspiration.

From *Field & Stream*'s Editor, Anthony Licata
I would like to thank Weldon Owen publisher Roger Shaw, executive editor Mariah Bear, and art director Iain Morris, who have put together a book filled with skills that have stood the test of time—in a package that should do the same. I'd also like to thank Eric Zinczenko, *Field & Stream* VP and Group Publisher, for championing the Total Outdoorsman concept in all its forms. This great collection of skills would not have been possible without the hard work of the entire *Field & Stream* team, and I'd particularly like to thank Art Director Sean Johnston, Photo Editor Amy Berkley, former Art Director Neil Jamieson, Executive Editor Mike Toth, Managing Editor Jean McKenna, Deputy Editor Jay Cassell, Senior Editor Colin Kearn, and Associate Editor Joe Cermele. I'd also like to thank Sid Evans for his role in creating the Total Outdoorsmen concept. Finally, I'd like to thank my father, Joseph Licata, who first brought me into the fields and streams and showed me what being a total outdoorsman really meant.

CREDITS

Photography courtesy of *Rick Adair:* 134, 161, 212, 234, 349 *Charles Alsheimer:* Hunting introduction (deer) *Barry and Cathy Beck:* 88, 109, 139, 148, 163 *Denver Bryan:* 204 *Bill Buckley:* contents (hunter on mountain), introduction (fisherman reeling, fisherman holding fish), Fishing introduction (fishermen catching fish), 154, 166, 215, 216 (turkey), 220, 265, 292, 296, 312, Survival introduction (hand holding compass) *Wally Eberhart:* 169 *Eric Engbretson:* 69, 106, 117 *Cliff Gardiner and John Keller:* 2, 5 (wire saw), 77, 124 (tube jig), 172, 225, 286, 324, 327, 328, 336 (a, c, d, f, k, l), 337, 344 (cedar bark, tinder fungus) *Google Earth:* 178 *Brian Grossenbacher:* foreword (fisherman casting), 78, 90, 153 *Brent Humphreys:* 18, 288 *iStock:* 38, 49, 175, 219, 256, 257, 274, 293, 342, 345, 358, imprint *Alexander Ivanov:* 37, 99, 150 (soft plastic, stickbait, spinnerbait, crank bait, surface lure), 177, 336 (g, j), 344 (duct tape, egg carton and sawdust, cotton balls and petroleum jelly, flare, tube, dryer lint, Spanish moss, birch bark, sagebrush bark, punk wood, cattail fluff) *Donald M. Jones:* introduction (elk), 199, 261, 269, 277, 297, 343 *Spencer Jones:* 5 (T-shirt, portable stove), 268 (cartridges) *Rich Kirchner:* 208 *Erika Larsen:* introduction (author and his children) *Anthony Licata:* foreword (photo of himself), 281 *Holly Lindem:* 270, 311 *Bill Lindner:* 133 *Minden Pictures/Chris Carey:* 73 *Neal and M.J. Mishler:* 221 *Pippa Morris:* 56, 66, 80 (gold ribbed hare's ear, black ant, popping bug, cricket, mini-tube spinner), 336 (h) *Ted Morrison:* 70, 150 (panfish), 162, 368 *Jay Nichols:* 131 *Jack Nickens:* 278 *T. Edward Nickens:* Camping introduction (cabin, hunter and child), 34, 67, 83, 93, 96, 179, 185, 233, 238, 287, 307, 308, F&S Field Report: Heart to Heart, 336 (i) *Travis Rathbone:* 22, 39, 46, 47, 60, 92, 147, 252, 317, 360 *Dan Saelinger:* contents (boots), Camping introduction (lantern), Fishing introduction (tackle box), 71, 102, 111, 114, 150 (walleye, pike, smallmouth, trout, striper), 158, 159, Hunting introduction (backpack), 194, 216 (box call), 236, Survival introduction (compass and dirt, hand holding match), 320 *Shutterstock:* 1, 8, 13, 16, 19, 24, 28, 29, 36, 44, 50, 58, 63, 80 (cricket, red wiggler), 104, 119, 124 (crayfish), 127, 142, 151, 180, 186, 187, 207, F&S Field Report: High Plains Showdown, 224, 229, 248, 267, 268 (animals), 280, 283, 294, 301, 303, Survival introduction (bear), 326, 329, 330, 332, 336 (b, e), 346, 354, 369, 371 *Dusan Smetana:* author photo on back cover, title page, introduction (author, hunters on horseback, pheasant), Camping introduction (tent), 42, Fishing introduction (fisherman on rocks, fishermen in boat, fisherman at dawn), 65, 115, 143, 144, 164, 171, Hunting introduction (elk, hunter), 183, 191, 202, 241, 250, 251, 273, 298, 316, Survival introduction (hunter and campfire), 365, 374 *Greg Sweney:* 197 *Mark Weiss:* 314

Illustrations courtesy of *Conor Buckley:* 70, 221, 239, 268 *flyingchilli.com:* 15, 195, 200, 264 *Hayden Foell:* 11, 173, 232 *Alan Kikuchi:* four section icons (Camping, Fishing, Hunting, Survival) *Kopp Illustration:* 146 *Raymond Larette:* 10, 12, 43, 89, 91, 134, 135, 164, 222, 227, 237, 284, 310, 314, 340, 366 *Andre Malok:* 120 *Daniel Marsiglio:* 4, 23, 30, 32, 46, 48, 59, 61, 62, 64, 72, 76, 79, 103, 108, 112, 128, 132, 138, 140, 160, 167, 182, 184, 188, 193, 206, 217, 243, 251, 253, 257, 302, 313, 317, 352, 353, 364, 370, 372, 373 *Will McDermott:* 2 *Samuel A. Minick:* 299 *Chris Philpot:* 147 *Robert L. Prince:* 6, 20, 51, 276 *Jameson Simpson:* 33, 85, 95, 176, 306, 321, 325 *Jeff Soto:* 14 *Jamie Spinello:* 125, 322, 341, 348, 356 *Peter Sucheski:* 114, 153, 246, 266 *Mike Sudal:* 68, 152, 170, 174, 196, 218 *Bryon Thompson:* 98, 113, 133, 205, 260, 277, 282, 323, 362 *Lauren Towner:* 17, 25, 35, 40, 52, 74, 94, 105, 110, 155, 203, 210, 214, 249, 272, 275, 359, 367, 368 *Paul Williams:* 21, 27, 116, 291, 365

Weldon Owen would like to thank Harry Bates, Kagan McLeod, and Steve Sanford for work done to accompany the original magazine articles.

FIELD & STREAM

Editor Anthony Licata
VP, Group Publisher Eric Zinczenko

2 Park Avenue
New York, NY 10016
www.fieldandstream.com

weldon**owen**

President, CEO Terry Newell
VP, Publisher Roger Shaw
VP, Sales and New Business Development Amy Kaneko
Executive Editor Mariah Bear
Editor Lucie Parker
Project Editor Amy Bauman
Editorial Assistant Emelie Griffin
Creative Director Kelly Booth
Art Director Iain R. Morris
Designers Jennifer Durrant and Meghan Hildebrand
Illustration Coordinator Conor Buckley
Production Director Chris Hemesath
Production Manager Michelle Duggan
Color Manager Teri Bell

Weldon Owen would also like to thank Bryn Walls for design development,
Kendra DeMoura, Michael Alexander Eros, Katharine Moore, Gail Nelson-
Bonebrake, and Charles Wormhoudt for editorial assistance; Marianna
Monaco for the index; and Michael Toussaint and Darryl & Terry Penry of
Petaluma Gun & Reloading Supply for prop assistance.

Field & Stream and Weldon Owen are divisions of
BONNIER

Library of Congress Control Number on file with the publisher

Flexi Edition ISBN 978-1-61628-061-1
Hardcover Edition ISBN 978-1-61628-178-6

10 9 8 7 6 5 4 3 2

2011 2012 2013 2014

Printed in the USA by RR Donnelley